Dog eat Doug

It's a Good Thing They're Cute

by Brian Anderson

Andrews McMeel
Publishing, LLC

Kansas City

08 09 10 11 12 TWP 10 9 8 7 6 5 4 3 2 1

ISBN-13: 978-0-7407-7366-2
ISBN-10: 0-7407-7366-6

Library of Congress Control Number: 2008921599

www.andrewsmcmeel.com

ATTENTION: SCHOOLS AND BUSINESSES

Andrews McMeel books are available at quantity discounts with bulk purchase for educational, business, or sales promotional use. For information, please write to: Special Sales Department, Andrews McMeel Publishing, LLC, 1130 Walnut Street, Kansas City, Missouri 64106.

For Mom and Dad

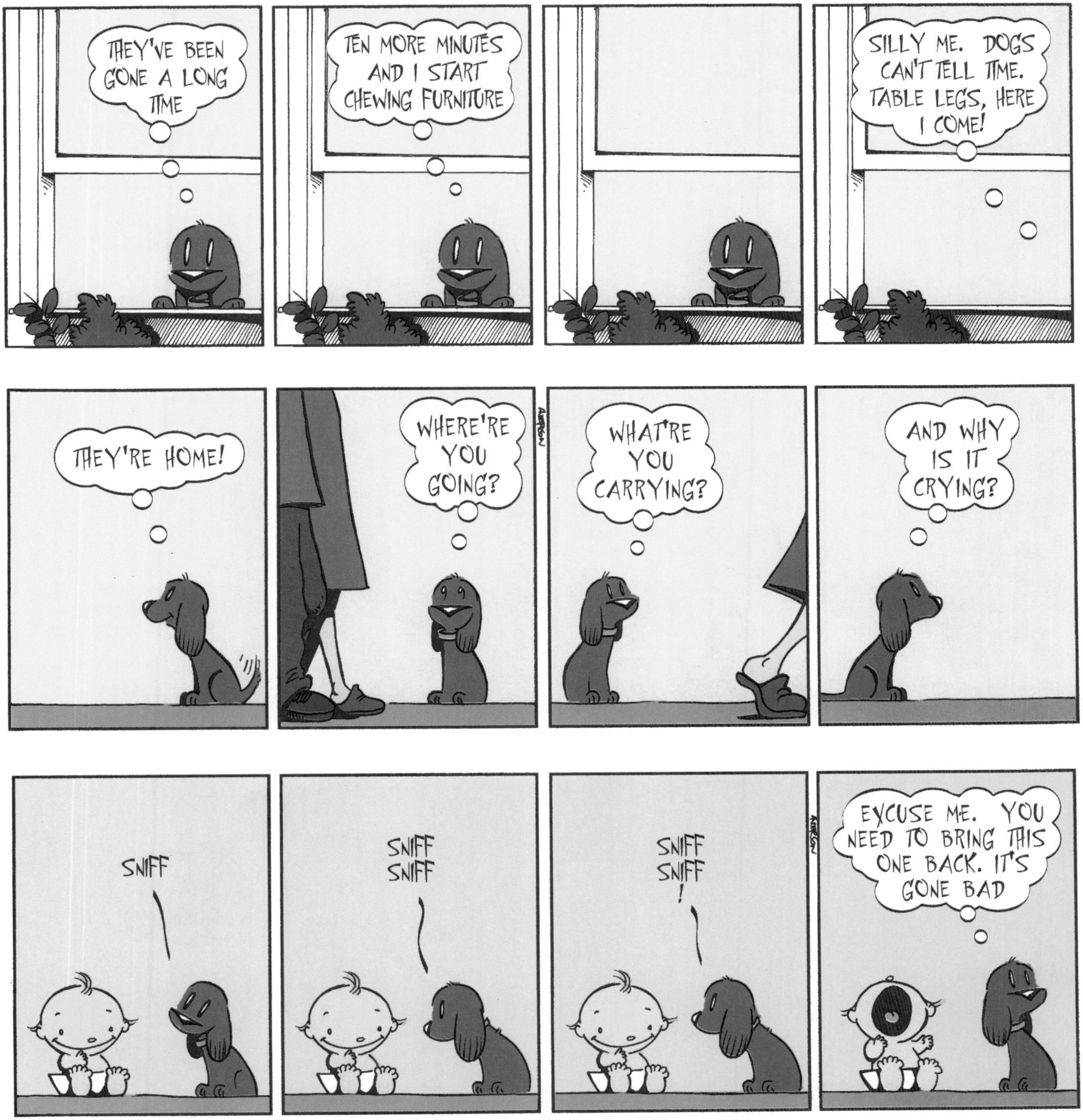
THEY'VE BEEN GONE A LONG TIME
TEN MORE MINUTES AND I START CHEWING FURNITURE
SILLY ME. DOGS CAN'T TELL TIME. TABLE LEGS, HERE I COME!
THEY'RE HOME!
WHERE'RE YOU GOING?
WHAT'RE YOU CARRYING?
AND WHY IS IT CRYING?
SNIFF
SNIFF SNIFF
SNIFF SNIFF !
EXCUSE ME. YOU NEED TO BRING THIS ONE BACK. IT'S GONE BAD

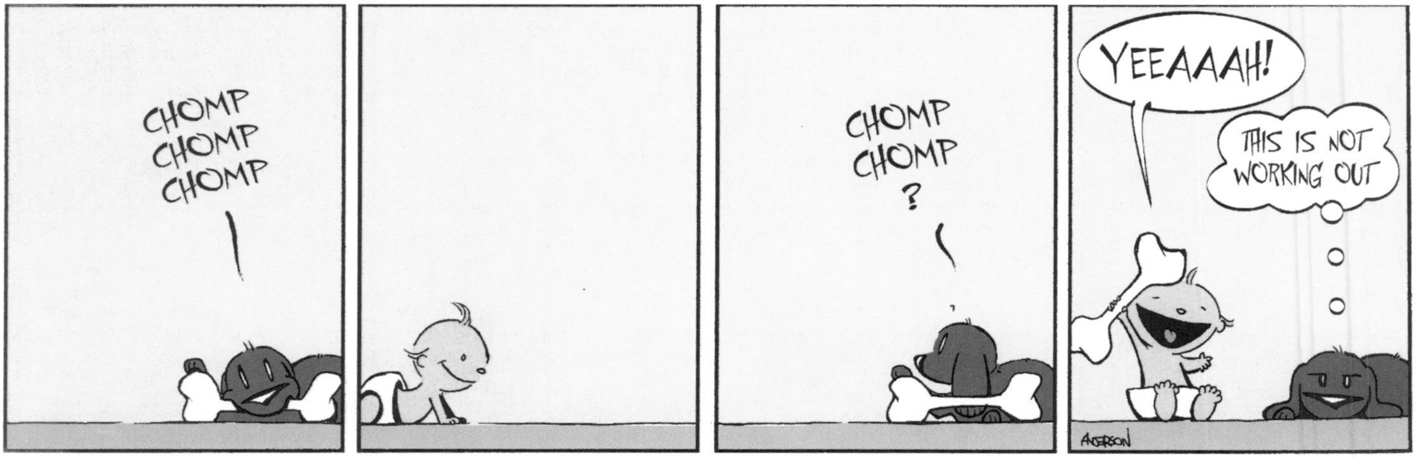
CHOMP CHOMP CHOMP
CHOMP CHOMP ?
YEEAAAH!
THIS IS NOT WORKING OUT

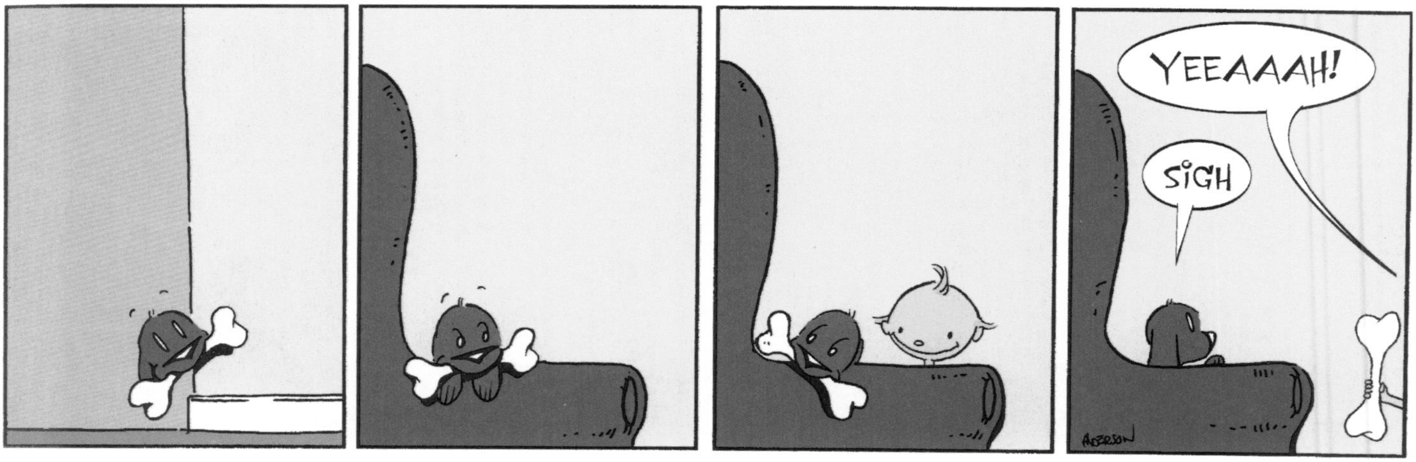
YEEAAAH!
SIGH

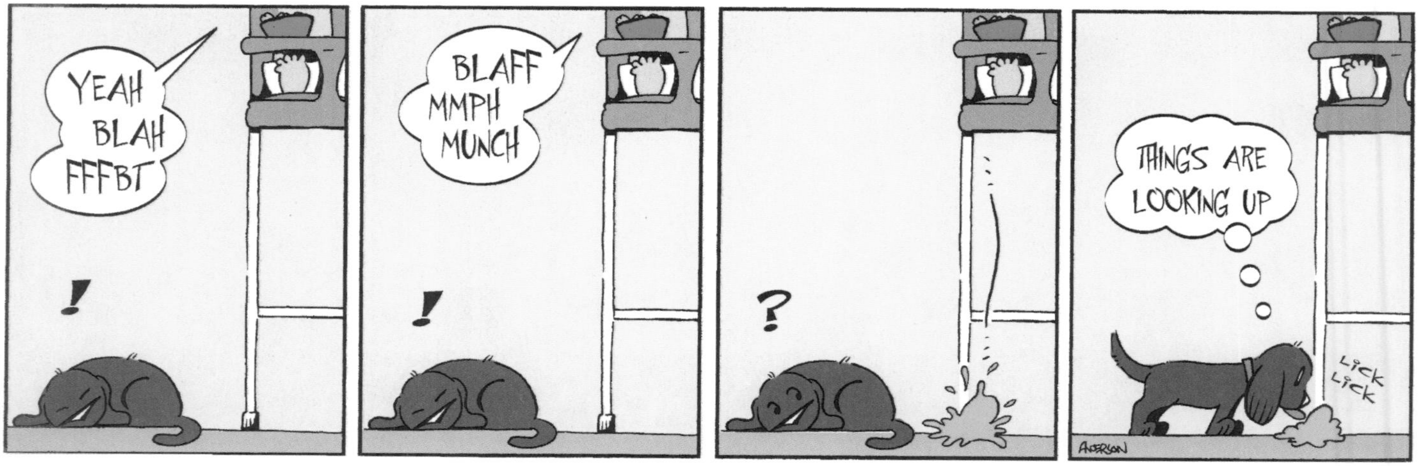
YEAH BLAH FFFBT
!
BLAFF MMPH MUNCH
!
?
THINGS ARE LOOKING UP
LICK LICK

ZING!
ZING!
ZING!
ZING!
SOPHIE! GO OUTSIDE AND PLAY!
Z
ADDISON

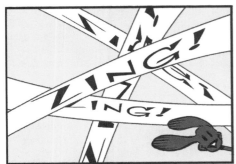

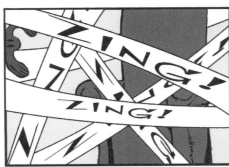

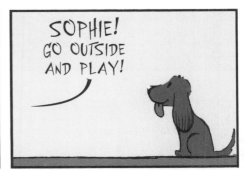

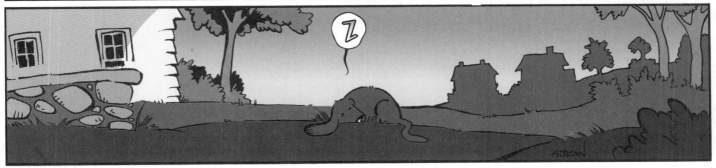

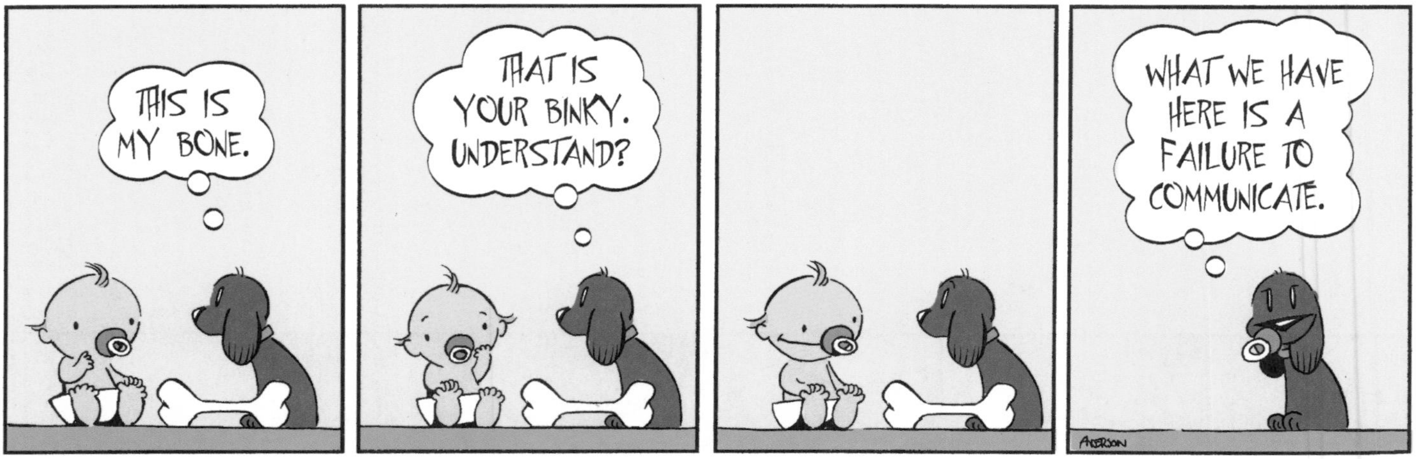
THIS IS MY BONE.
THAT IS YOUR BINKY. UNDERSTAND?
WHAT WE HAVE HERE IS A FAILURE TO COMMUNICATE.

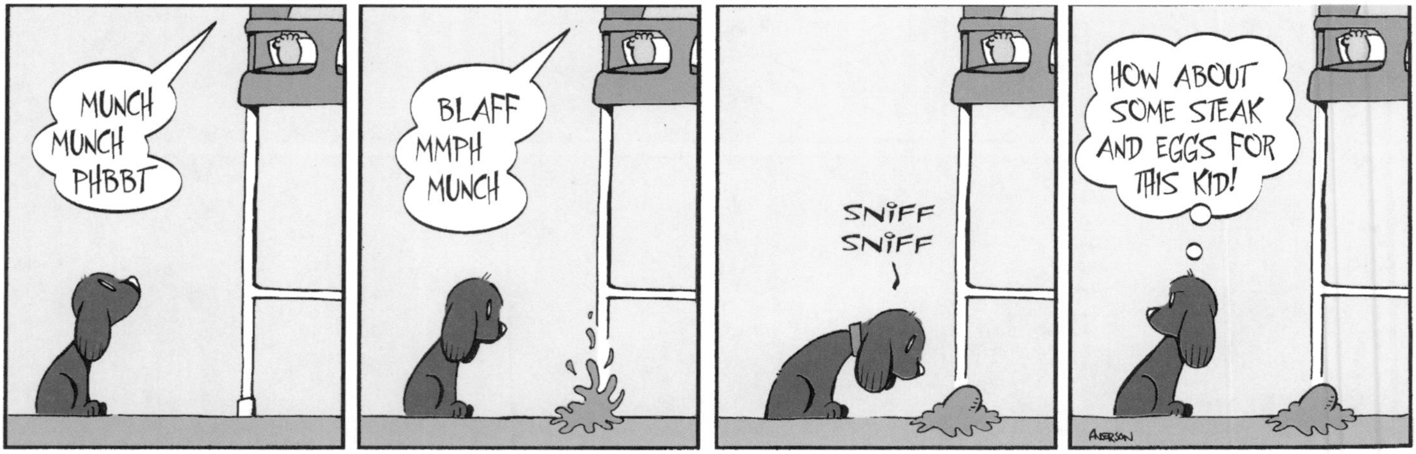
MUNCH MUNCH PHBBT
BLAFF MMPH MUNCH
SNIFF SNIFF
HOW ABOUT SOME STEAK AND EGGS FOR THIS KID!

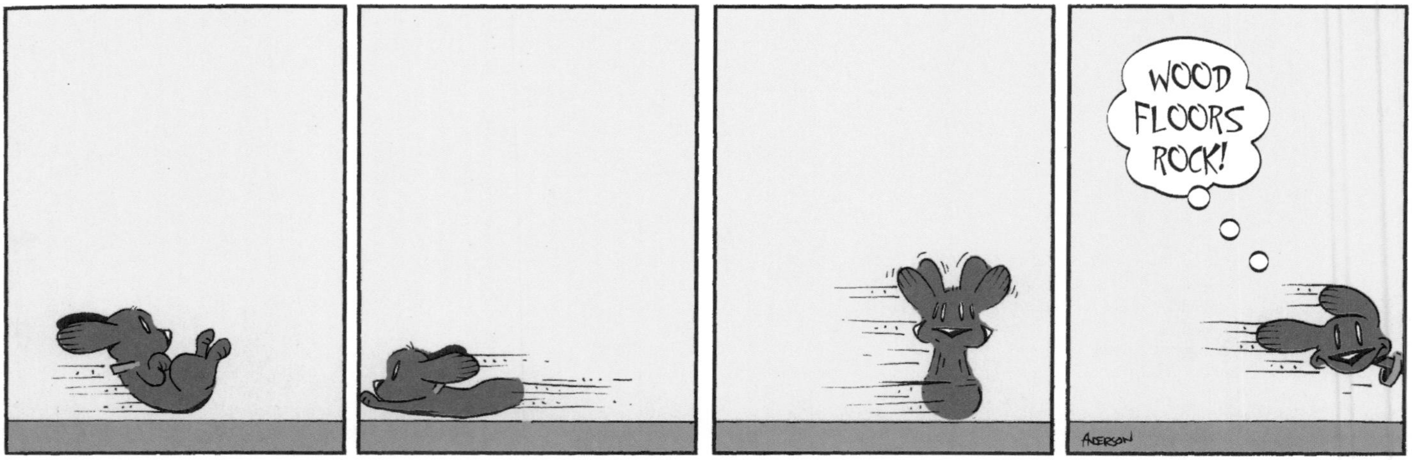
WOOD FLOORS ROCK!

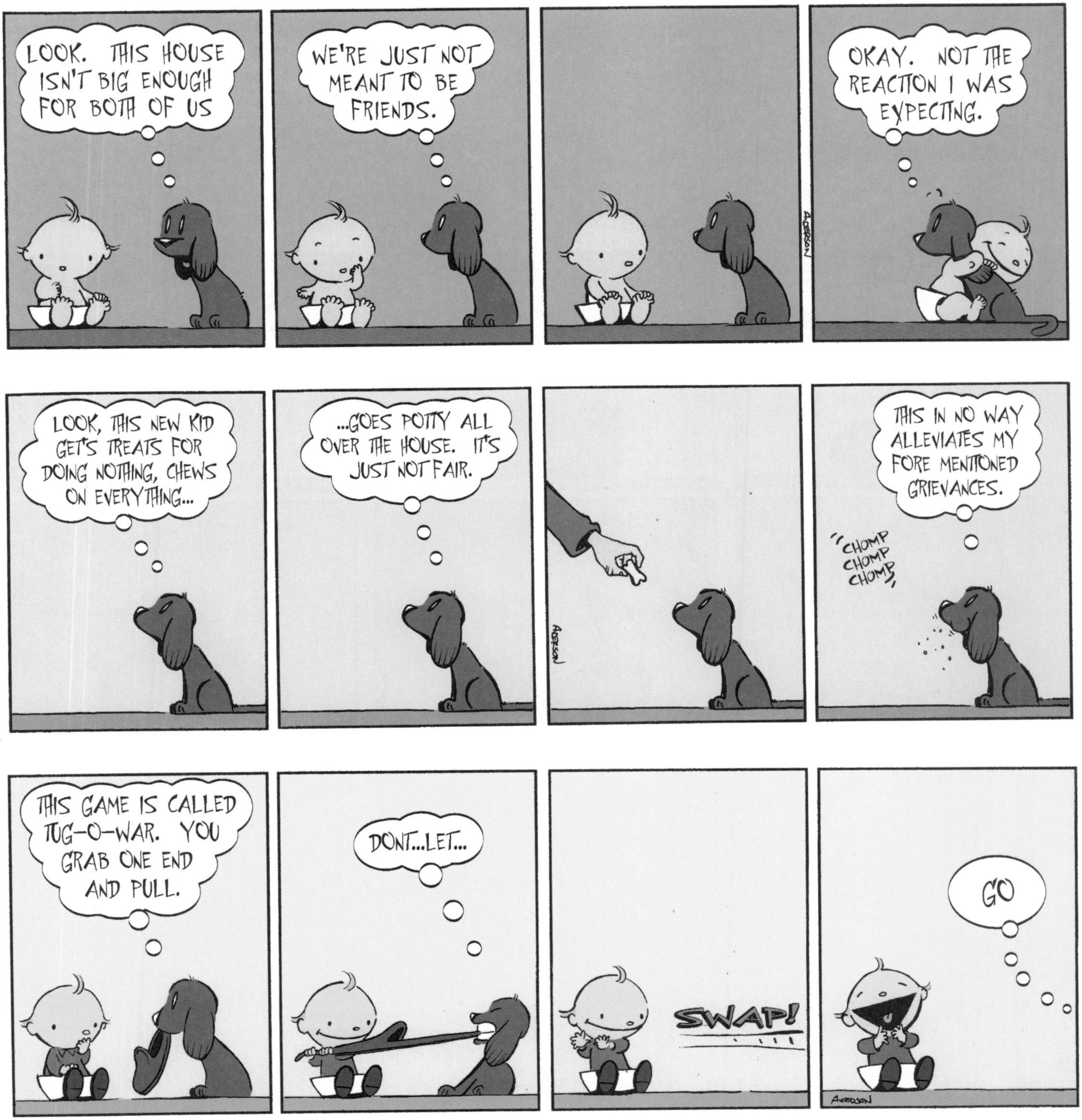
LOOK. THIS HOUSE ISN'T BIG ENOUGH FOR BOTH OF US
WE'RE JUST NOT MEANT TO BE FRIENDS.
OKAY. NOT THE REACTION I WAS EXPECTING.
LOOK, THIS NEW KID GET'S TREATS FOR DOING NOTHING, CHEWS ON EVERYTHING...
...GOES POTTY ALL OVER THE HOUSE. IT'S JUST NOT FAIR.
CHOMP CHOMP CHOMP
THIS IN NO WAY ALLEVIATES MY FORE MENTIONED GRIEVANCES.
THIS GAME IS CALLED TUG-O-WAR. YOU GRAB ONE END AND PULL.
DONT...LET...
SWAP!
GO

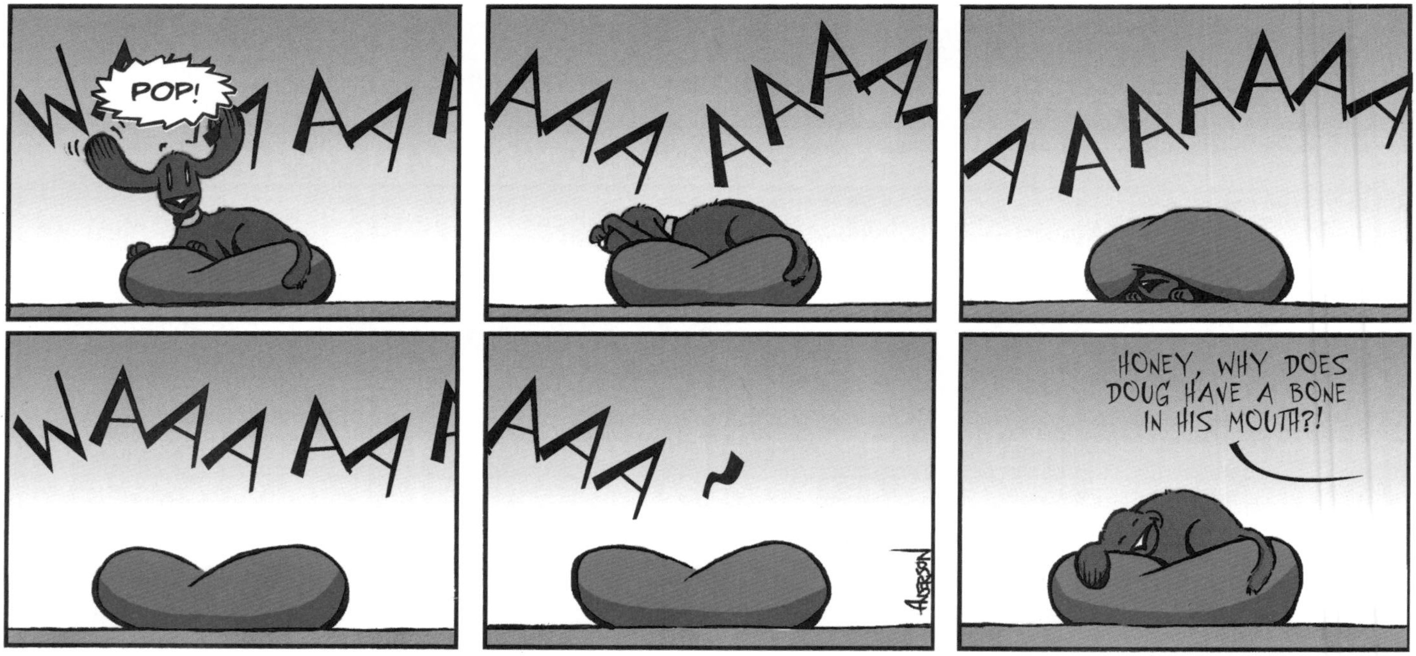
POP!
WAAAAAAAAAAAAAAAAAAAAAAAAAAA
WAAAAAAAAAA~
ANDERSON
HONEY, WHY DOES DOUG HAVE A BONE IN HIS MOUTH?!

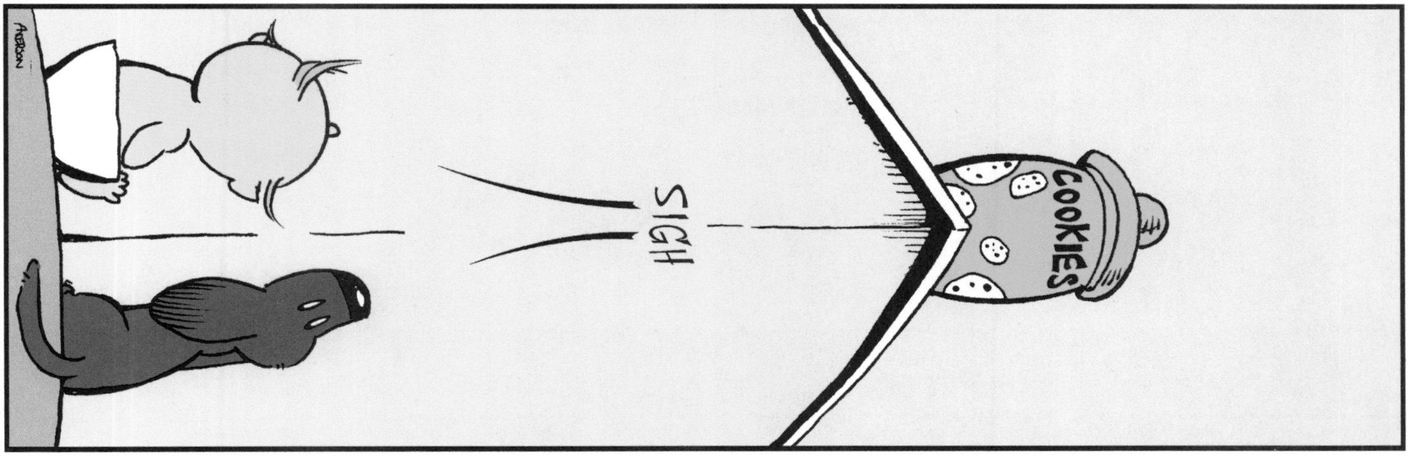
ANDERSON
SIGH
COOKIES

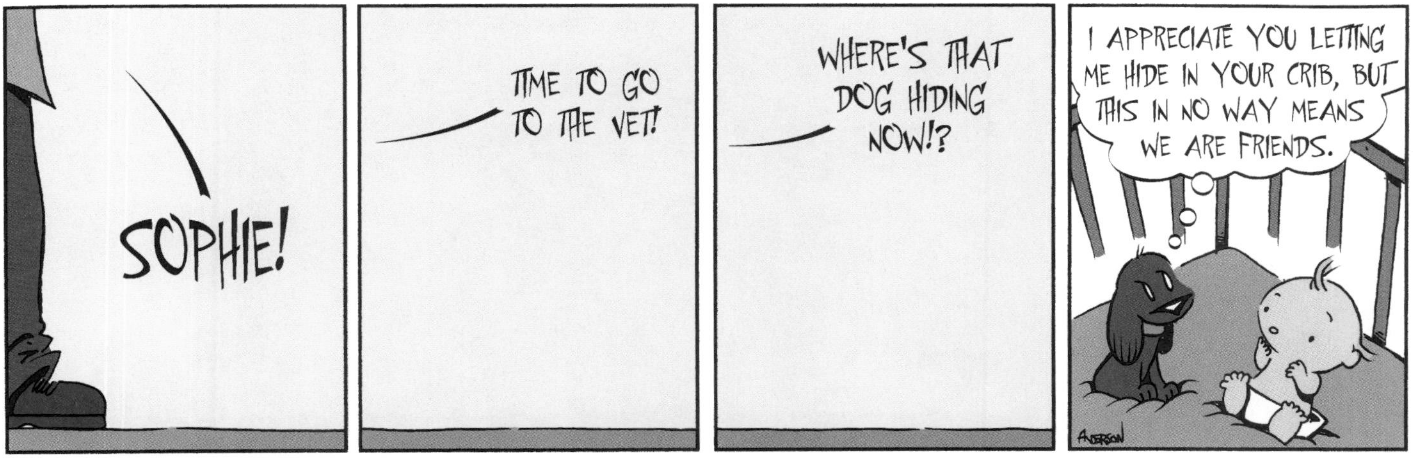
SOPHIE!
TIME TO GO TO THE VET!
WHERE'S THAT DOG HIDING NOW!?
I APPRECIATE YOU LETTING ME HIDE IN YOUR CRIB, BUT THIS IN NO WAY MEANS WE ARE FRIENDS.
ANDERSON

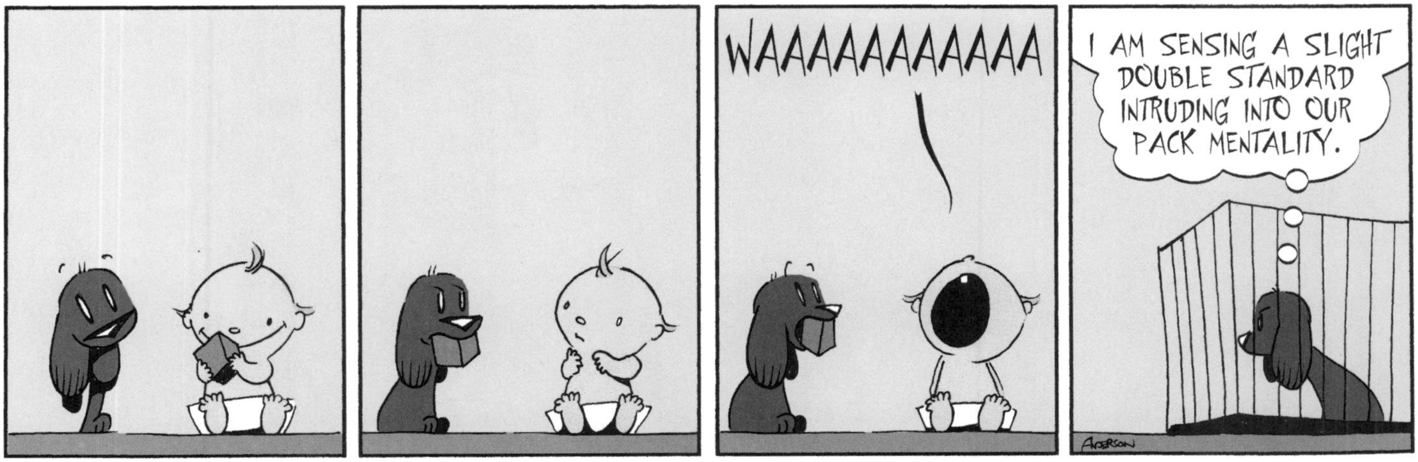
WAAAAAAAAAA
I AM SENSING A SLIGHT DOUBLE STANDARD INTRUDING INTO OUR PACK MENTALITY.
ANDERSON

UNDER THE BED. MY LAST REFUGE.

NO USURPING, TYRANNICAL BABY CAN...

SNIFF?

I SMELL PAMPERS

YEEAAAH!

ANDERSON

DON'T THINK I DON'T KNOW THE GAME YOU'RE PLAYING.

YOUR LITTLE "HELPLESS" ACT CAN ONLY GO ON SO LONG.

ENJOY IT WHILE YOU CAN

THEY'LL LEAVE US HOME ALONE SOMEDAY.

ANDERSON

OF COURSE YOU CAN!

I DO IT ALL THE TIME.

RIGHT BY THAT BUSH IS FINE.

DOUG! WHAT ARE YOU DOING?!

WHEN YA GOTTA GO, YA GOTTA GO.

ANDERSON

WHAT'S SO SPECIAL ABOUT BABIES?!
THEY JUST LIE AROUND ALL DAY
CAN'T FETCH, CAN'T PLAY CHASE.
BABY'S DON'T HAVE ONE REDEEMABLE QUALITY!
SMOOOCH!
SHEESH! JUST WHEN YOU THINK YOU KNOW SOMEONE!

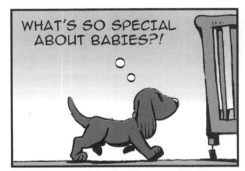

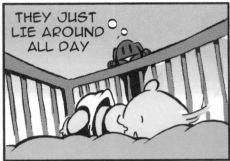

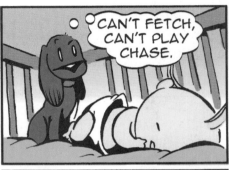

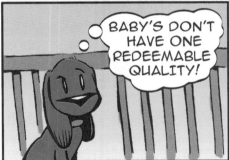

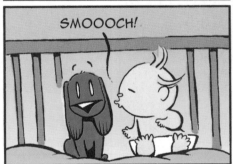

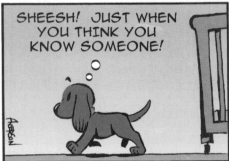

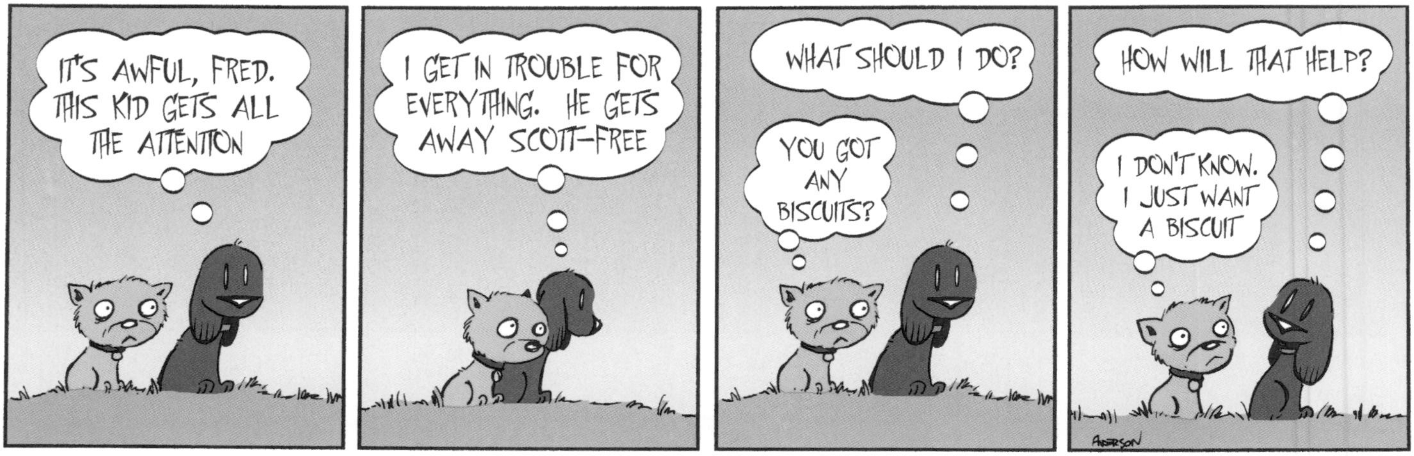
IT'S AWFUL, FRED. THIS KID GETS ALL THE ATTENTION
I GET IN TROUBLE FOR EVERYTHING. HE GETS AWAY SCOTT-FREE
WHAT SHOULD I DO?
YOU GOT ANY BISCUITS?
HOW WILL THAT HELP?
I DON'T KNOW. I JUST WANT A BISCUIT
ANDERSON

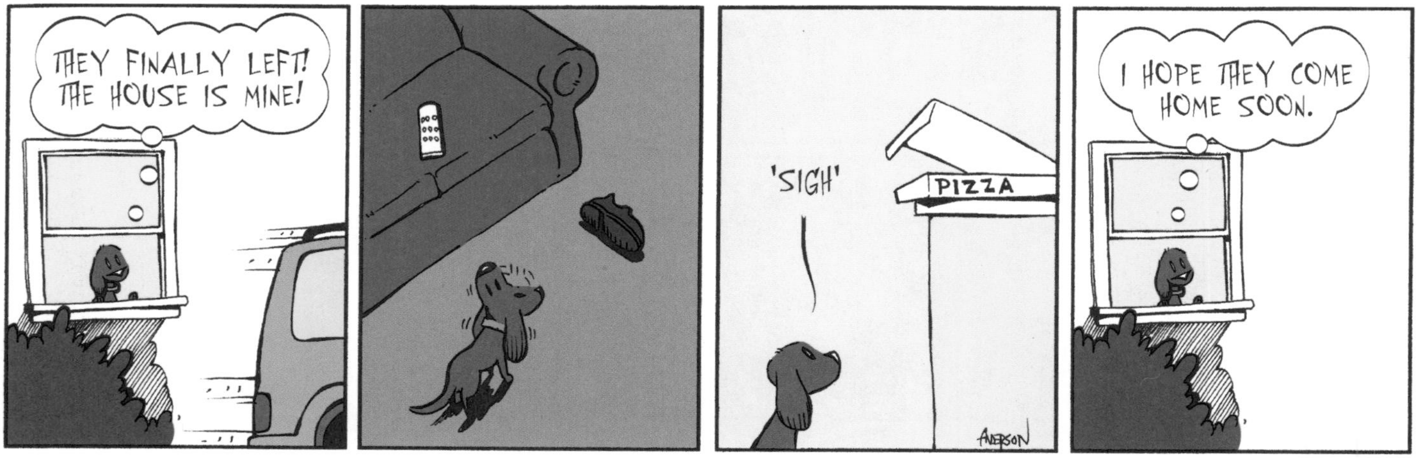
THEY FINALLY LEFT! THE HOUSE IS MINE!
'SIGH'
PIZZA
ANDERSON
I HOPE THEY COME HOME SOON.

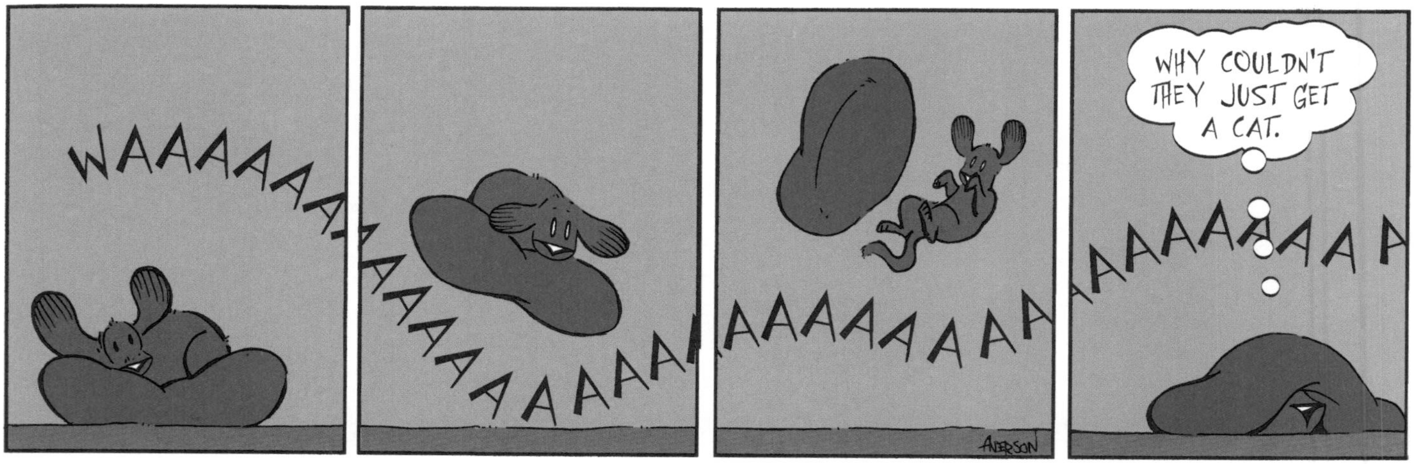
WAAAAAA
AAAAAAAAAAA
AAAAAAAAA
AAAAAAAAA
ANDERSON
WHY COULDN'T THEY JUST GET A CAT.

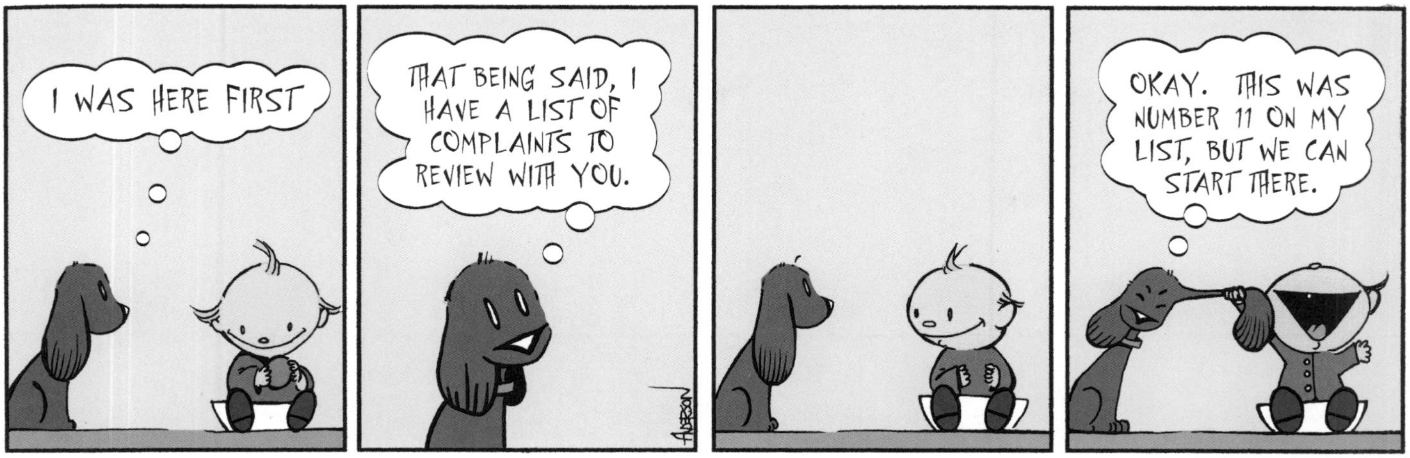
I WAS HERE FIRST
THAT BEING SAID, I HAVE A LIST OF COMPLAINTS TO REVIEW WITH YOU.
OKAY. THIS WAS NUMBER 11 ON MY LIST, BUT WE CAN START THERE.

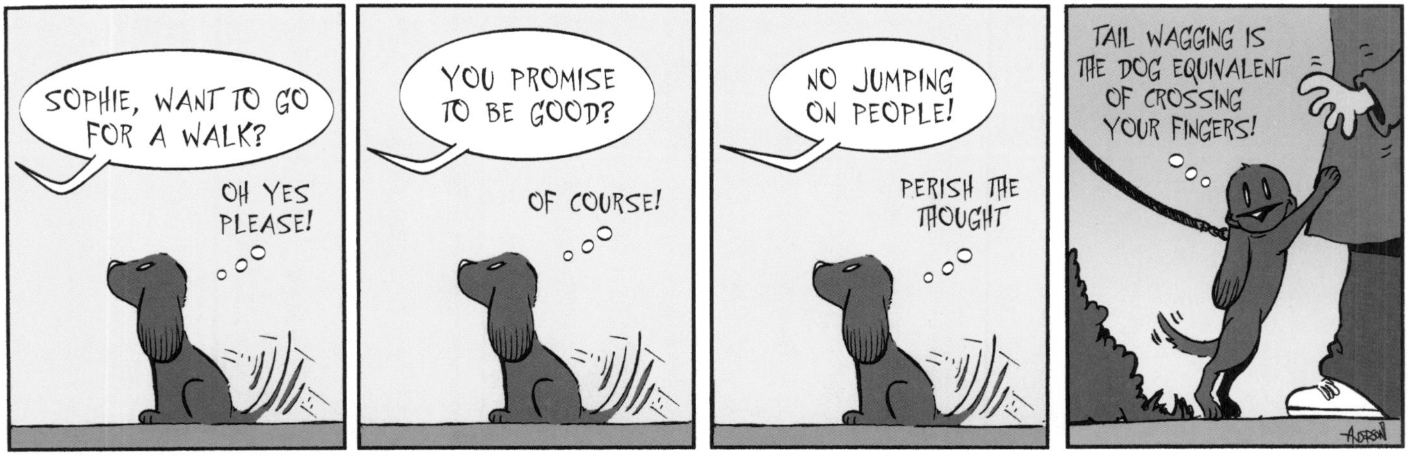
SOPHIE, WANT TO GO FOR A WALK?
OH YES PLEASE!
YOU PROMISE TO BE GOOD?
OF COURSE!
NO JUMPING ON PEOPLE!
PERISH THE THOUGHT
TAIL WAGGING IS THE DOG EQUIVALENT OF CROSSING YOUR FINGERS!

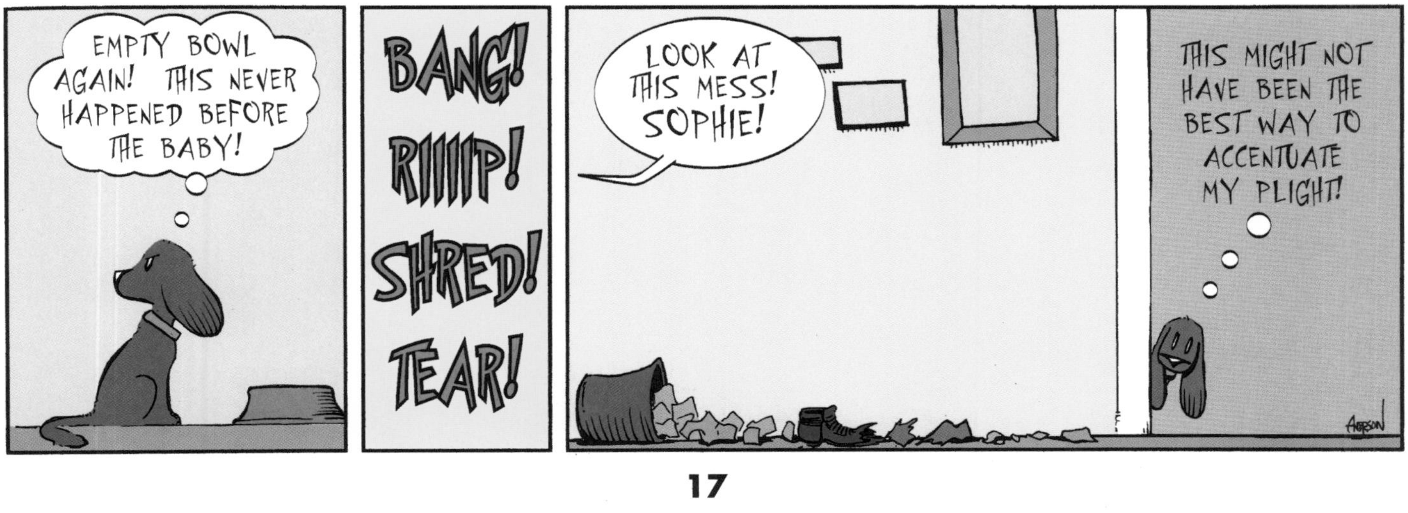
EMPTY BOWL AGAIN! THIS NEVER HAPPENED BEFORE THE BABY!
BANG! RIIIP! SHRED! TEAR!
LOOK AT THIS MESS! SOPHIE!
THIS MIGHT NOT HAVE BEEN THE BEST WAY TO ACCENTUATE MY PLIGHT!

SOPHIE, SIT!
ROLLOVER.
STAND UP!
LIE DOWN.
GOOD GIRL!
IT'S A LOT OF WORK, BUT THOSE TREATS SURE ARE WORTH IT!
MUNCH! MUNCH! MUNCH!
ANDERSON

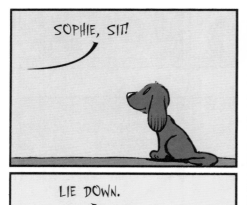

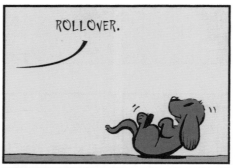

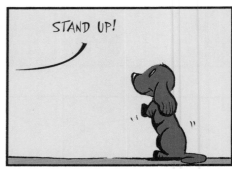

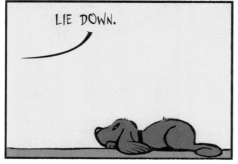

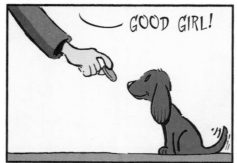

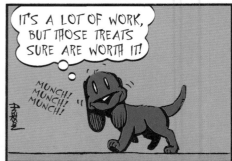

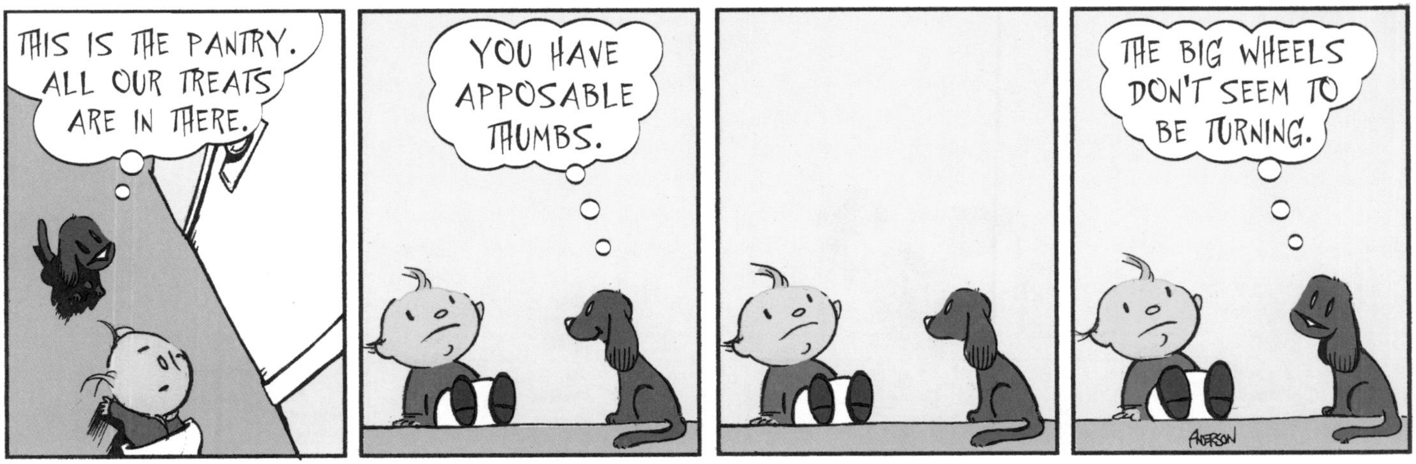
THIS IS THE PANTRY. ALL OUR TREATS ARE IN THERE.
YOU HAVE APPOSABLE THUMBS.
THE BIG WHEELS DON'T SEEM TO BE TURNING.

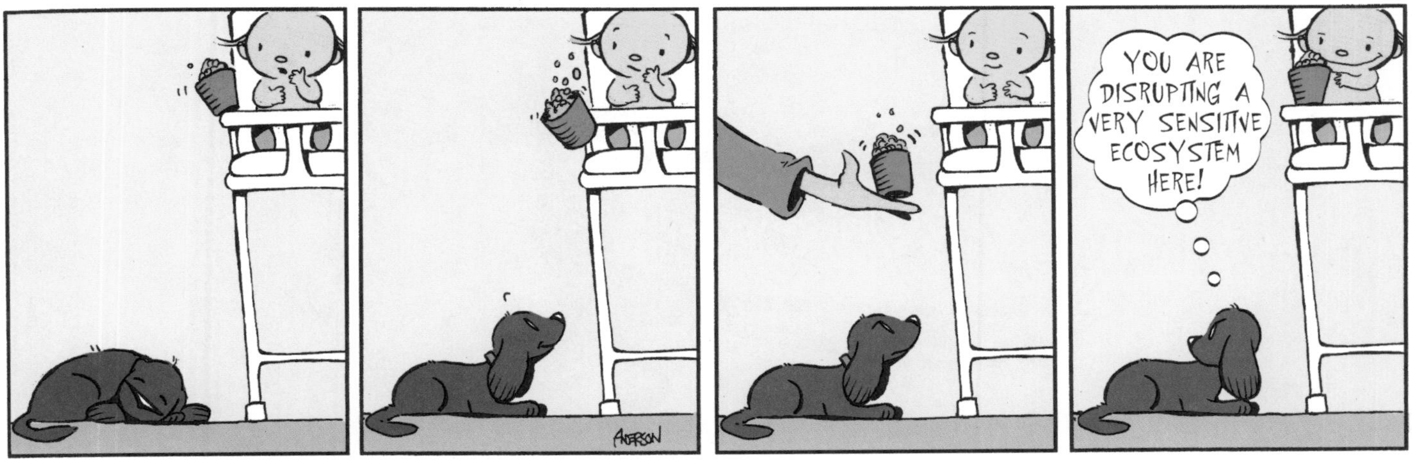
YOU ARE DISRUPTING A VERY SENSITIVE ECOSYSTEM HERE!

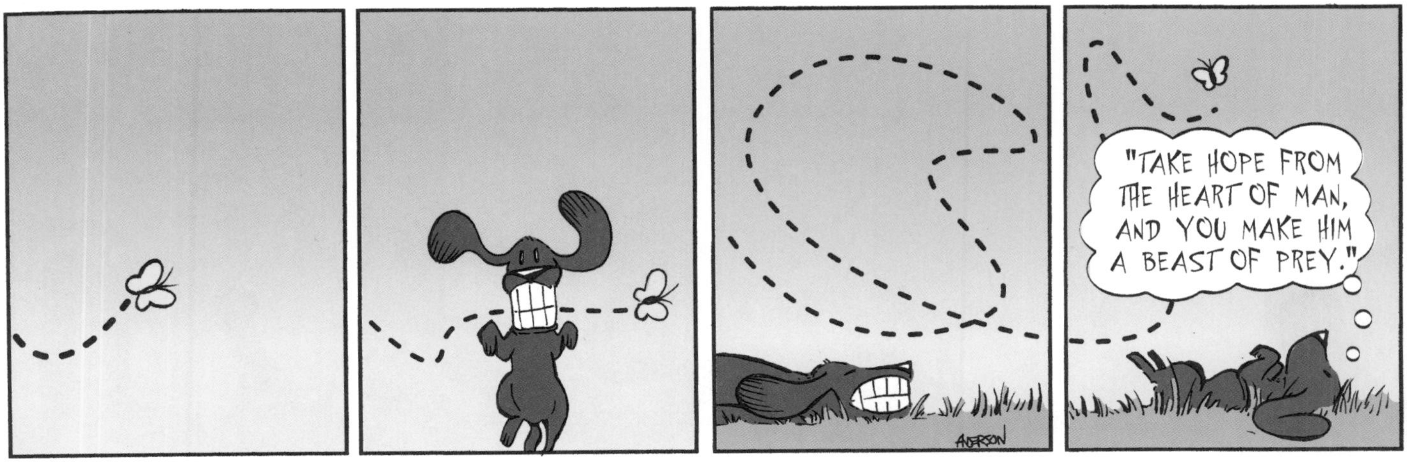
"TAKE HOPE FROM THE HEART OF MAN, AND YOU MAKE HIM A BEAST OF PREY."

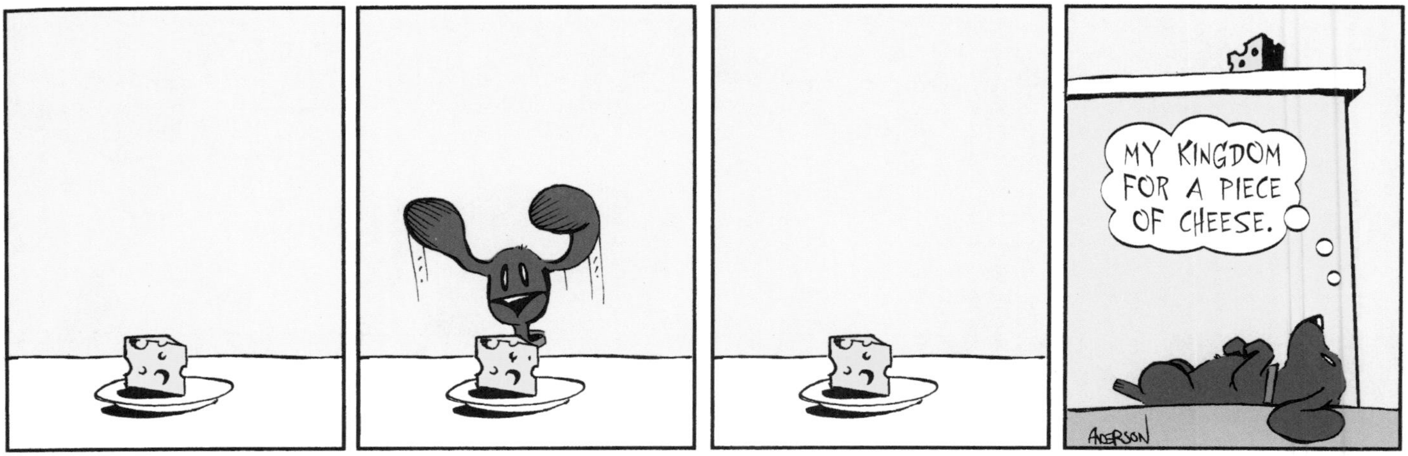
MY KINGDOM FOR A PIECE OF CHEESE.
ANDERSON

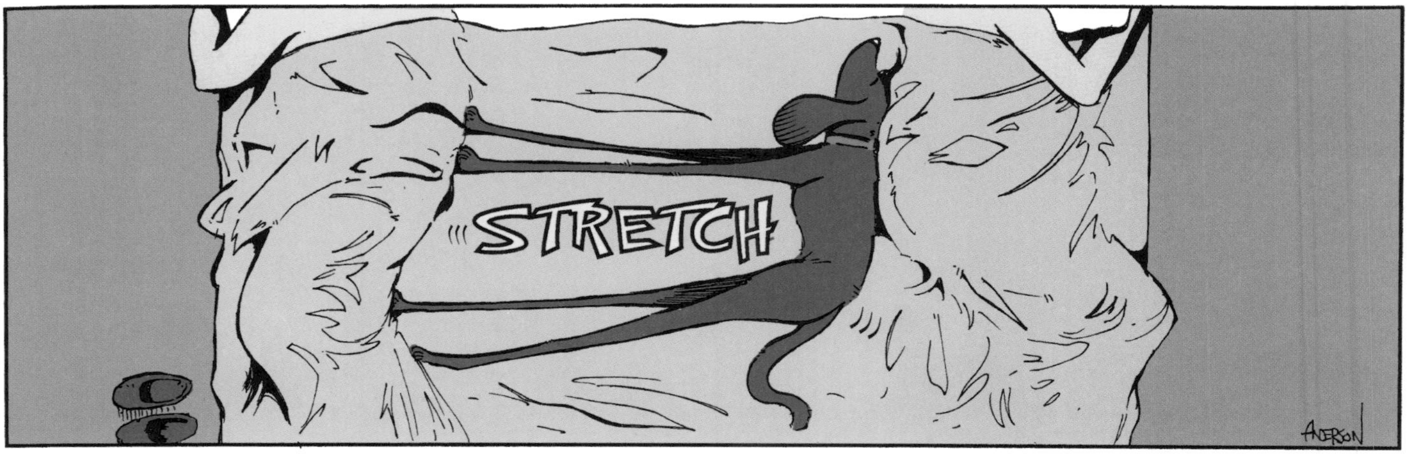
STRETCH
ANDERSON

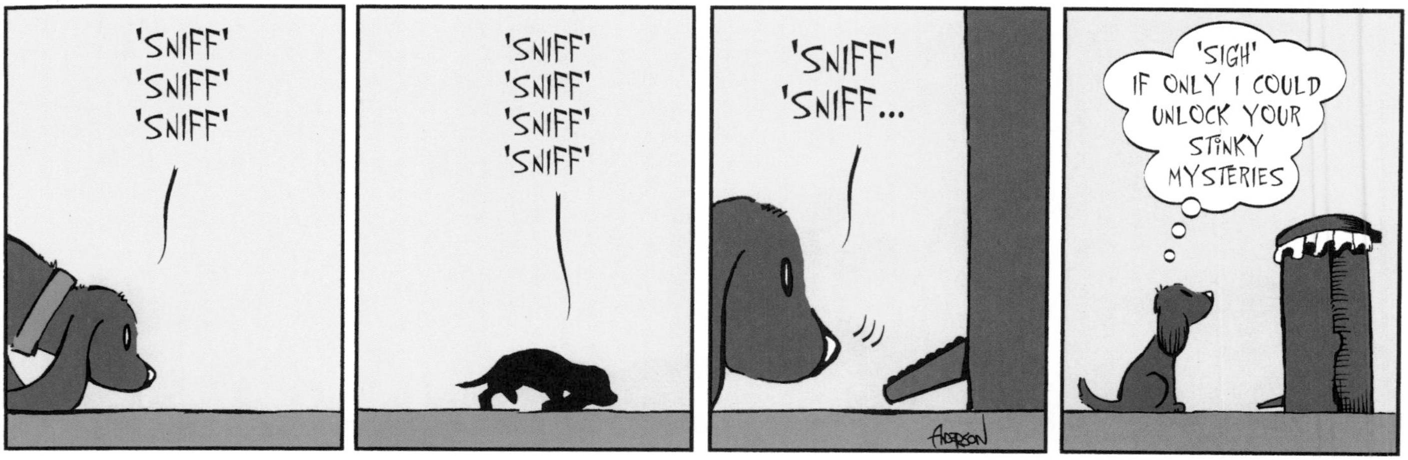
'SNIFF' 'SNIFF' 'SNIFF'
'SNIFF' 'SNIFF' 'SNIFF' 'SNIFF'
'SNIFF' 'SNIFF...
'SIGH' IF ONLY I COULD UNLOCK YOUR STINKY MYSTERIES
ANDERSON

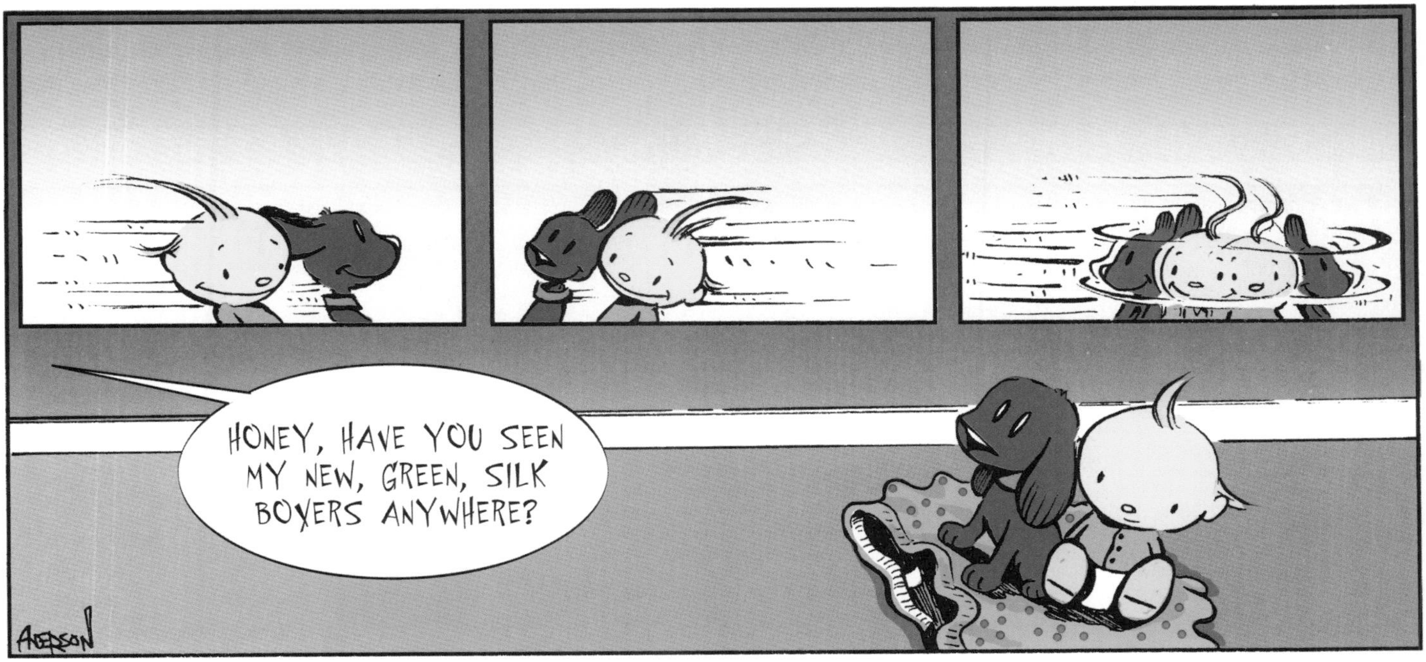
HONEY, HAVE YOU SEEN MY NEW, GREEN, SILK BOXERS ANYWHERE?
ANDERSON

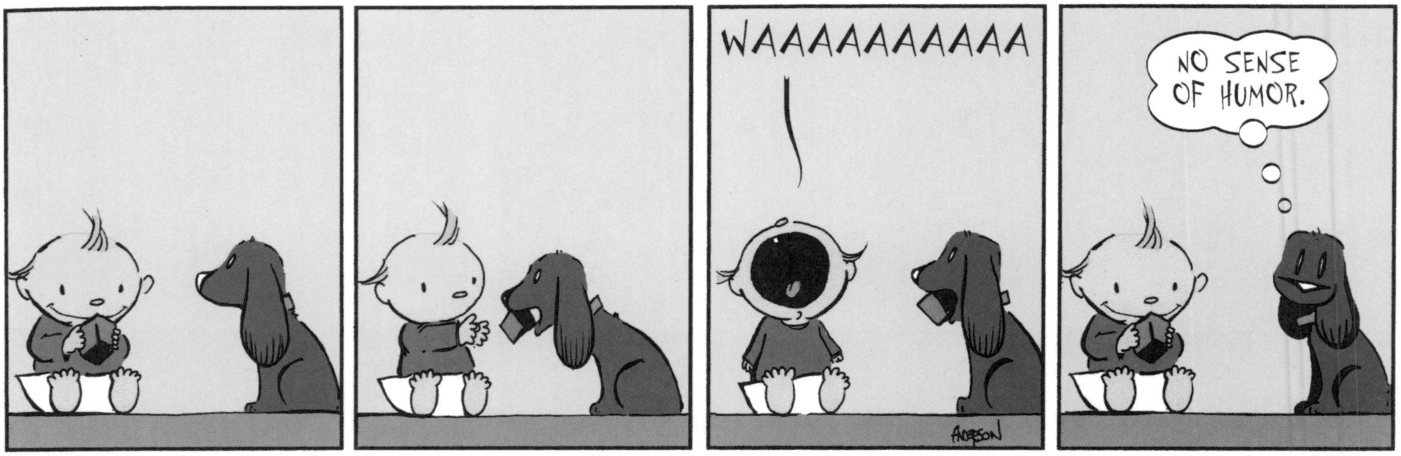
WAAAAAAAAAA
NO SENSE OF HUMOR.
ANDERSON

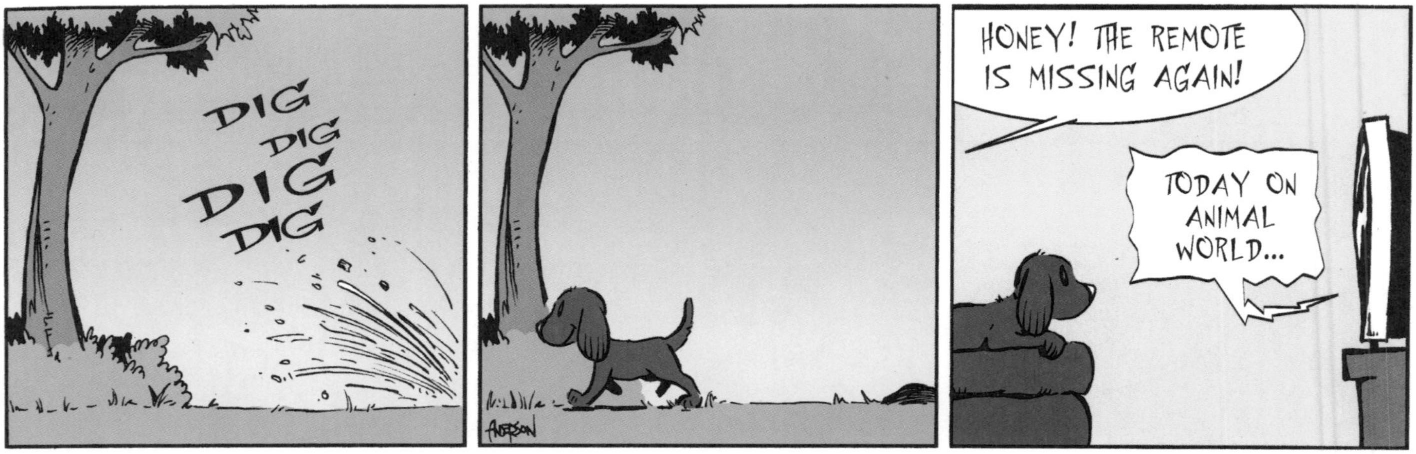
DIG DIG DIG DIG
ANDERSON
HONEY! THE REMOTE IS MISSING AGAIN!
TODAY ON ANIMAL WORLD...

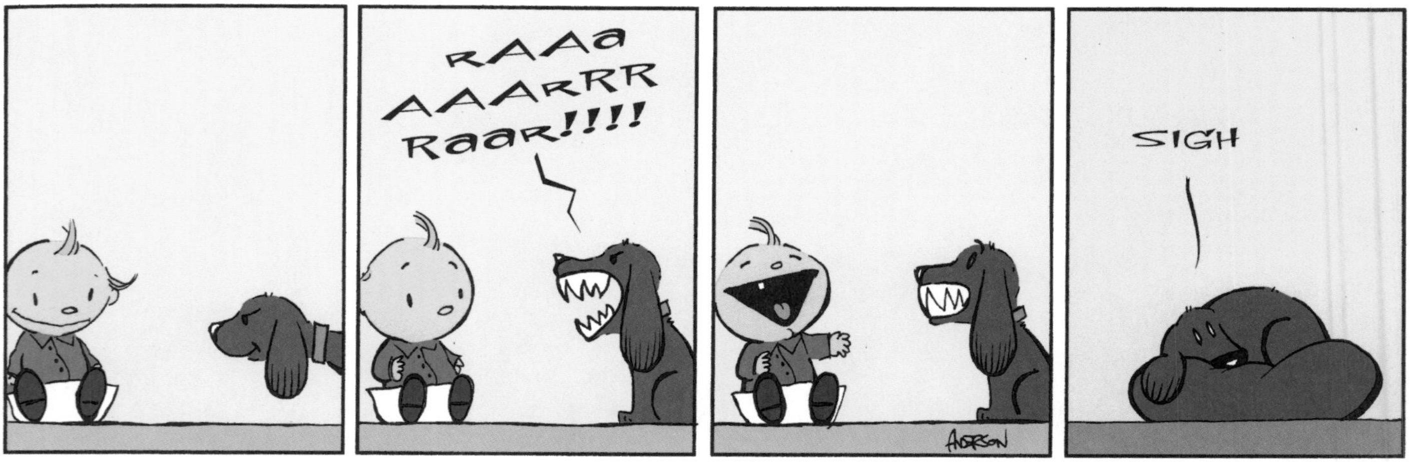
RAAa AAARRR Raar!!!!
ANDERSON
SIGH

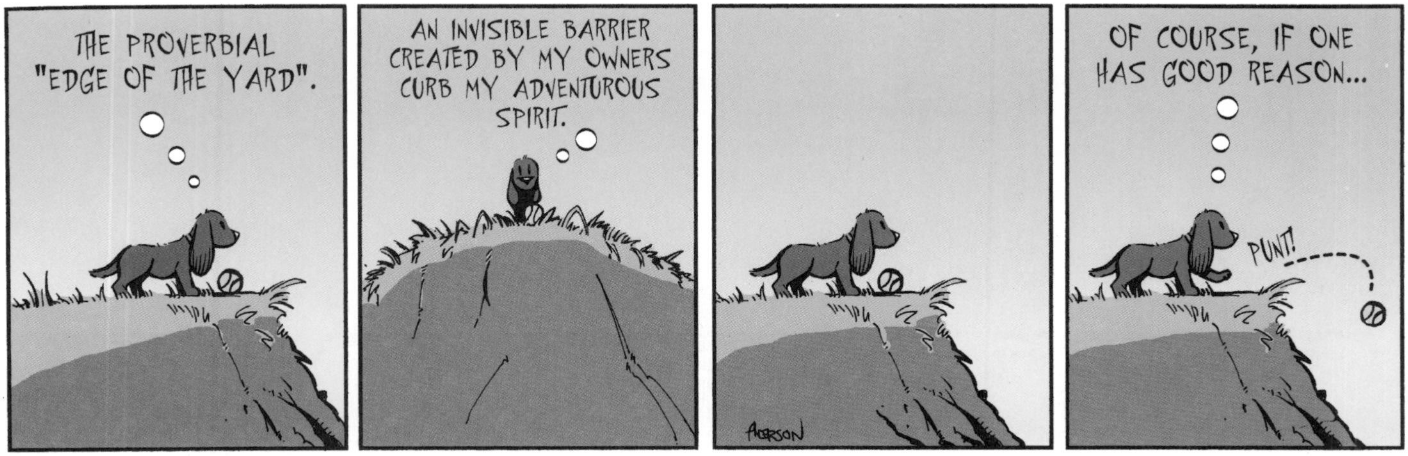
THE PROVERBIAL "EDGE OF THE YARD".
AN INVISIBLE BARRIER CREATED BY MY OWNERS CURB MY ADVENTUROUS SPIRIT.
OF COURSE, IF ONE HAS GOOD REASON...
PUNT!

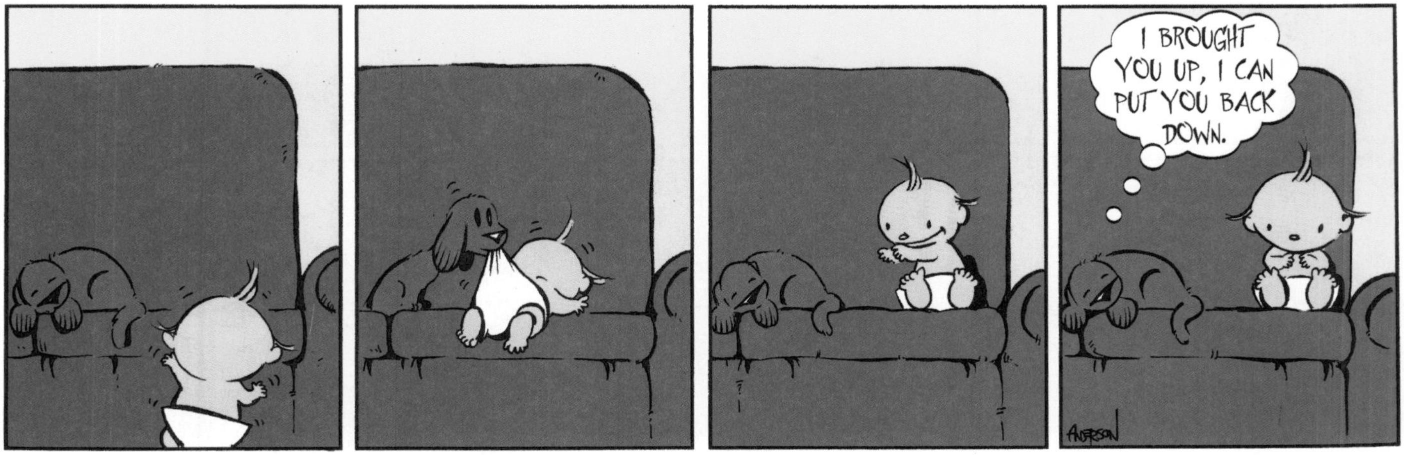
I BROUGHT YOU UP, I CAN PUT YOU BACK DOWN.

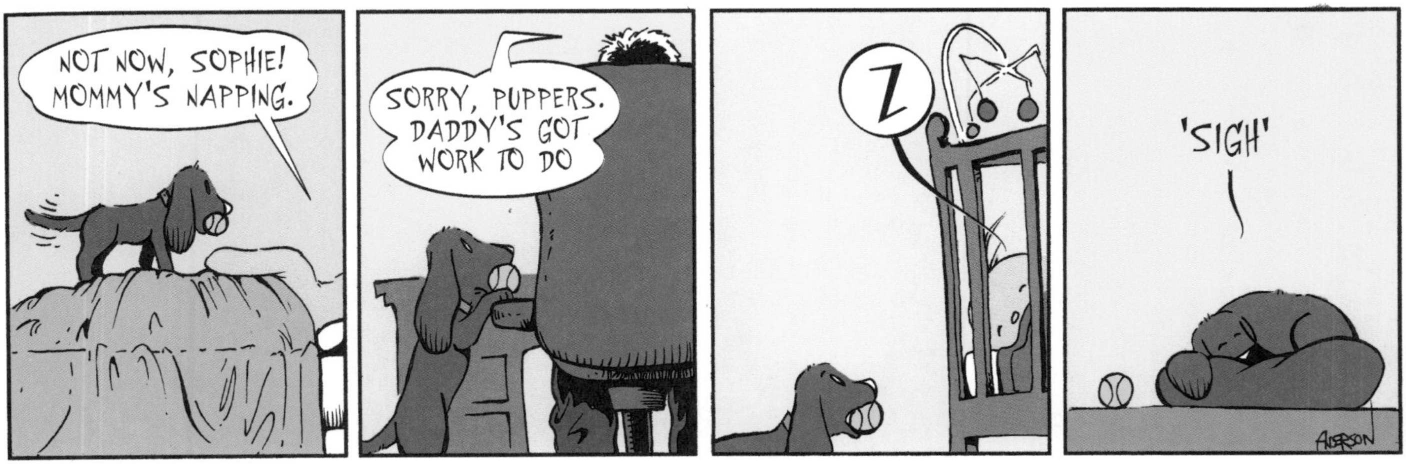
NOT NOW, SOPHIE! MOMMY'S NAPPING.
SORRY, PUPPERS. DADDY'S GOT WORK TO DO
Z
'SIGH'

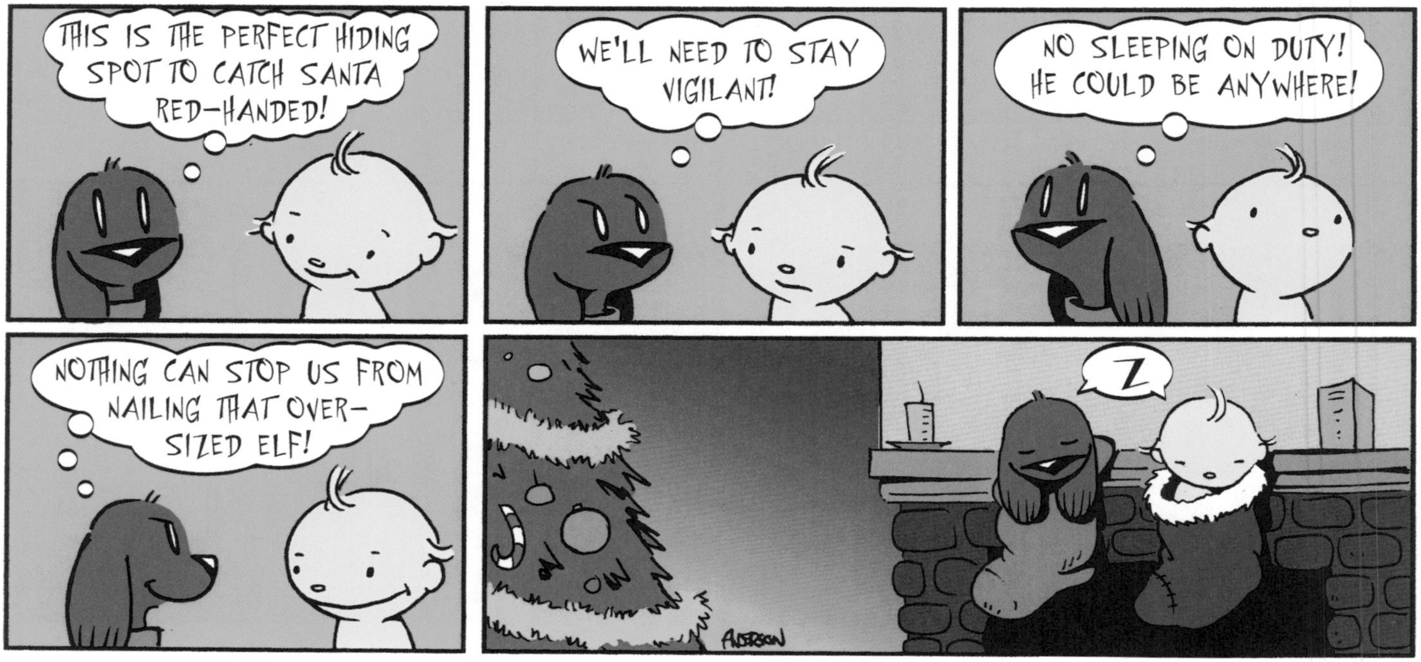
THIS IS THE PERFECT HIDING SPOT TO CATCH SANTA RED-HANDED!
WE'LL NEED TO STAY VIGILANT!
NO SLEEPING ON DUTY! HE COULD BE ANYWHERE!
NOTHING CAN STOP US FROM NAILING THAT OVER-SIZED ELF!
Z
ANDERSON

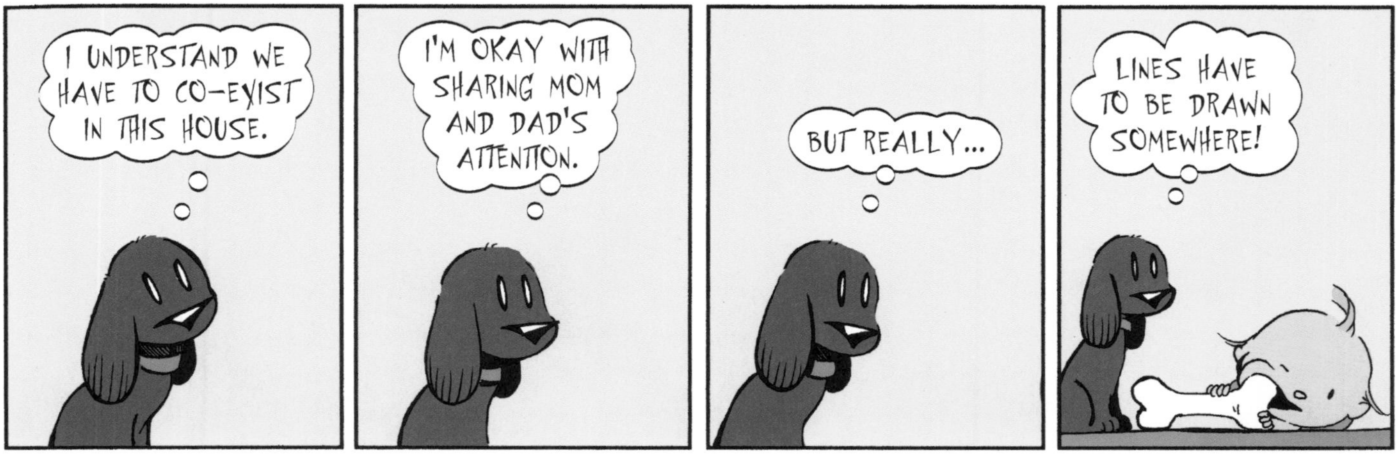
I UNDERSTAND WE HAVE TO CO-EXIST IN THIS HOUSE.
I'M OKAY WITH SHARING MOM AND DAD'S ATTENTION.
BUT REALLY...
LINES HAVE TO BE DRAWN SOMEWHERE!

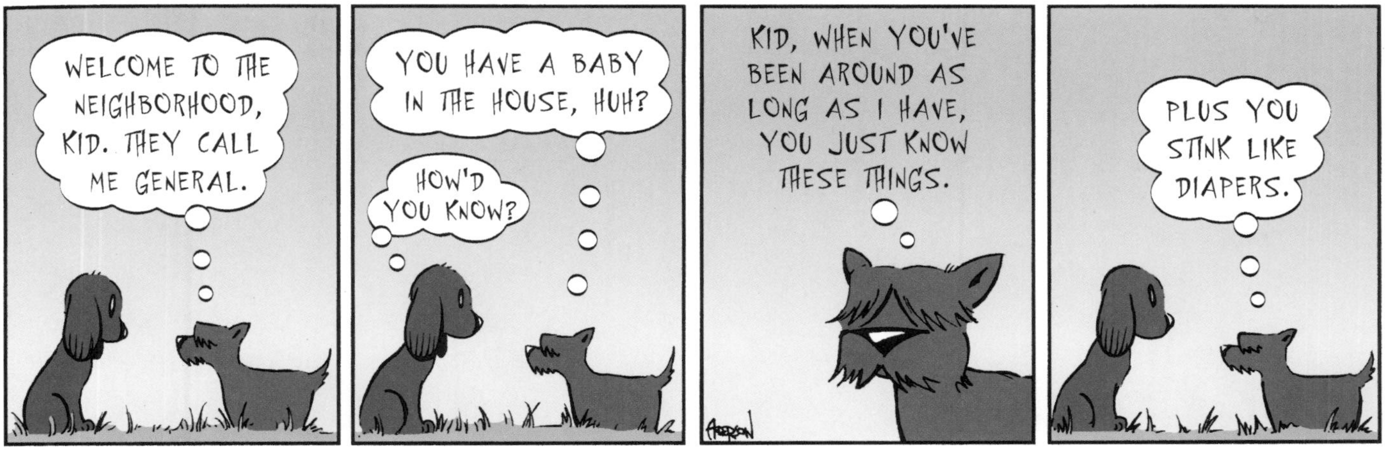
WELCOME TO THE NEIGHBORHOOD, KID. THEY CALL ME GENERAL.
YOU HAVE A BABY IN THE HOUSE, HUH?
HOW'D YOU KNOW?
KID, WHEN YOU'VE BEEN AROUND AS LONG AS I HAVE, YOU JUST KNOW THESE THINGS.
PLUS YOU STINK LIKE DIAPERS.

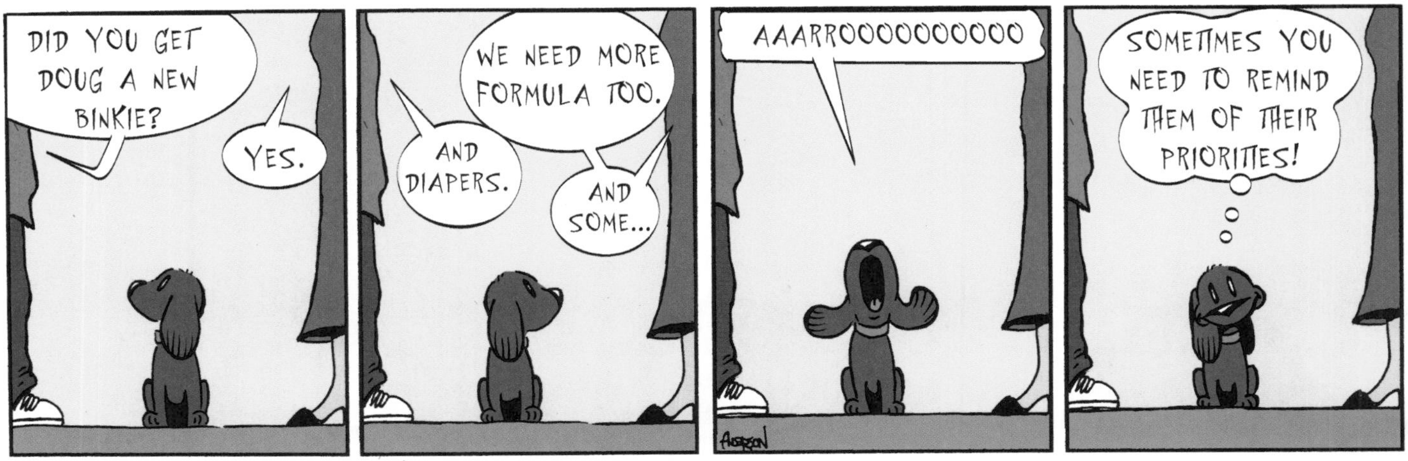
DID YOU GET DOUG A NEW BINKIE?
YES.
WE NEED MORE FORMULA TOO.
AND DIAPERS.
AND SOME...
AAARROOOOOOOOOOO
SOMETIMES YOU NEED TO REMIND THEM OF THEIR PRIORITIES!

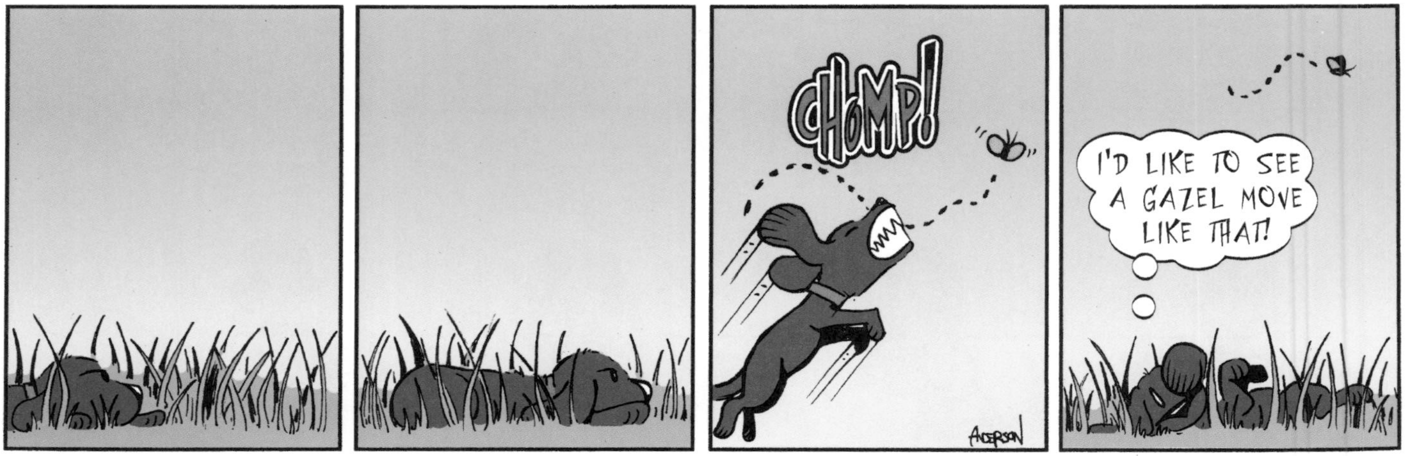
CHOMP!
ANDERSON
I'D LIKE TO SEE A GAZEL MOVE LIKE THAT!

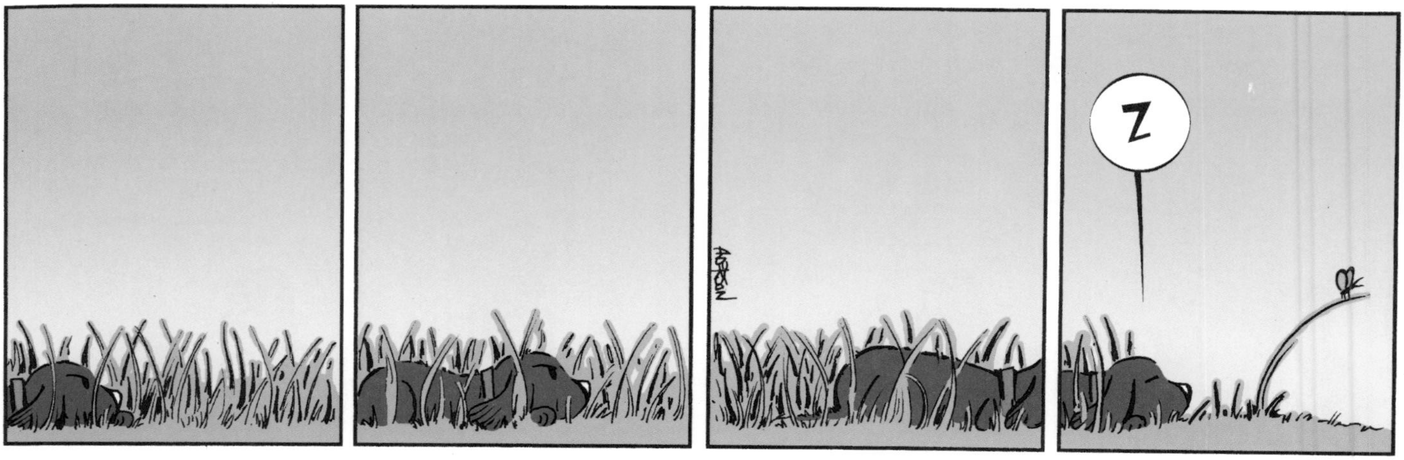
ANDERSON
Z

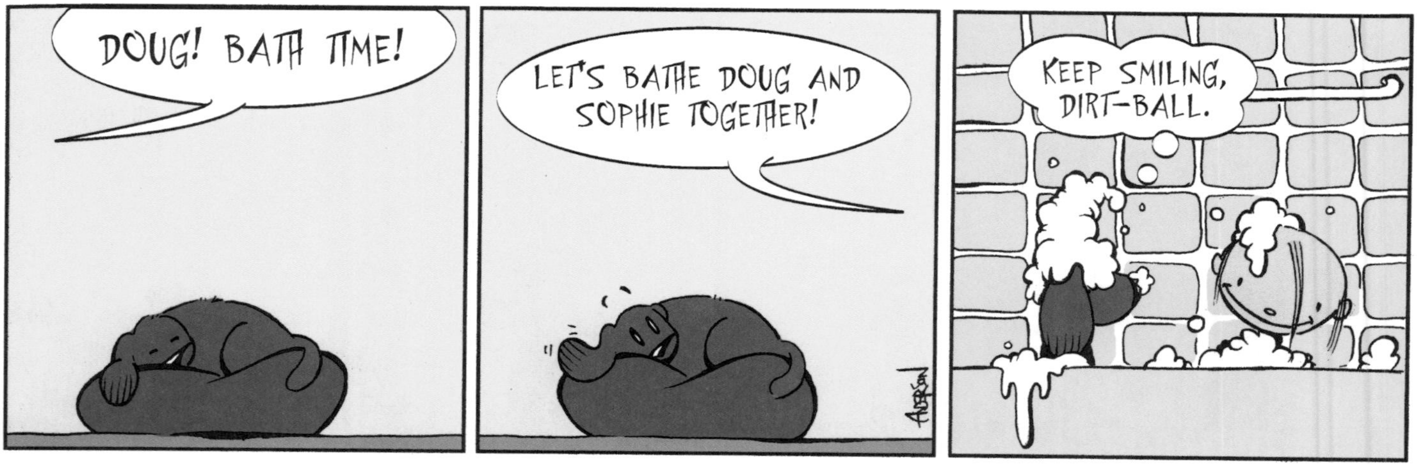
DOUG! BATH TIME!
LET'S BATHE DOUG AND SOPHIE TOGETHER!
ANDERSON
KEEP SMILING, DIRT-BALL.

THEY'RE NOT IN HERE.
NOTHING.
ANY LUCK?
TOYS
DAD SAID TO FIND THEM, BUT I DON'T SEE OUR PATIENCE ANYWHERE.

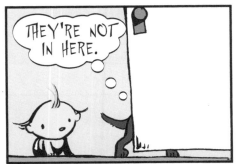

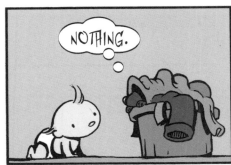

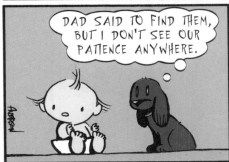

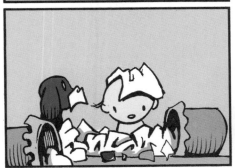

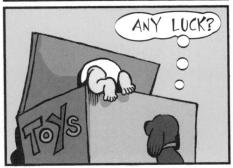

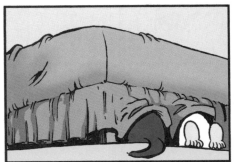

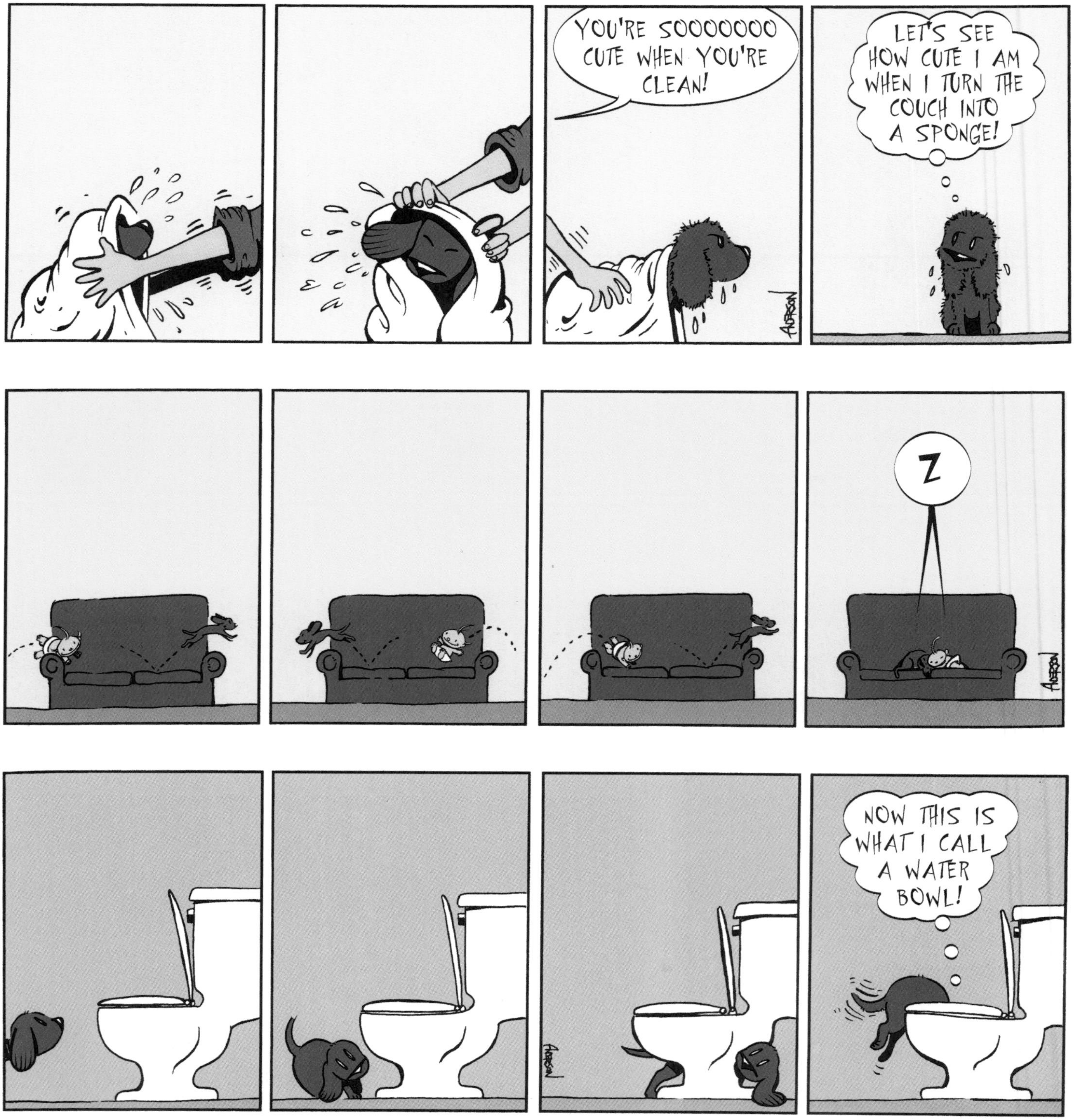
YOU'RE SOOOOOOO CUTE WHEN YOU'RE CLEAN!
LET'S SEE HOW CUTE I AM WHEN I TURN THE COUCH INTO A SPONGE!
Z
NOW THIS IS WHAT I CALL A WATER BOWL!

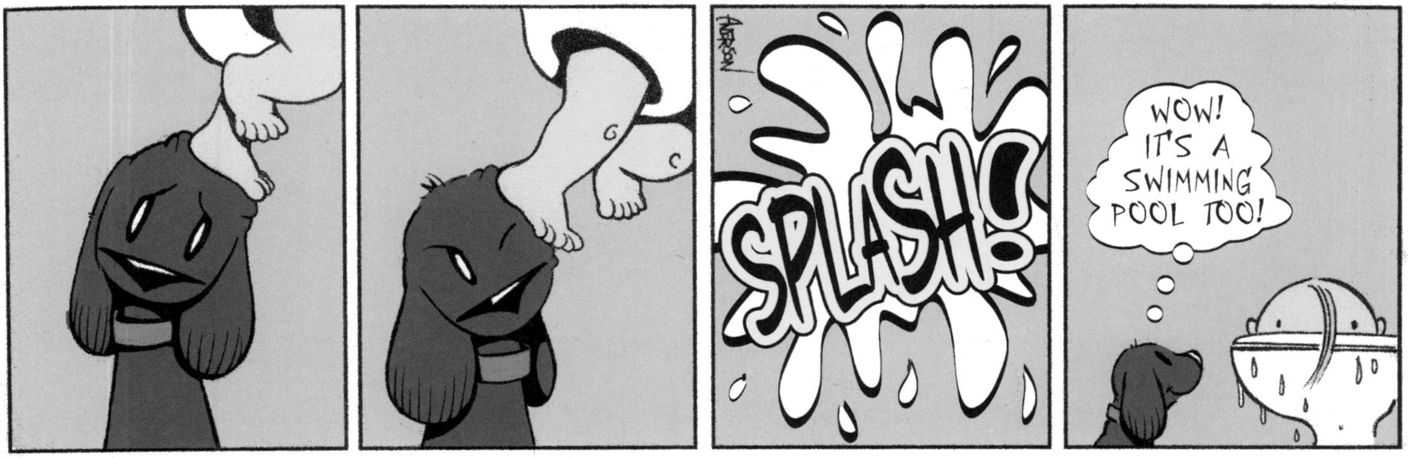
SPLASH!
WOW! IT'S A SWIMMING POOL TOO!

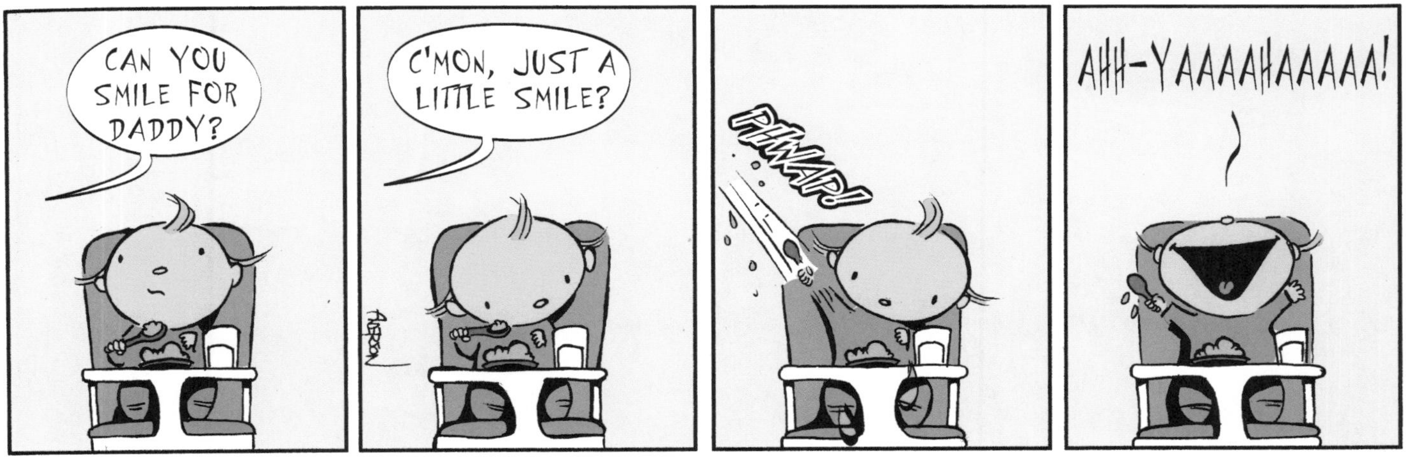
CAN YOU SMILE FOR DADDY?
C'MON, JUST A LITTLE SMILE?
PHWAP!
AHH-YAAAAHAAAAA!

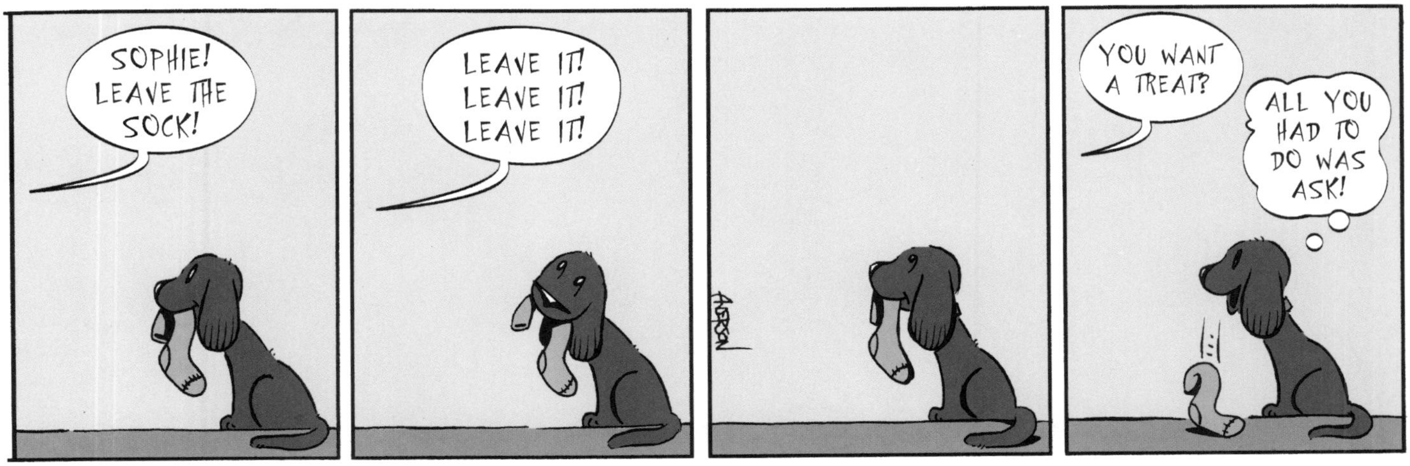
SOPHIE! LEAVE THE SOCK!
LEAVE IT! LEAVE IT! LEAVE IT!
YOU WANT A TREAT?
ALL YOU HAD TO DO WAS ASK!

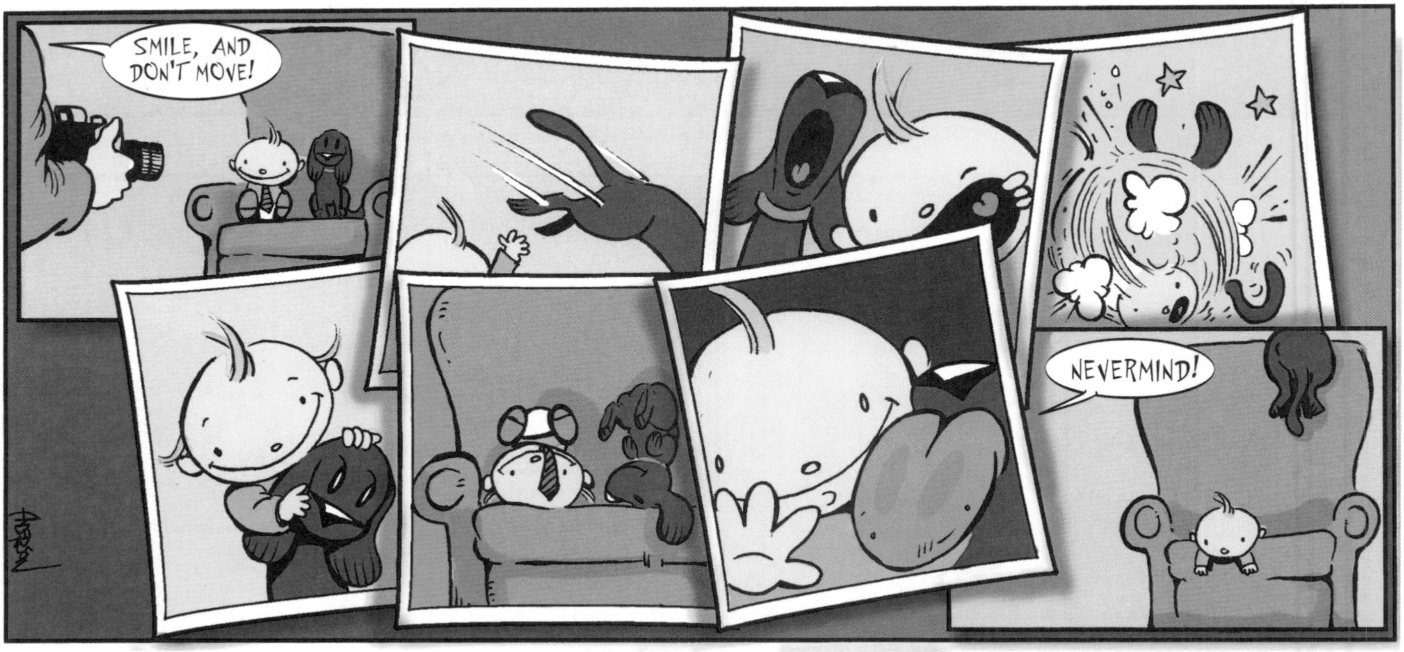
SMILE, AND DON'T MOVE!
NEVERMIND!

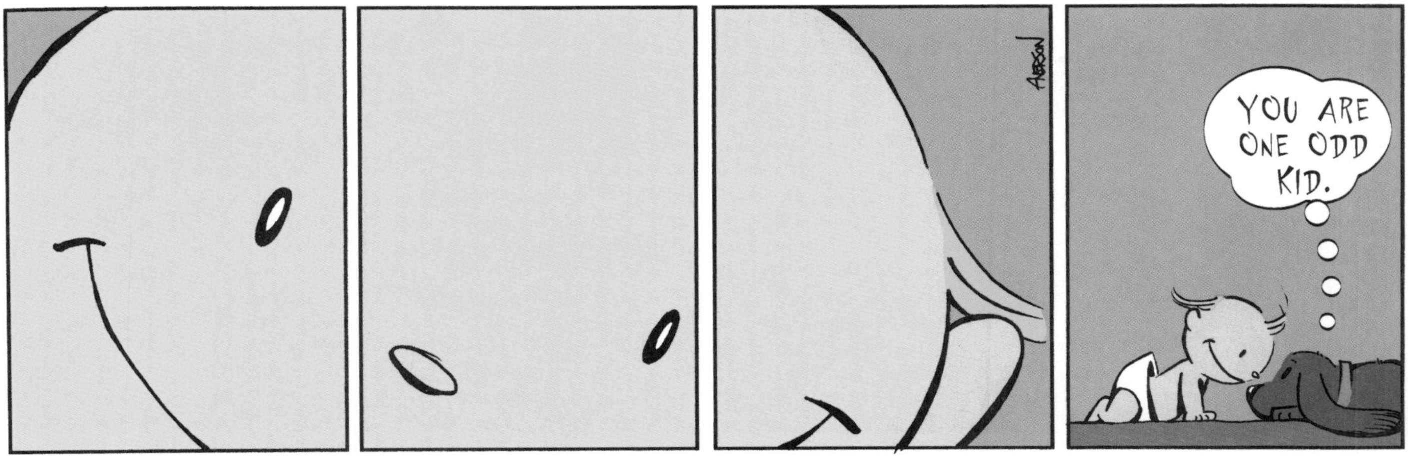
YOU ARE ONE ODD KID.

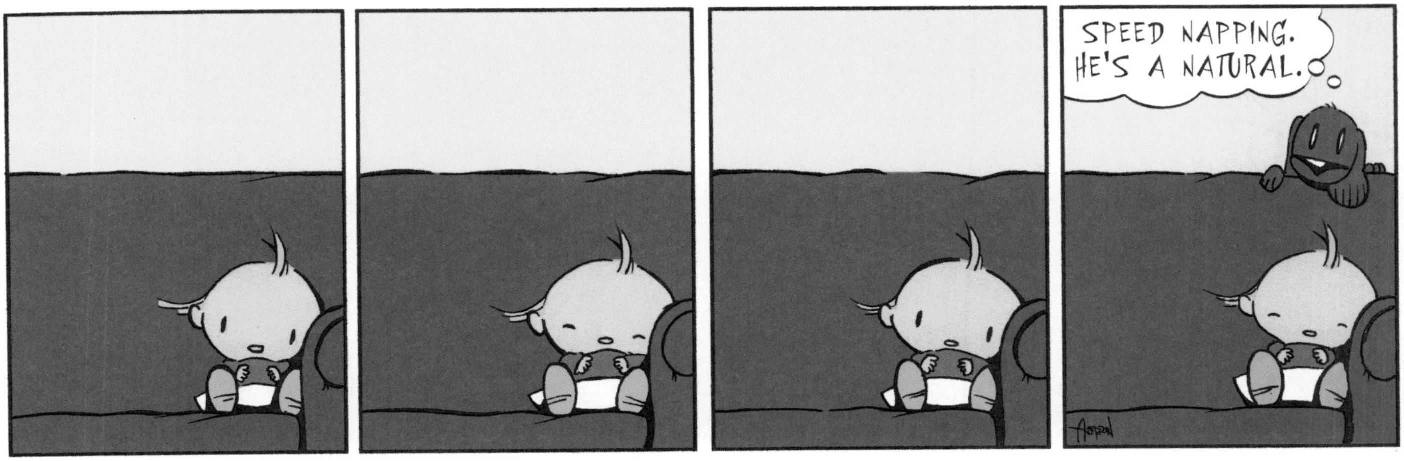
SPEED NAPPING. HE'S A NATURAL.

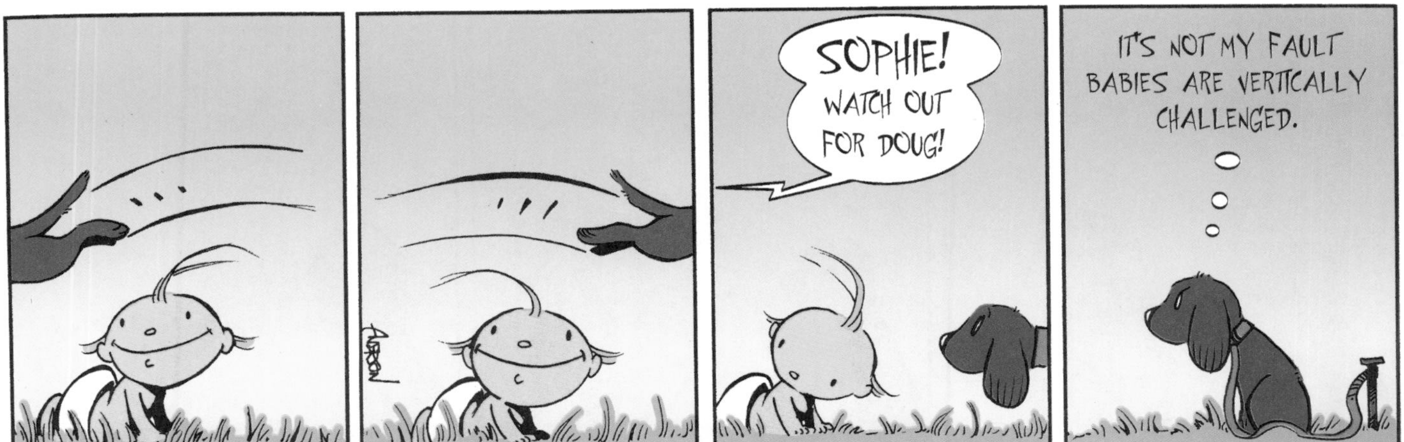
SOPHIE! WATCH OUT FOR DOUG!
IT'S NOT MY FAULT BABIES ARE VERTICALLY CHALLENGED.

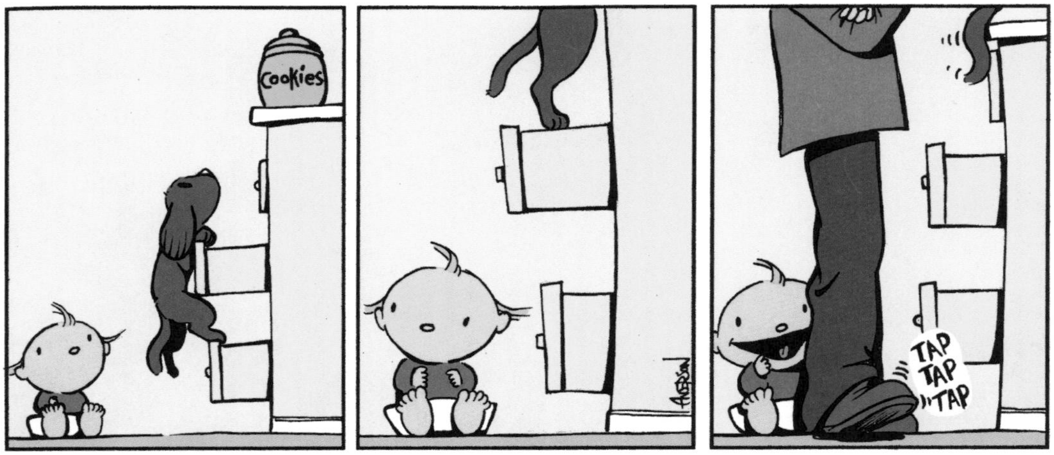
Cookies
TAP
TAP
TAP
NEXT TIME, I'LL BE THE LOOKOUT!

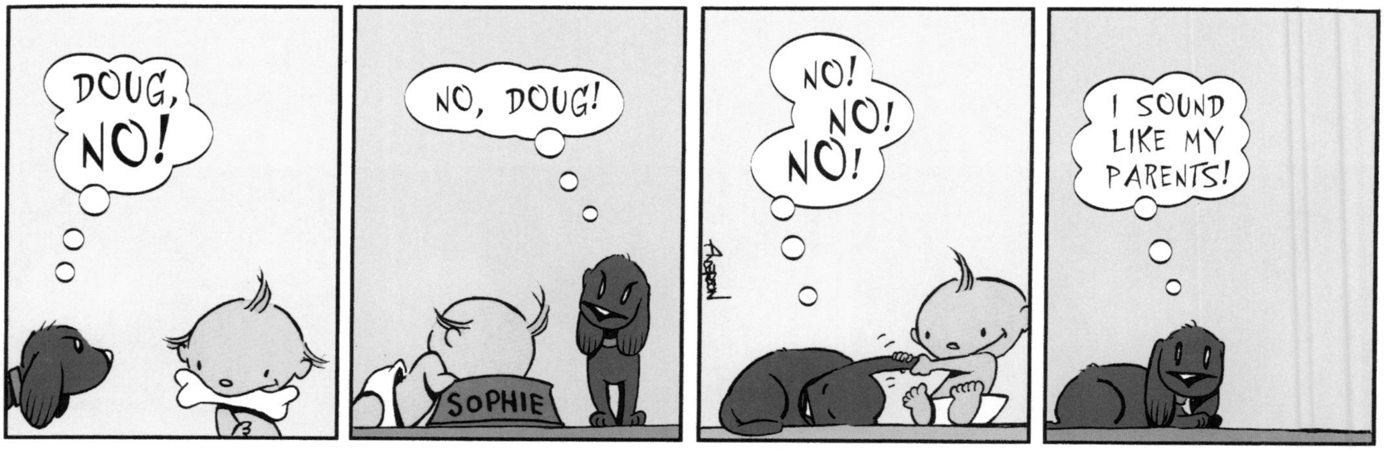
DOUG, NO!
SOPHIE
NO, DOUG!
NO! NO! NO!
I SOUND LIKE MY PARENTS!

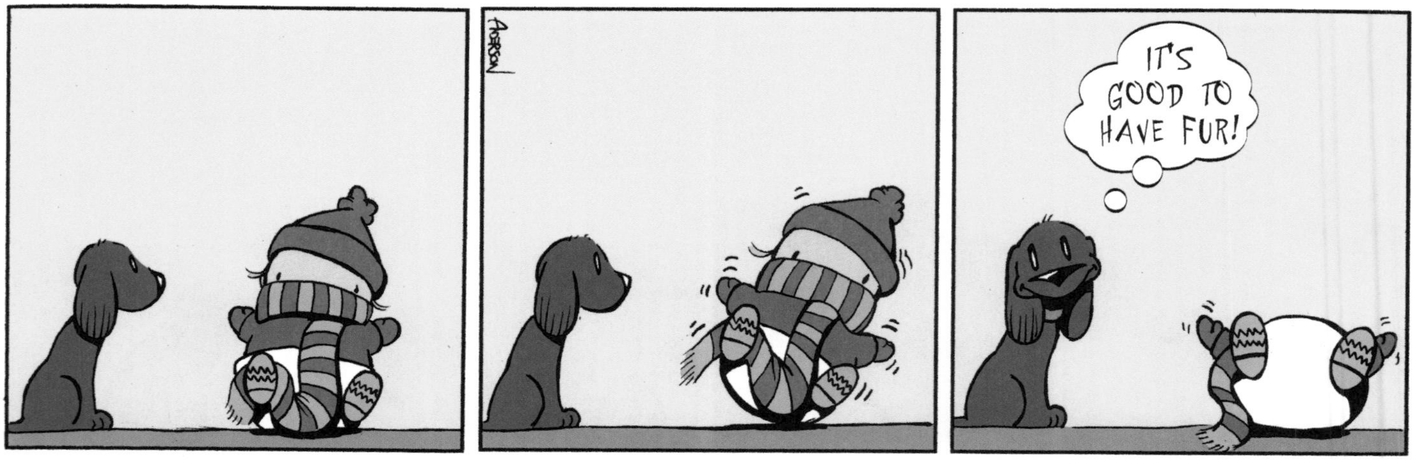
IT'S GOOD TO HAVE FUR!

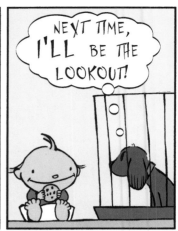

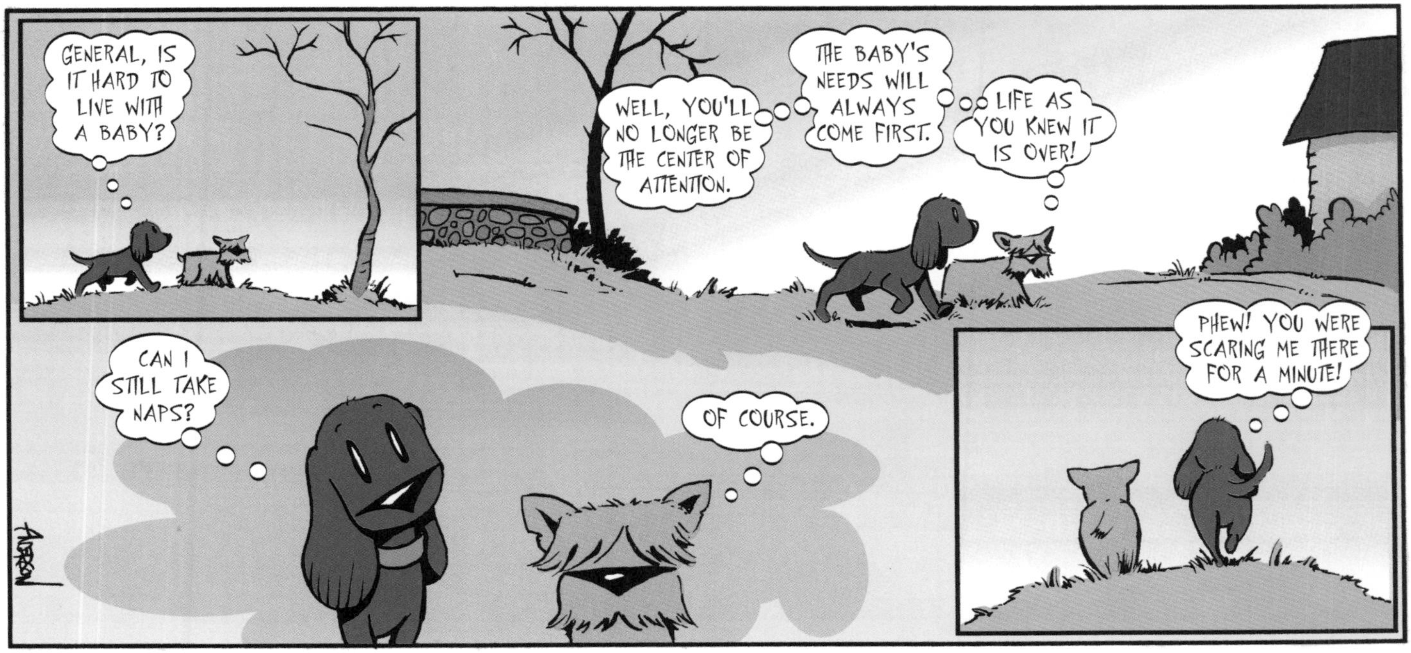
GENERAL, IS IT HARD TO LIVE WITH A BABY?
WELL, YOU'LL NO LONGER BE THE CENTER OF ATTENTION.
THE BABY'S NEEDS WILL ALWAYS COME FIRST.
LIFE AS YOU KNEW IT IS OVER!
CAN I STILL TAKE NAPS?
OF COURSE.
PHEW! YOU WERE SCARING ME THERE FOR A MINUTE!

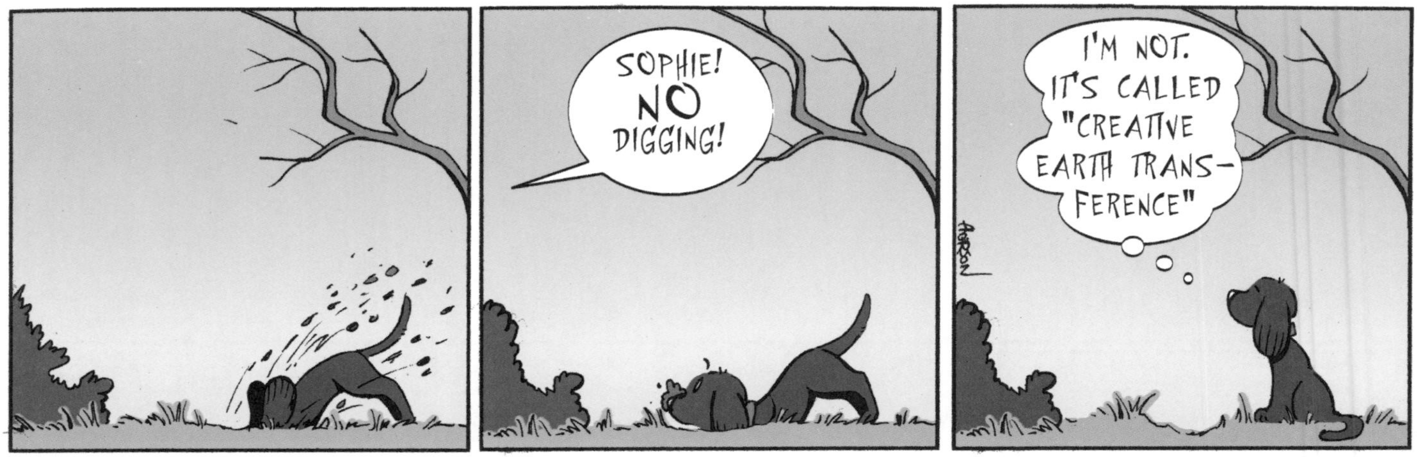
SOPHIE! NO DIGGING!
I'M NOT. IT'S CALLED "CREATIVE EARTH TRANS-FERENCE"

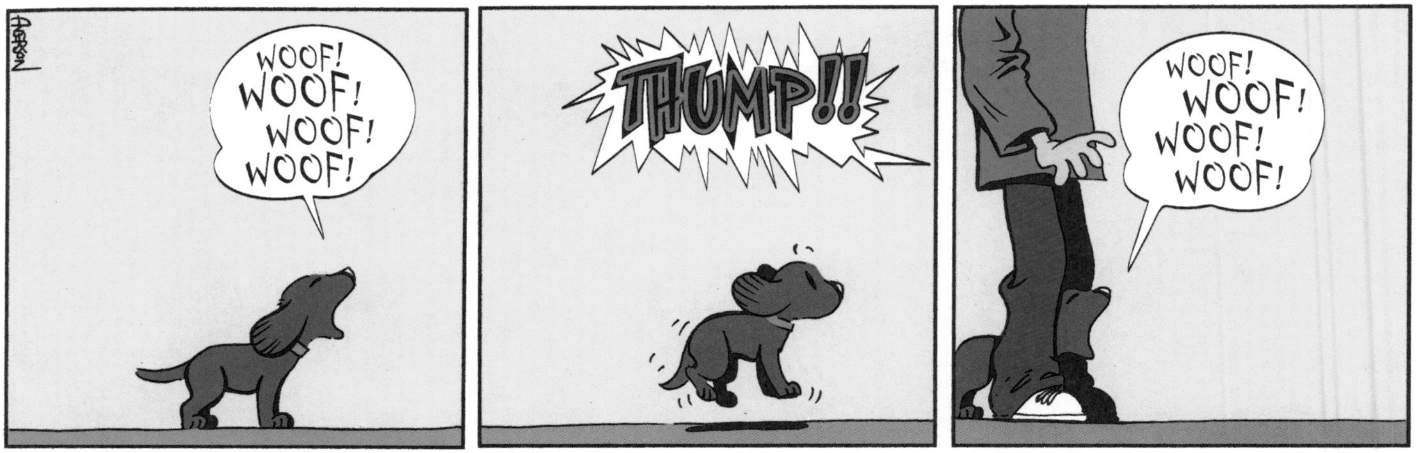
WOOF! WOOF! WOOF! WOOF!
THUMP!!
WOOF! WOOF! WOOF! WOOF!

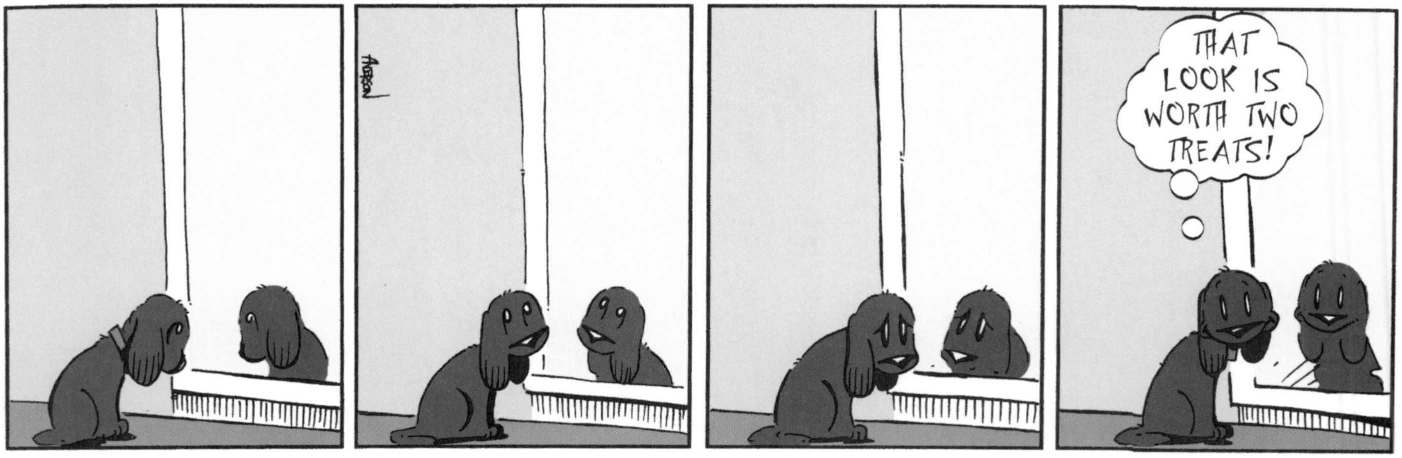
THAT LOOK IS WORTH TWO TREATS!

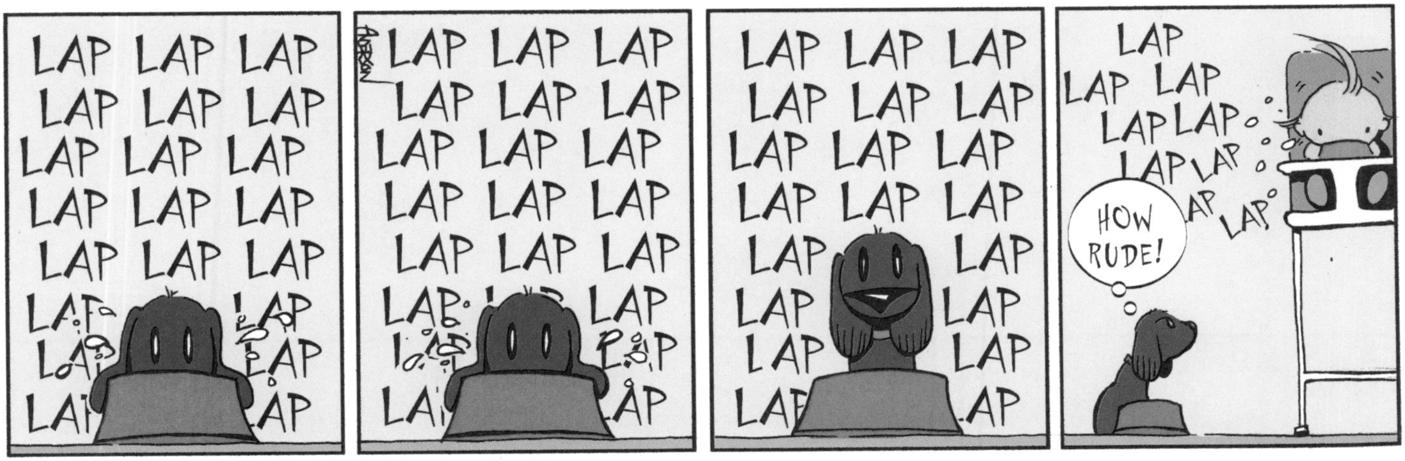
LAP LAP LAP
LAP LAP LAP
LAP LAP LAP
LAP LAP LAP
LAP LAP LAP
LAP LAP LAP
LAP LAP LAP
LAP LAP LAP
LAP LAP LAP
LAP LAP LAP
LAP LAP LAP
LAP LAP LAP
LAP LAP LAP
LAP LAP LAP
LAP LAP LAP
LAP LAP LAP
LAP LAP LAP LAP LAP LAP LAP
HOW RUDE!

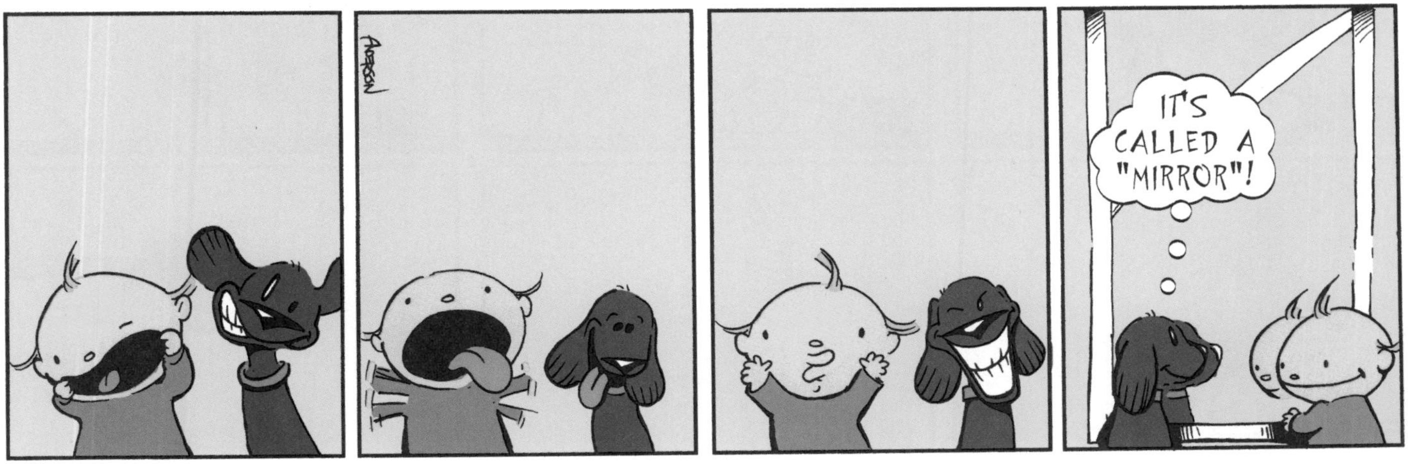
IT'S CALLED A "MIRROR"!

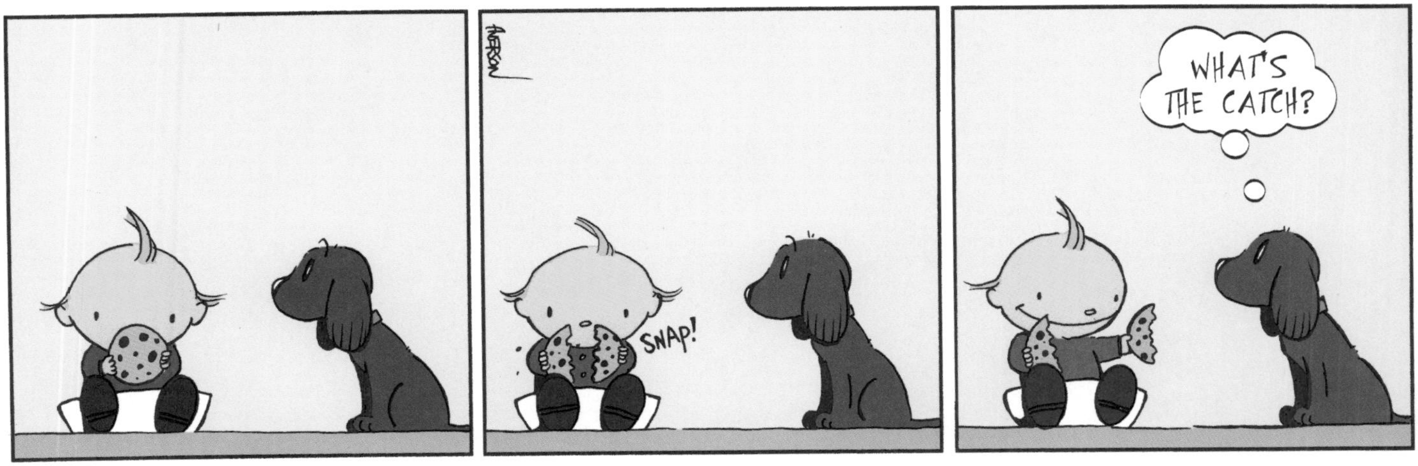
SNAP!
WHAT'S THE CATCH?

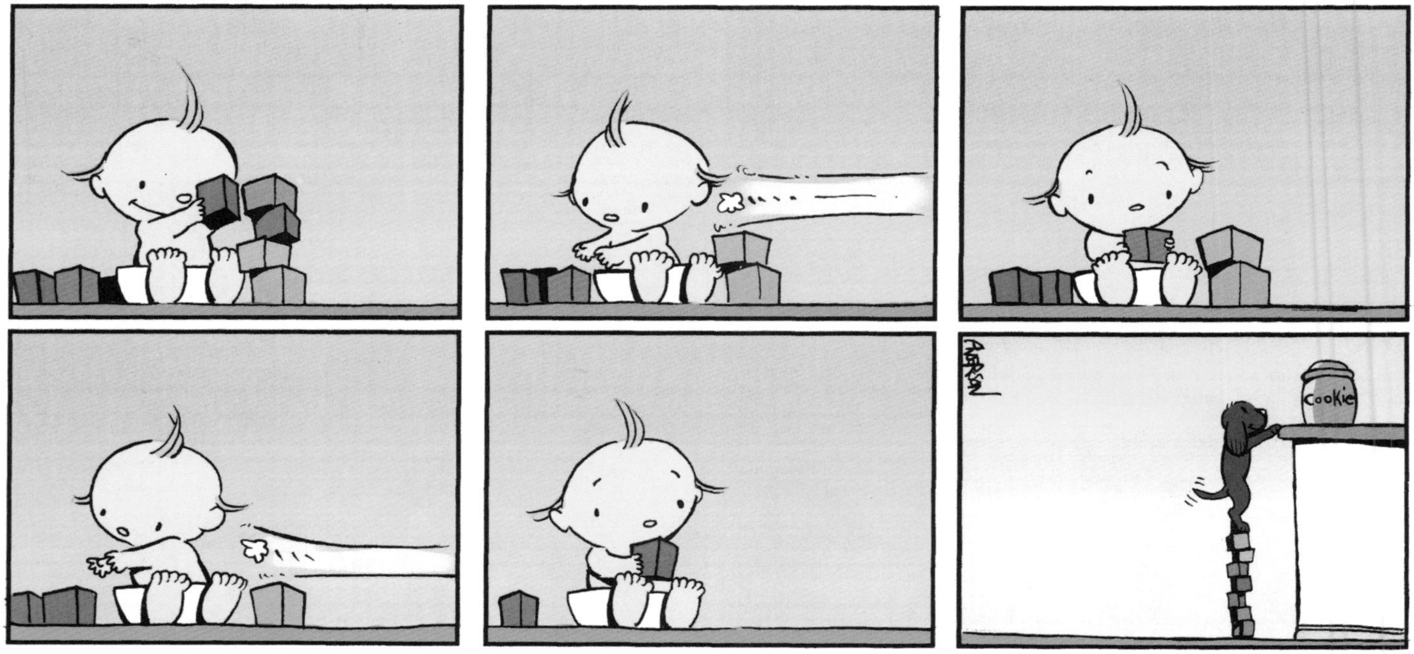
cookie

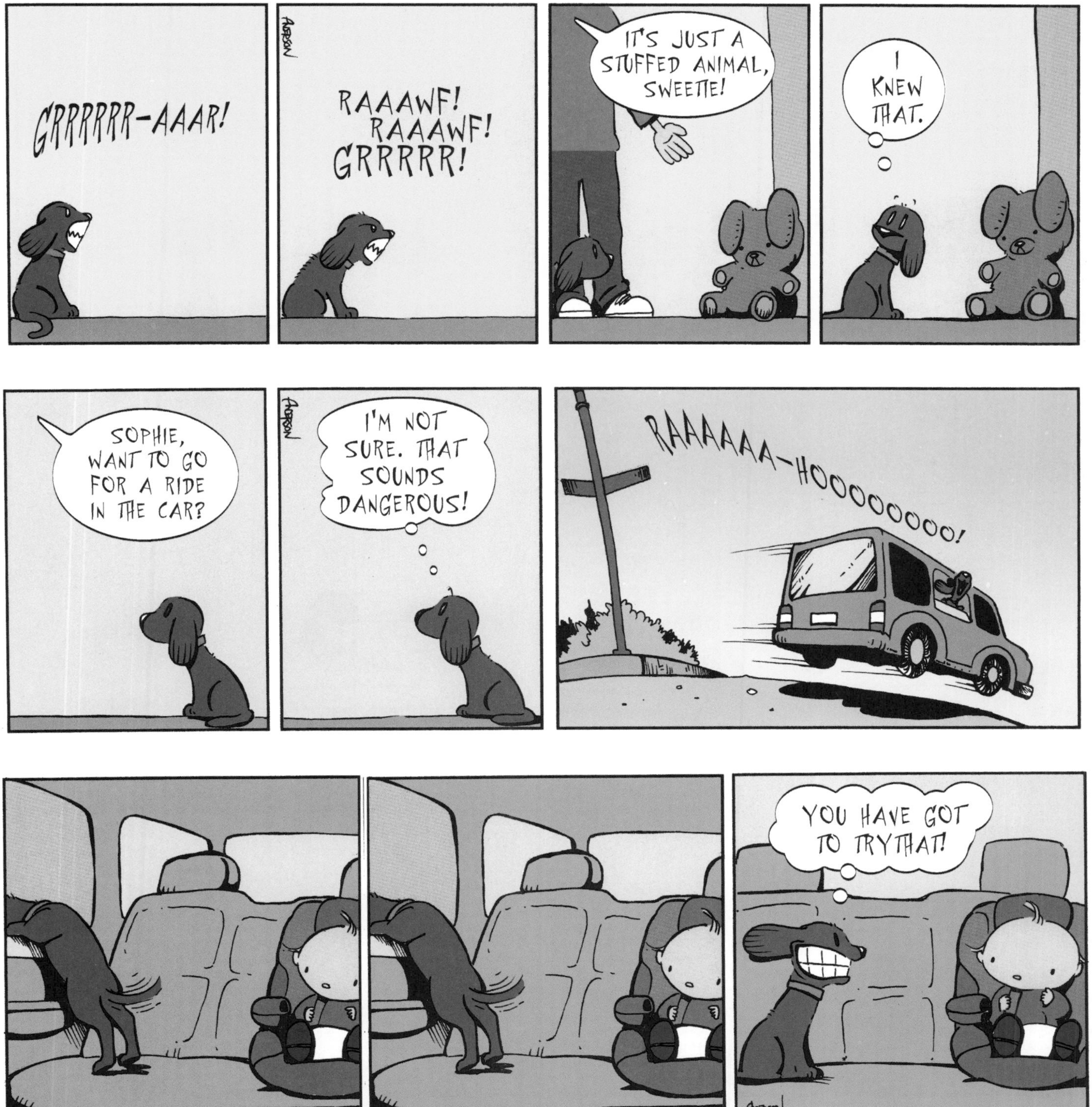
GRRRRRR-AAAR!
ANDERSON
RAAAWF! RAAAWF! GRRRRR!
IT'S JUST A STUFFED ANIMAL, SWEETIE!
I KNEW THAT.
SOPHIE, WANT TO GO FOR A RIDE IN THE CAR?
ANDERSON
I'M NOT SURE. THAT SOUNDS DANGEROUS!
RAAAAAA-HOOOOOOOOO!
YOU HAVE GOT TO TRY THAT!
ANDERSON

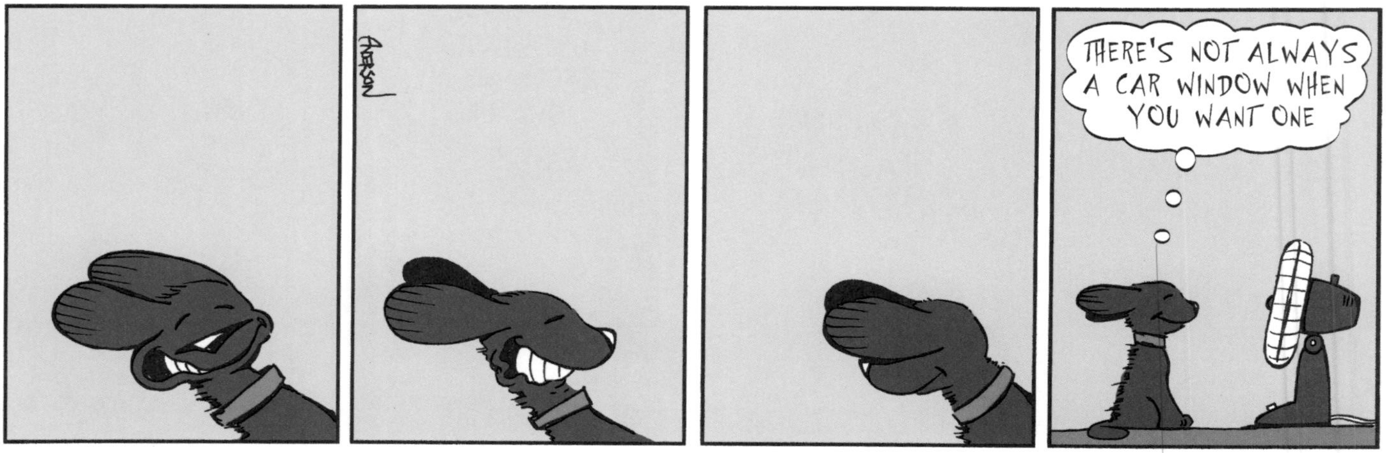
THERE'S NOT ALWAYS A CAR WINDOW WHEN YOU WANT ONE

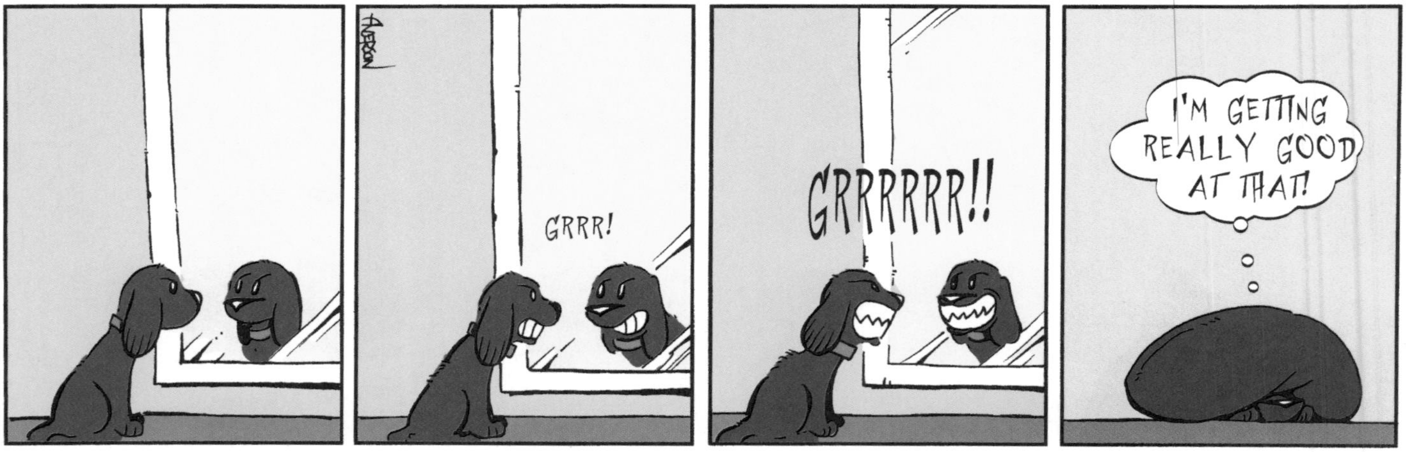
GRRR!
GRRRRRR!!
I'M GETTING REALLY GOOD AT THAT!

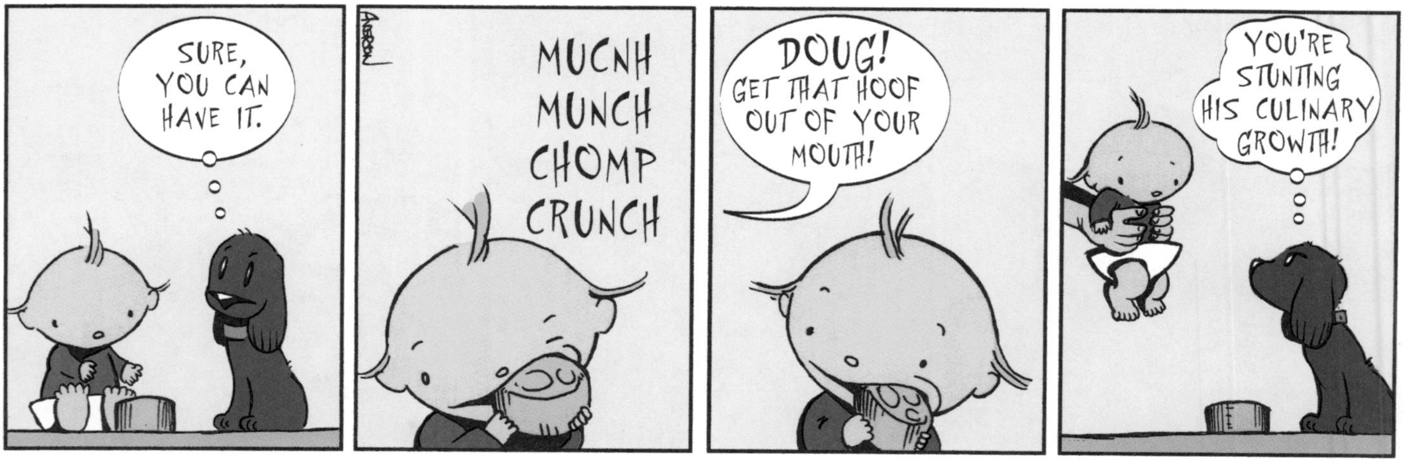
SURE, YOU CAN HAVE IT.
MUCNH
MUNCH
CHOMP
CRUNCH
DOUG! GET THAT HOOF OUT OF YOUR MOUTH!
YOU'RE STUNTING HIS CULINARY GROWTH!

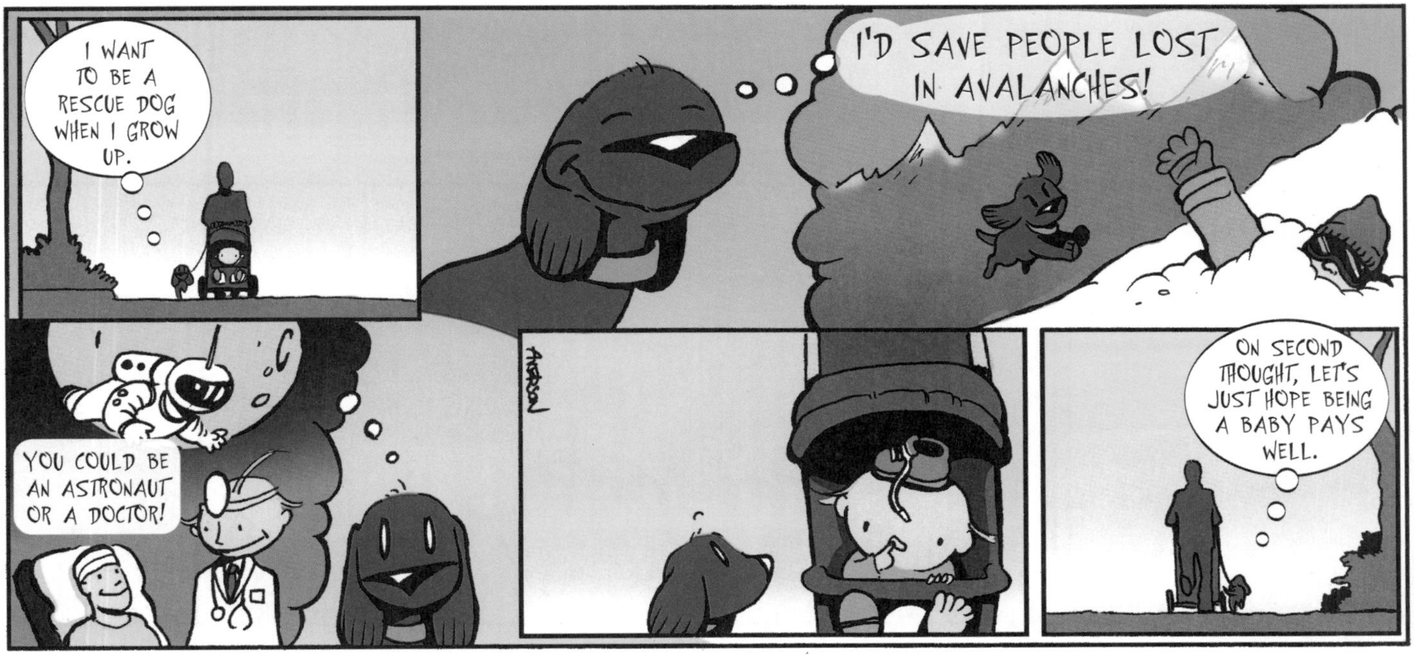
I WANT TO BE A RESCUE DOG WHEN I GROW UP.
I'D SAVE PEOPLE LOST IN AVALANCHES!
YOU COULD BE AN ASTRONAUT OR A DOCTOR!
ON SECOND THOUGHT, LET'S JUST HOPE BEING A BABY PAYS WELL.

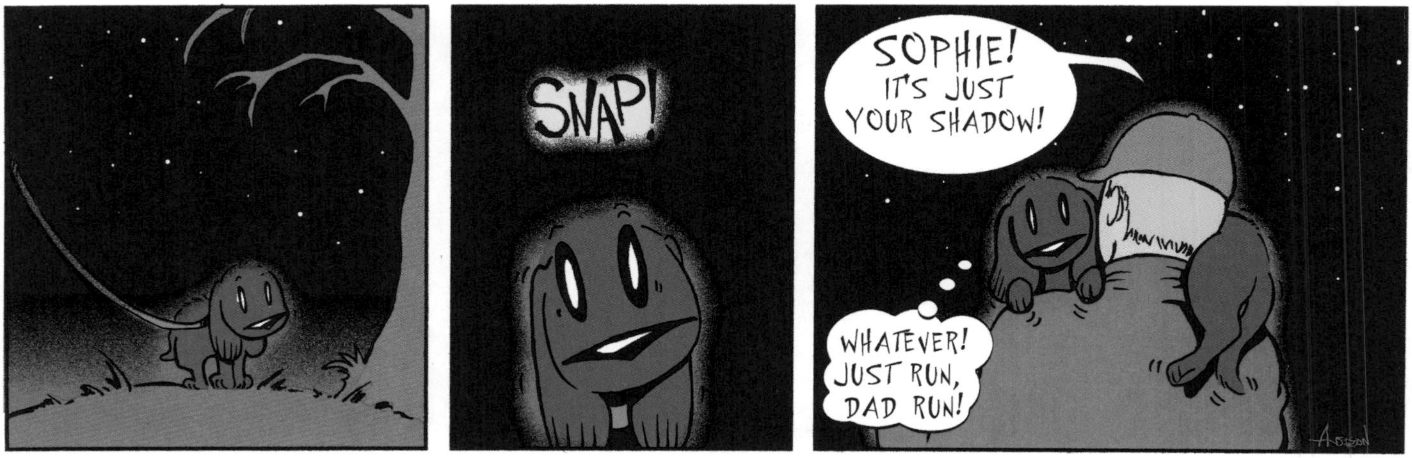
SNAP!
SOPHIE! IT'S JUST YOUR SHADOW!
WHATEVER! JUST RUN, DAD RUN!

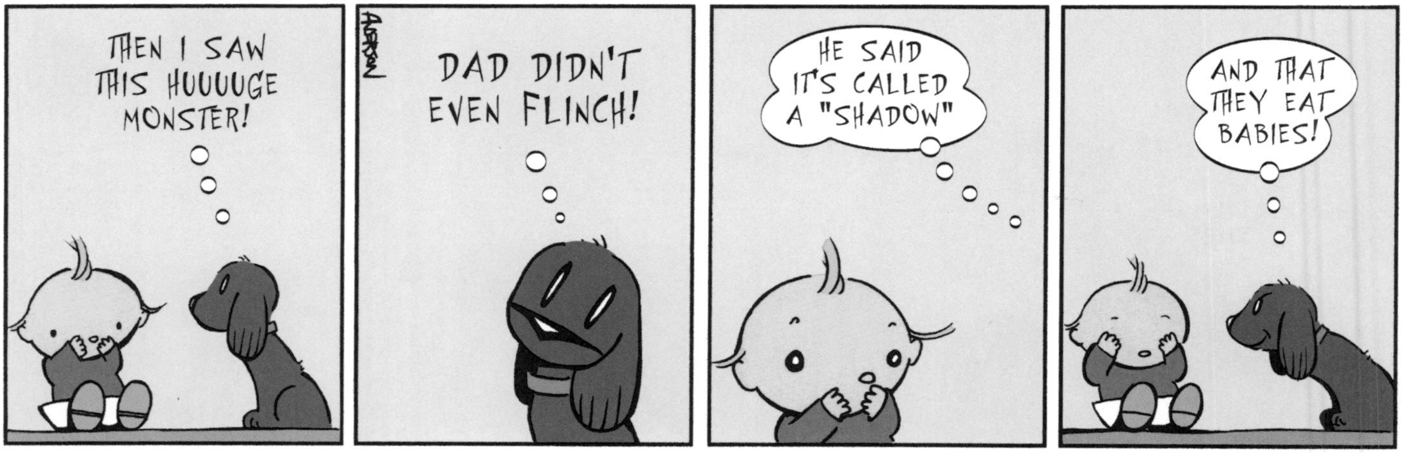
THEN I SAW THIS HUUUUGE MONSTER!
DAD DIDN'T EVEN FLINCH!
HE SAID IT'S CALLED A "SHADOW"
AND THAT THEY EAT BABIES!

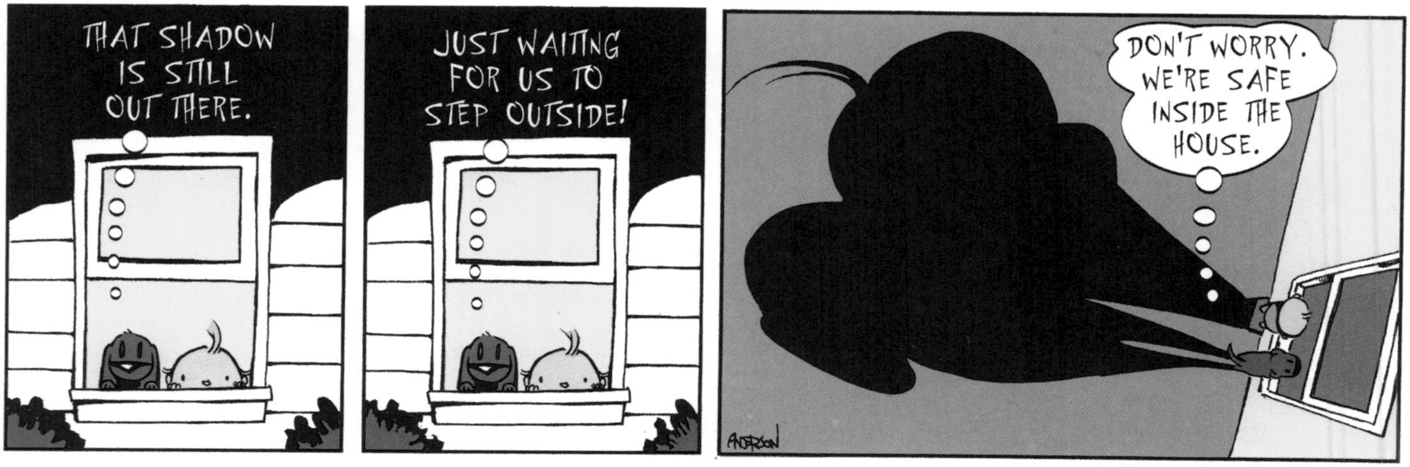
THAT SHADOW IS STILL OUT THERE.
JUST WAITING FOR US TO STEP OUTSIDE!
DON'T WORRY. WE'RE SAFE INSIDE THE HOUSE.

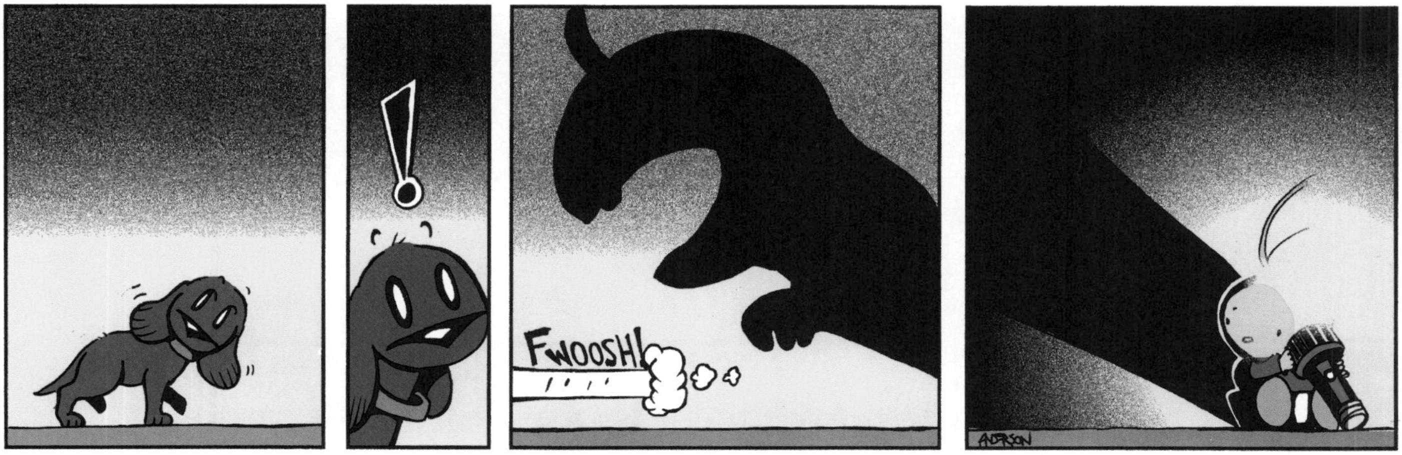
FWOOSH!

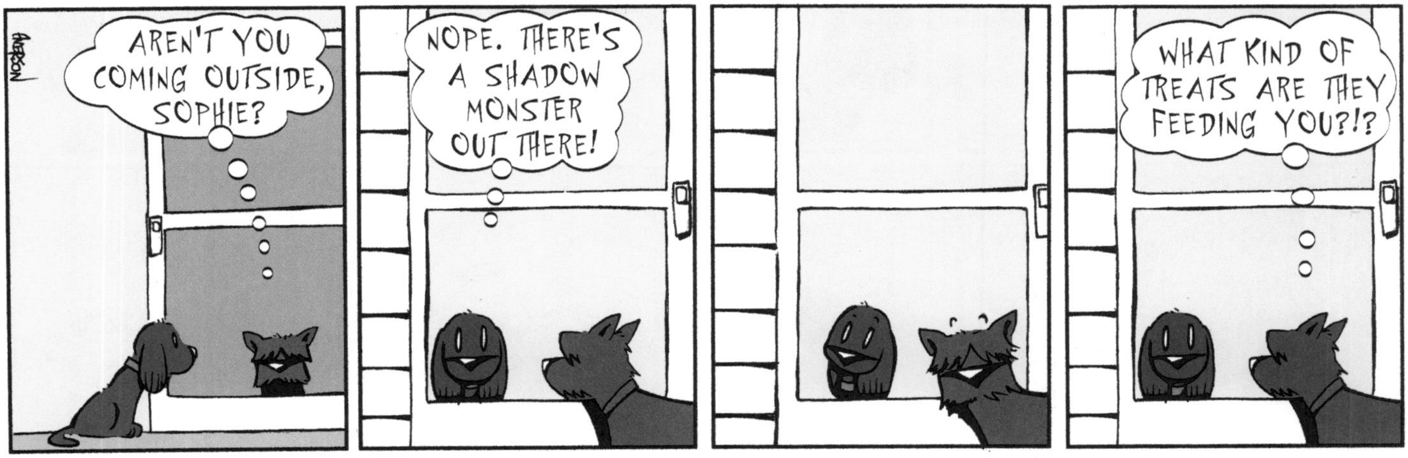
AREN'T YOU COMING OUTSIDE, SOPHIE?
NOPE. THERE'S A SHADOW MONSTER OUT THERE!
WHAT KIND OF TREATS ARE THEY FEEDING YOU?!?

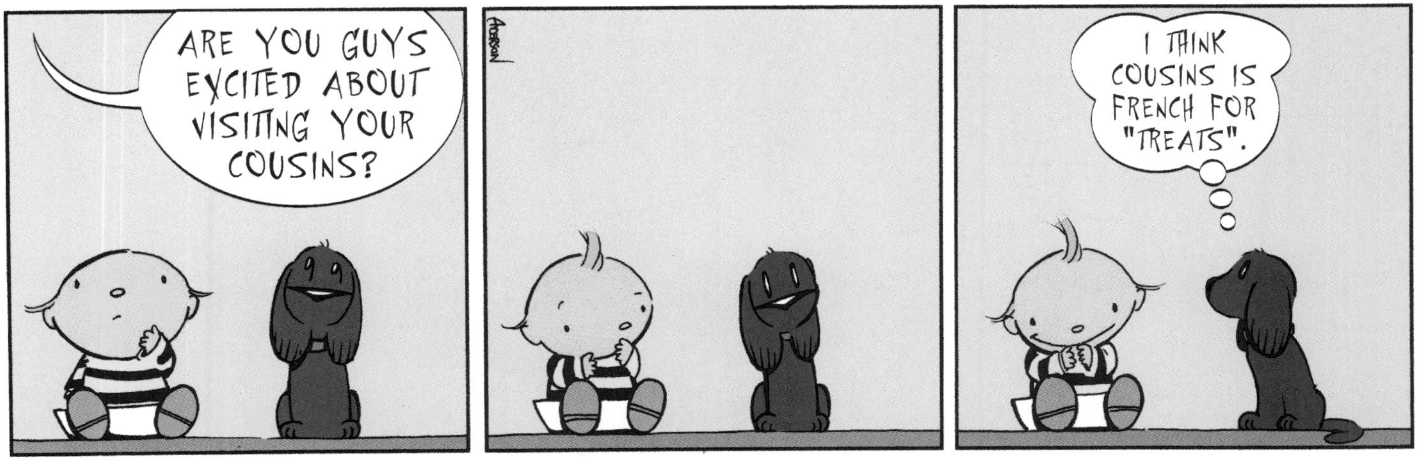
ARE YOU GUYS EXCITED ABOUT VISITING YOUR COUSINS?
I THINK COUSINS IS FRENCH FOR "TREATS".

LOOK WHAT MOMMY GOT YOU, DOUGIE!
HA! HA! HA! HA! HA! HA! HA!
WOW. THAT'S A GREAT LOOK...FOR A SEA URCHIN!
YOU LOOK LIKE A CLOWN WITH NO SENSE OF FASHION!
MOMMY DIDN'T FORGET YOU, SOPHIE!
THE IRONY IS BITING, ISN'T IT?
ANDERSON

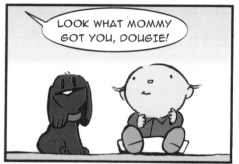

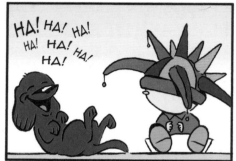

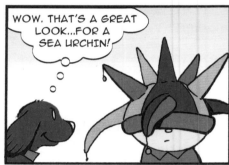

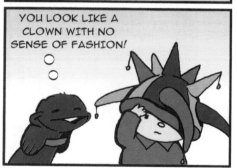

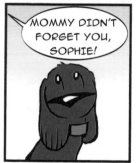

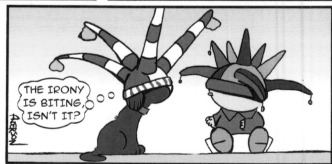

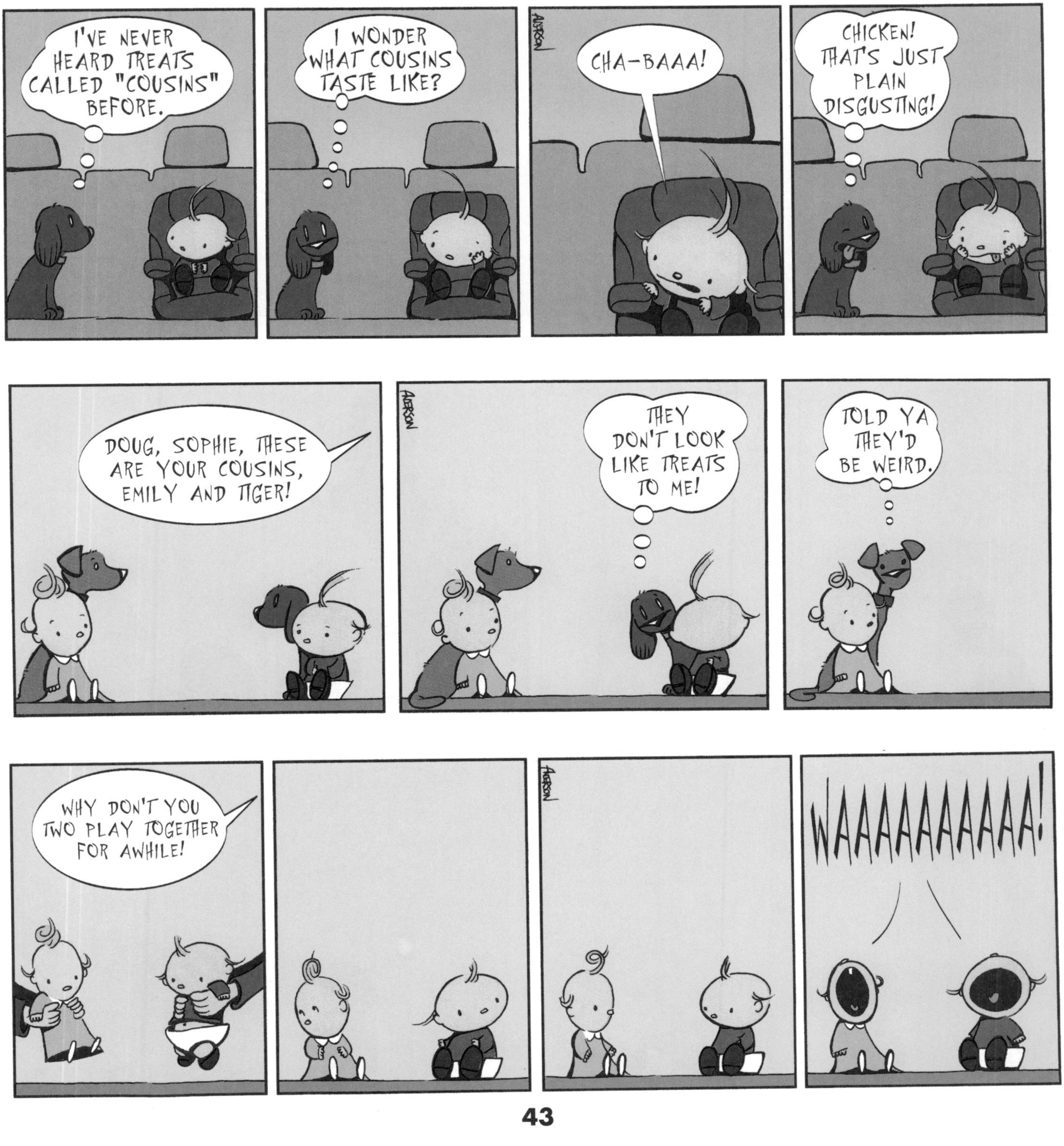
I'VE NEVER HEARD TREATS CALLED "COUSINS" BEFORE.
I WONDER WHAT COUSINS TASTE LIKE?
CHA-BAAA!
CHICKEN! THAT'S JUST PLAIN DISGUSTING!
DOUG, SOPHIE, THESE ARE YOUR COUSINS, EMILY AND TIGER!
THEY DON'T LOOK LIKE TREATS TO ME!
TOLD YA THEY'D BE WEIRD.
WHY DON'T YOU TWO PLAY TOGETHER FOR AWHILE!
WAAAAAAAAAA!

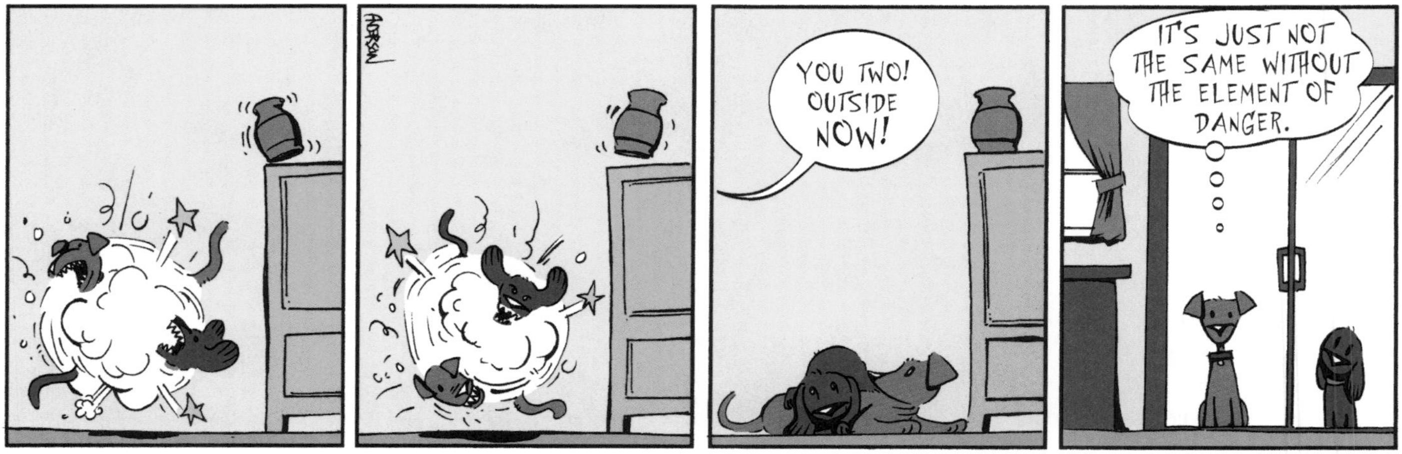
YOU TWO! OUTSIDE NOW!
IT'S JUST NOT THE SAME WITHOUT THE ELEMENT OF DANGER.

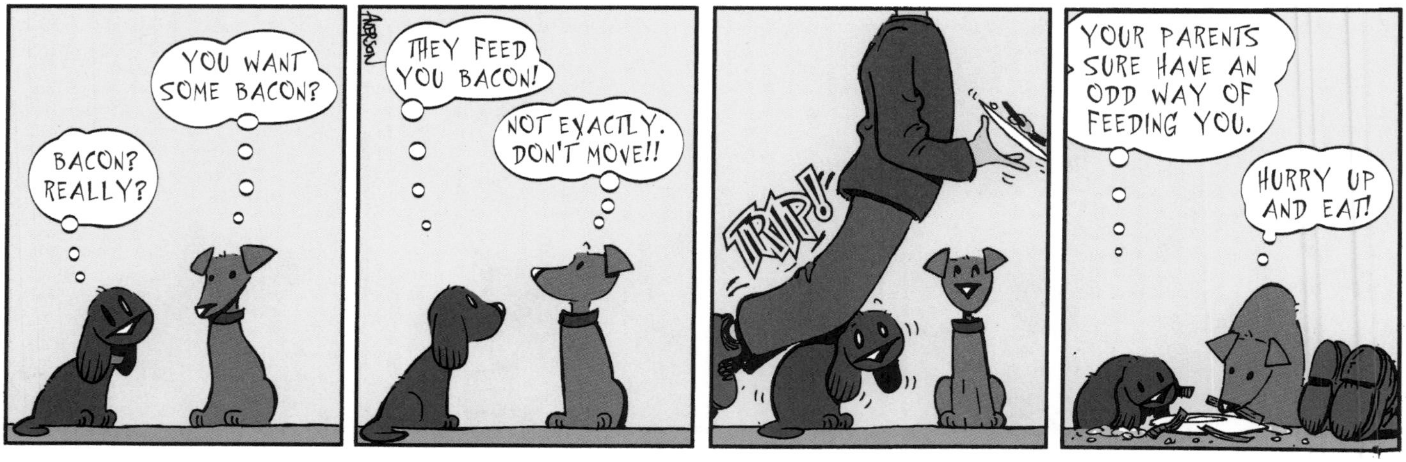
YOU WANT SOME BACON?
BACON? REALLY?
THEY FEED YOU BACON!
NOT EXACTLY. DON'T MOVE!!
TRIP!
YOUR PARENTS SURE HAVE AN ODD WAY OF FEEDING YOU.
HURRY UP AND EAT!

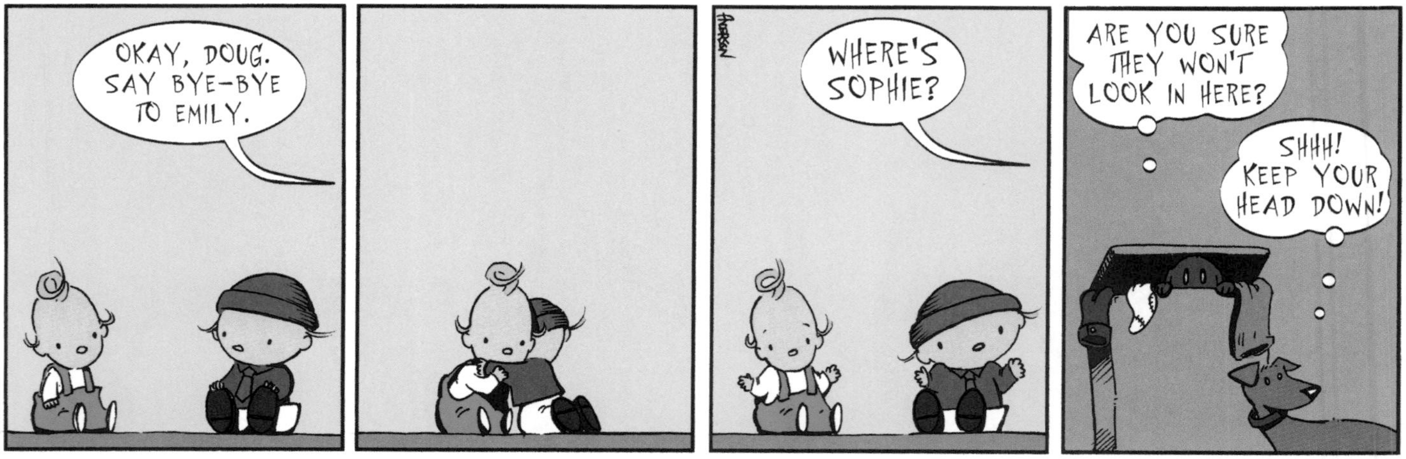
OKAY, DOUG. SAY BYE-BYE TO EMILY.
WHERE'S SOPHIE?
ARE YOU SURE THEY WON'T LOOK IN HERE?
SHHH! KEEP YOUR HEAD DOWN!

I'VE FIGURED YOU OUT, SHADOW!
YOU'RE ATTACHED TO ME!
AND YOU HAVE TO DO WHATEVER I WANT!
I'M NOT SCARED OF YOU ANYMORE!
SO-SO!
FWOOOSH!
HONEY, DID YOU KNOW SOPHIE COULD CLIMB TREES?!?

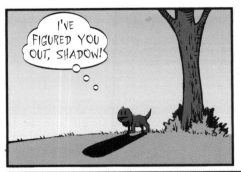

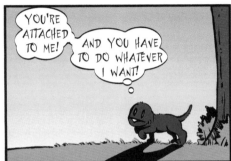

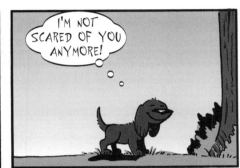

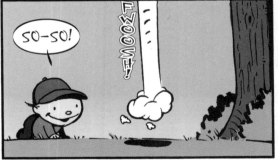

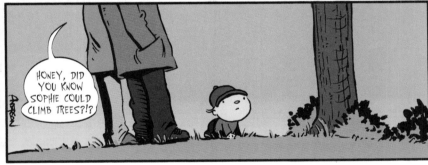

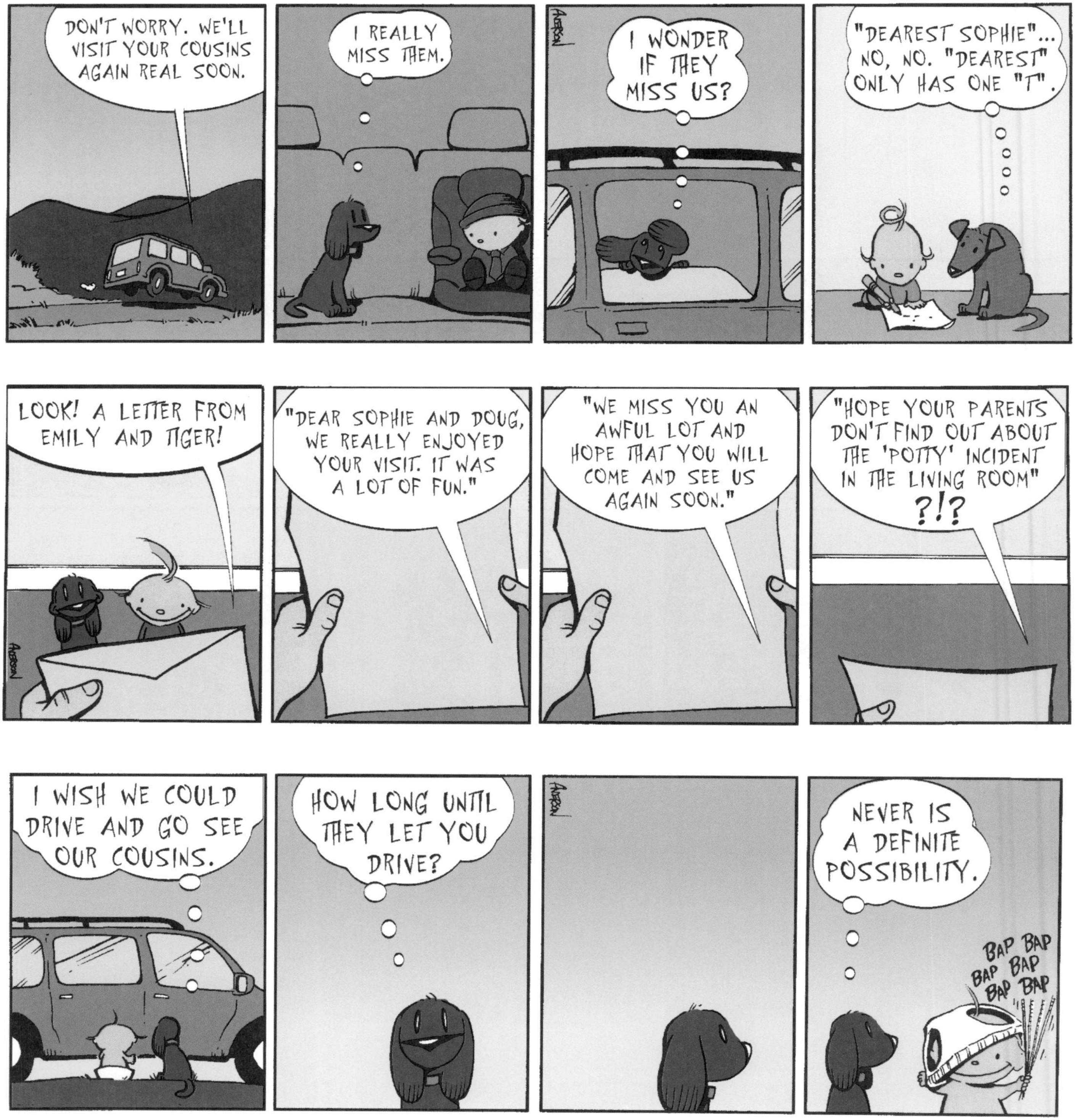
DON'T WORRY. WE'LL VISIT YOUR COUSINS AGAIN REAL SOON.
I REALLY MISS THEM.
I WONDER IF THEY MISS US?
"DEAREST SOPHIE"... NO, NO. "DEAREST" ONLY HAS ONE "T".
LOOK! A LETTER FROM EMILY AND TIGER!
"DEAR SOPHIE AND DOUG, WE REALLY ENJOYED YOUR VISIT. IT WAS A LOT OF FUN."
"WE MISS YOU AN AWFUL LOT AND HOPE THAT YOU WILL COME AND SEE US AGAIN SOON."
"HOPE YOUR PARENTS DON'T FIND OUT ABOUT THE 'POTTY' INCIDENT IN THE LIVING ROOM"
?!?
I WISH WE COULD DRIVE AND GO SEE OUR COUSINS.
HOW LONG UNTIL THEY LET YOU DRIVE?
NEVER IS A DEFINITE POSSIBILITY.
BAP BAP BAP BAP BAP BAP

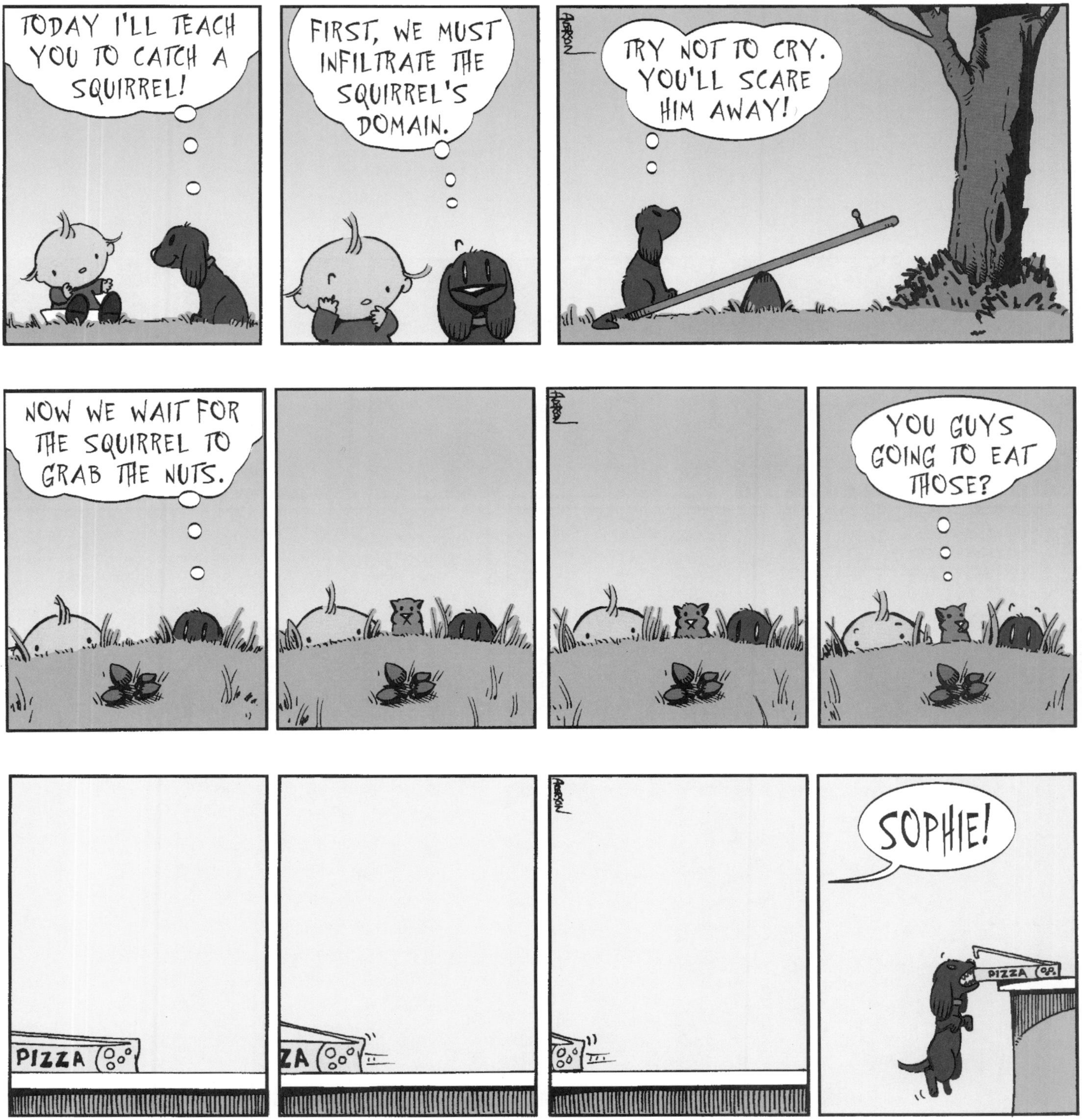
TODAY I'LL TEACH YOU TO CATCH A SQUIRREL!
FIRST, WE MUST INFILTRATE THE SQUIRREL'S DOMAIN.
TRY NOT TO CRY. YOU'LL SCARE HIM AWAY!
NOW WE WAIT FOR THE SQUIRREL TO GRAB THE NUTS.
YOU GUYS GOING TO EAT THOSE?
PIZZA
ZA
SOPHIE!
PIZZA

LET'S CATCH SOME SQUIRRELS.
COOL! I'VE NEVER DONE THAT!
REALLY? WHAT DO YOU HUNT AT HOME?
MOTHS!
QUITE THE PREDATOR, AREN'T WE.
YAH! YOU SHOULD SEE THEM MOVE!
YOU GO THAT WAY. DON'T WORRY IF YOU DON'T CATCH ANY THE FIRST TIME.
I CAUGHT ONE!
CONGRATULATIONS. YOU JUST BAGGED YOUR FIRST PLASTIC DEER.
ANDERSON

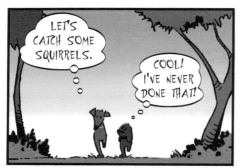

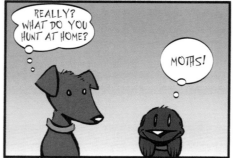

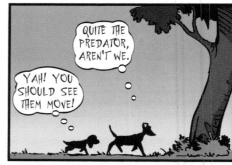

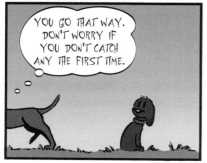

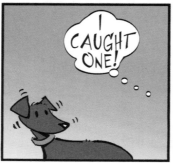

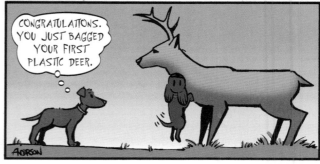

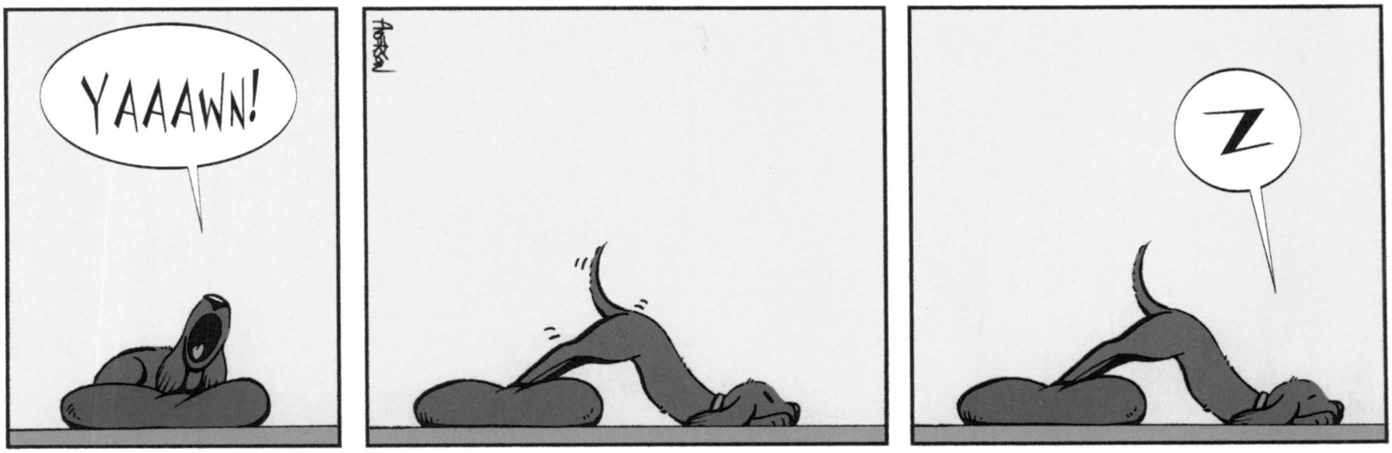
YAAAWN!
Z

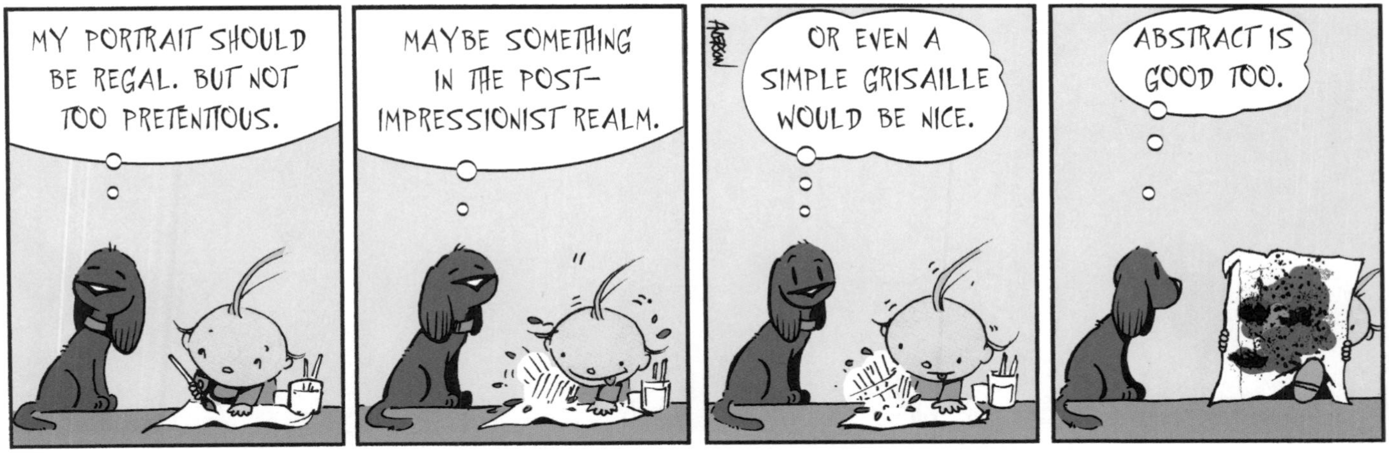
MY PORTRAIT SHOULD BE REGAL. BUT NOT TOO PRETENTIOUS.
MAYBE SOMETHING IN THE POST-IMPRESSIONIST REALM.
OR EVEN A SIMPLE GRISAILLE WOULD BE NICE.
ABSTRACT IS GOOD TOO.

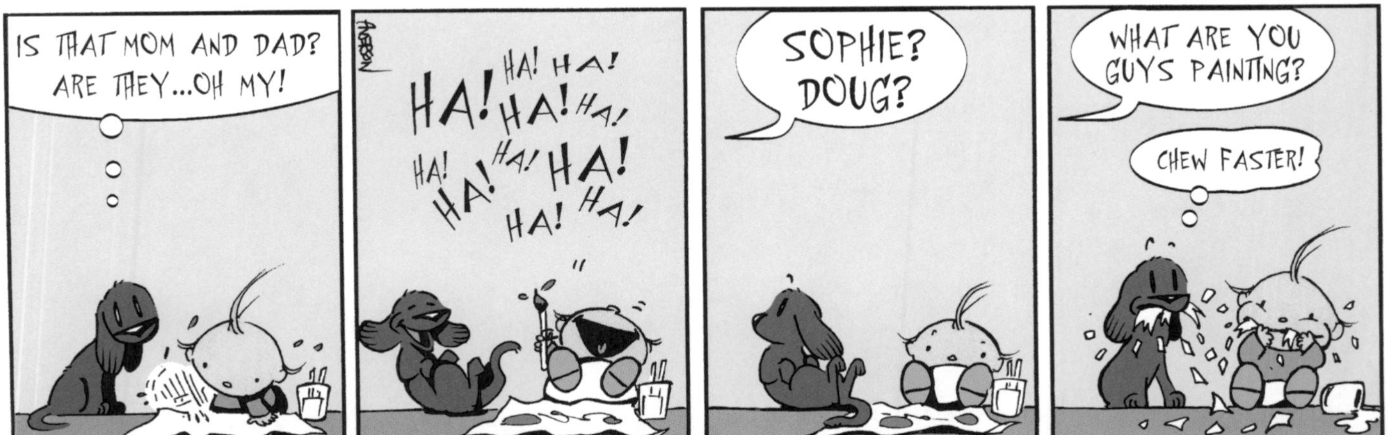
IS THAT MOM AND DAD? ARE THEY...OH MY!
HA! HA! HA! HA! HA! HA! HA! HA! HA! HA! HA! HA!
SOPHIE? DOUG?
WHAT ARE YOU GUYS PAINTING?
CHEW FASTER!

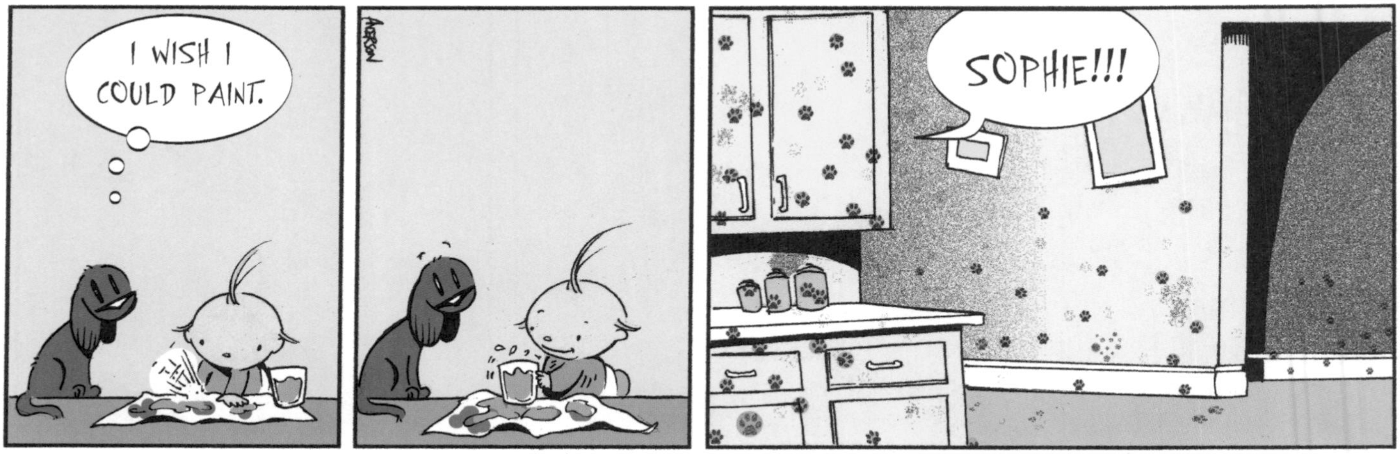
I WISH I COULD PAINT.
SOPHIE!!!

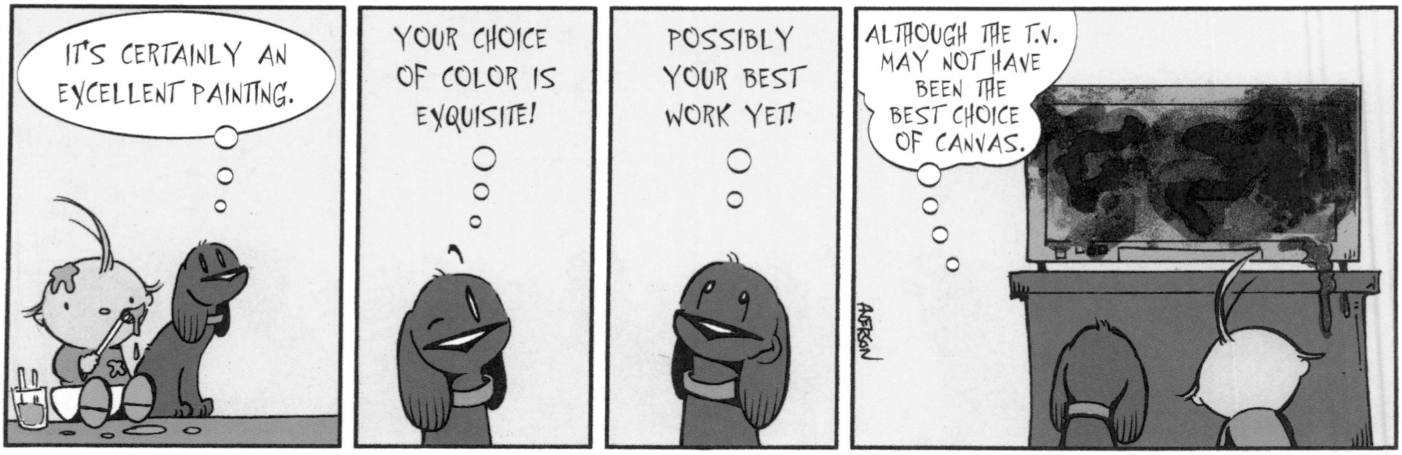
IT'S CERTAINLY AN EXCELLENT PAINTING.
YOUR CHOICE OF COLOR IS EXQUISITE!
POSSIBLY YOUR BEST WORK YET!
ALTHOUGH THE T.V. MAY NOT HAVE BEEN THE BEST CHOICE OF CANVAS.

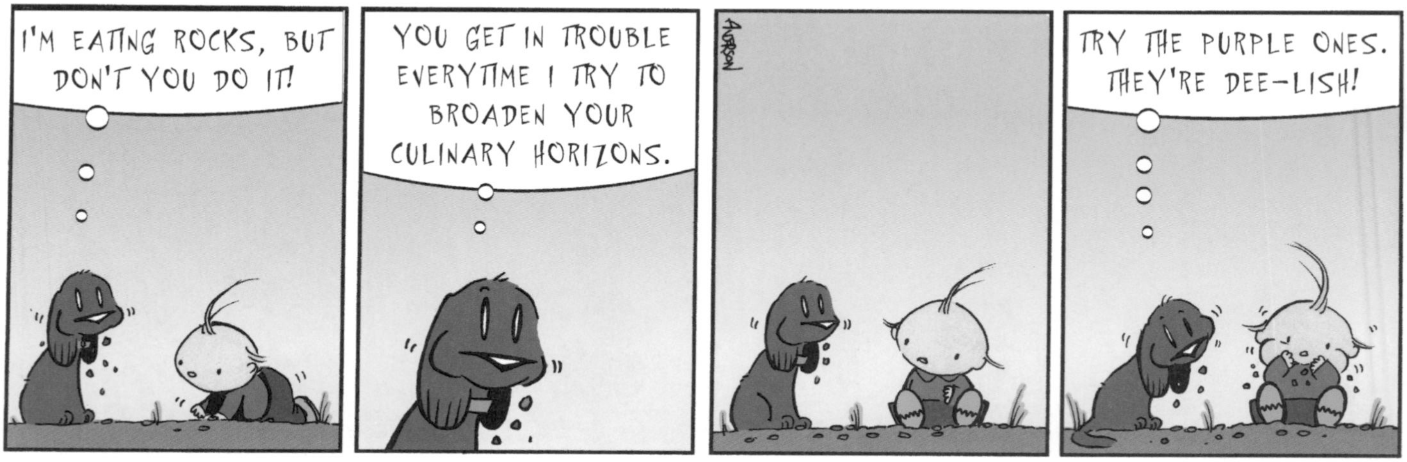
I'M EATING ROCKS, BUT DON'T YOU DO IT!
YOU GET IN TROUBLE EVERYTIME I TRY TO BROADEN YOUR CULINARY HORIZONS.
TRY THE PURPLE ONES. THEY'RE DEE-LISH!

WHAT ARE YOU GUYS DOING?
CATCHING A SQUIRREL.
DO YOU KNOW WHAT SQUIRRELS LOOK LIKE?
ANDERSON
DO YOU?
YAH. THERE'S ONE RIGHT OVER THERE!
THANKS! LET'S GO GET 'IM, DOUG!
GOOD LUCK!

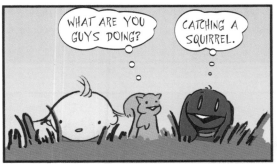

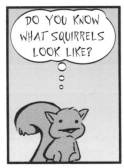

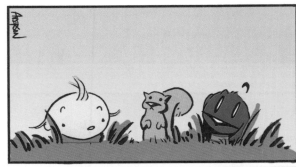

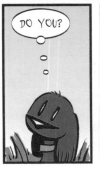

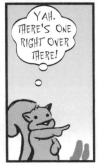

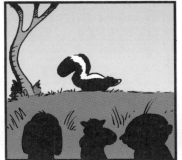

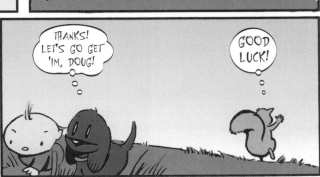

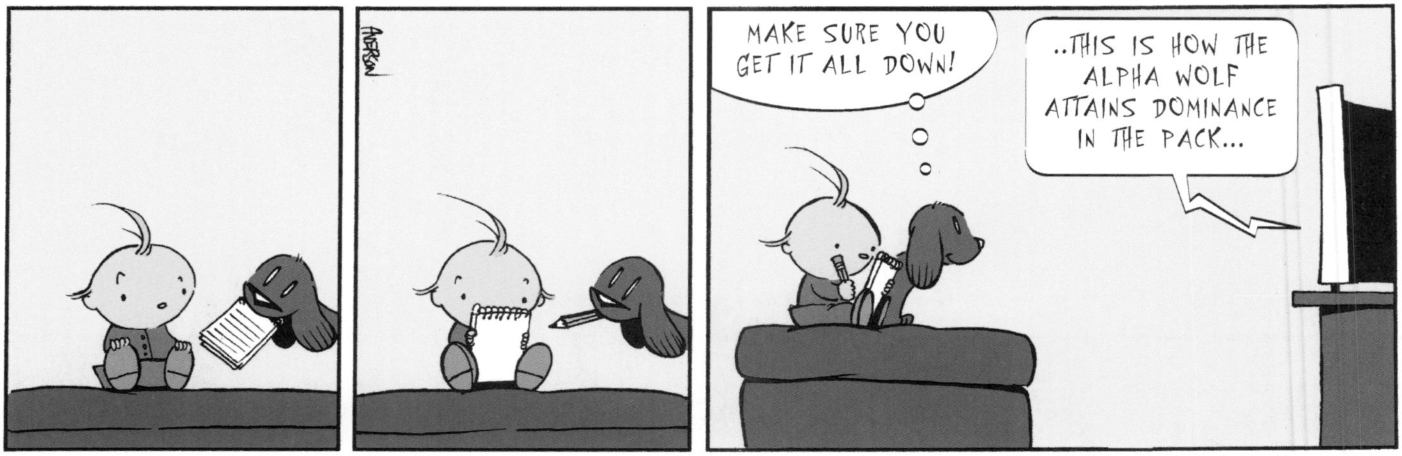
MAKE SURE YOU GET IT ALL DOWN!
..THIS IS HOW THE ALPHA WOLF ATTAINS DOMINANCE IN THE PACK...

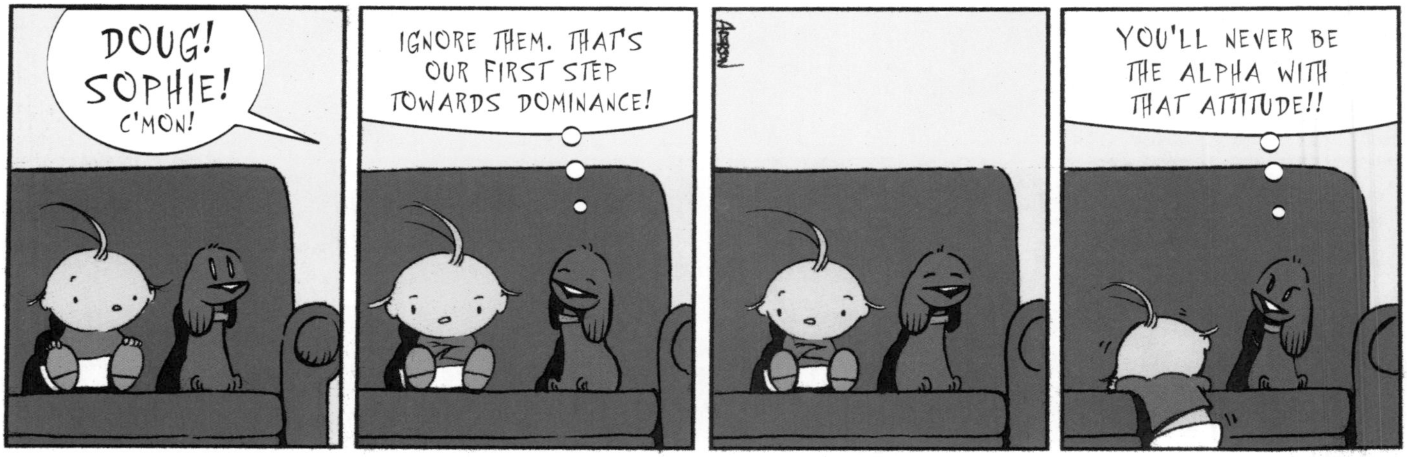
DOUG! SOPHIE! C'MON!
IGNORE THEM. THAT'S OUR FIRST STEP TOWARDS DOMINANCE!
YOU'LL NEVER BE THE ALPHA WITH THAT ATTITUDE!!

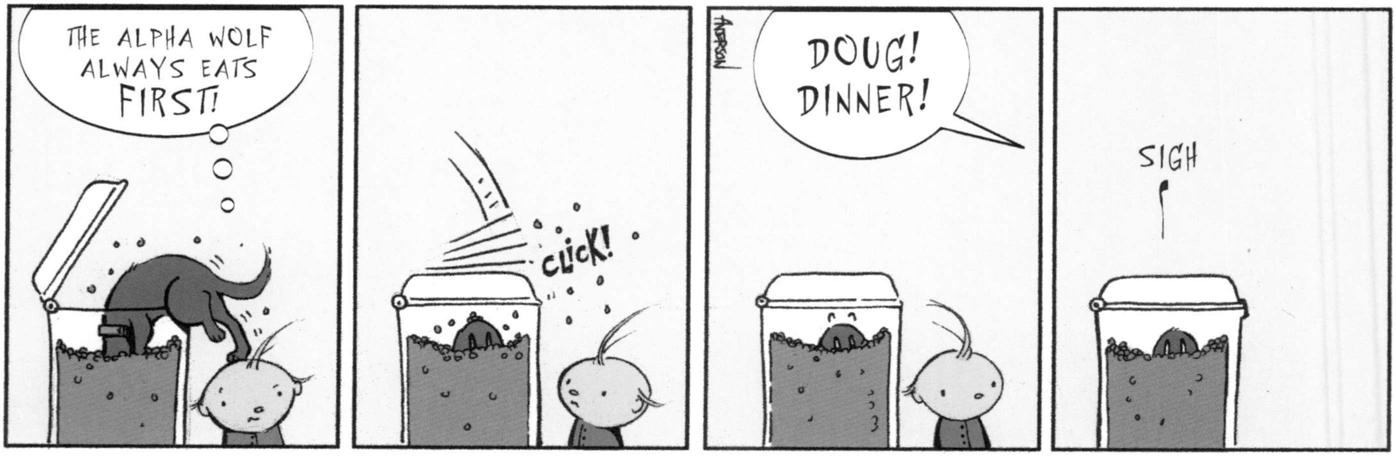
THE ALPHA WOLF ALWAYS EATS FIRST!
CLICK!
DOUG! DINNER!
SIGH

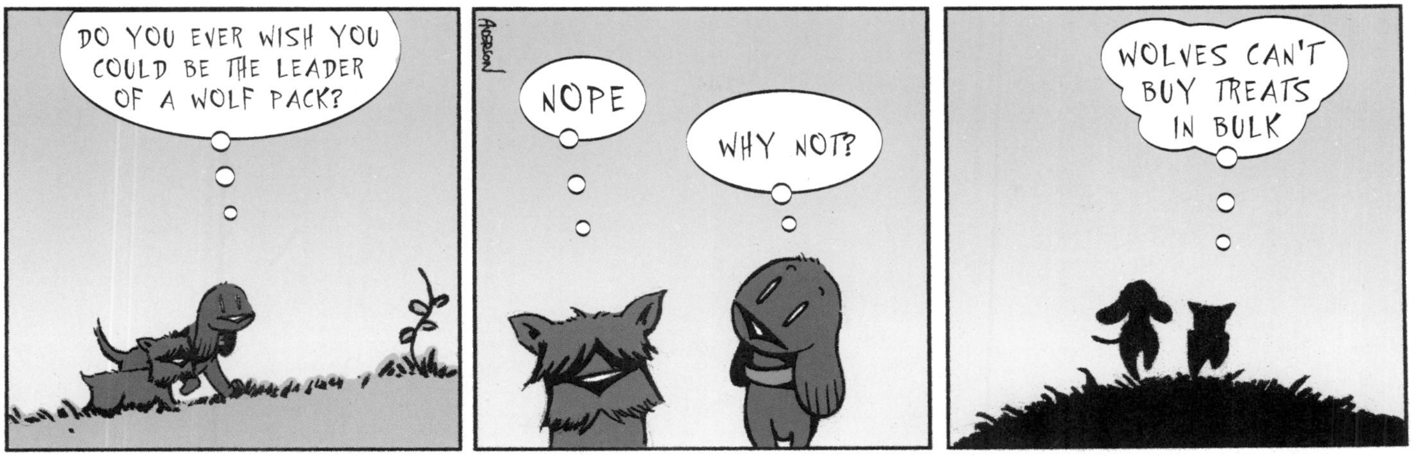
DO YOU EVER WISH YOU COULD BE THE LEADER OF A WOLF PACK?
NOPE
WHY NOT?
WOLVES CAN'T BUY TREATS IN BULK

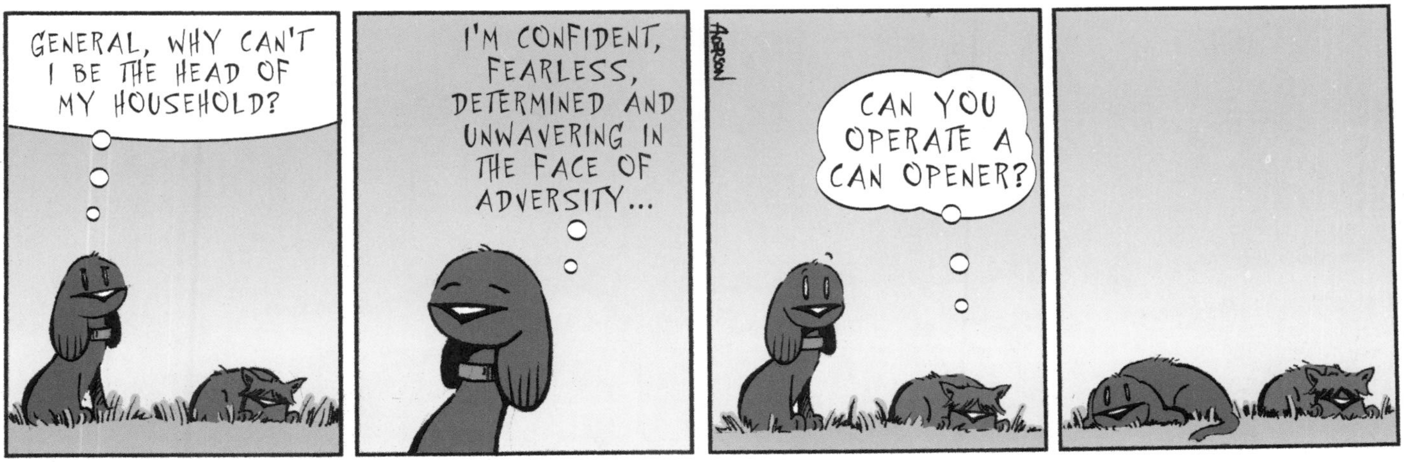
GENERAL, WHY CAN'T I BE THE HEAD OF MY HOUSEHOLD?
I'M CONFIDENT, FEARLESS, DETERMINED AND UNWAVERING IN THE FACE OF ADVERSITY...
CAN YOU OPERATE A CAN OPENER?

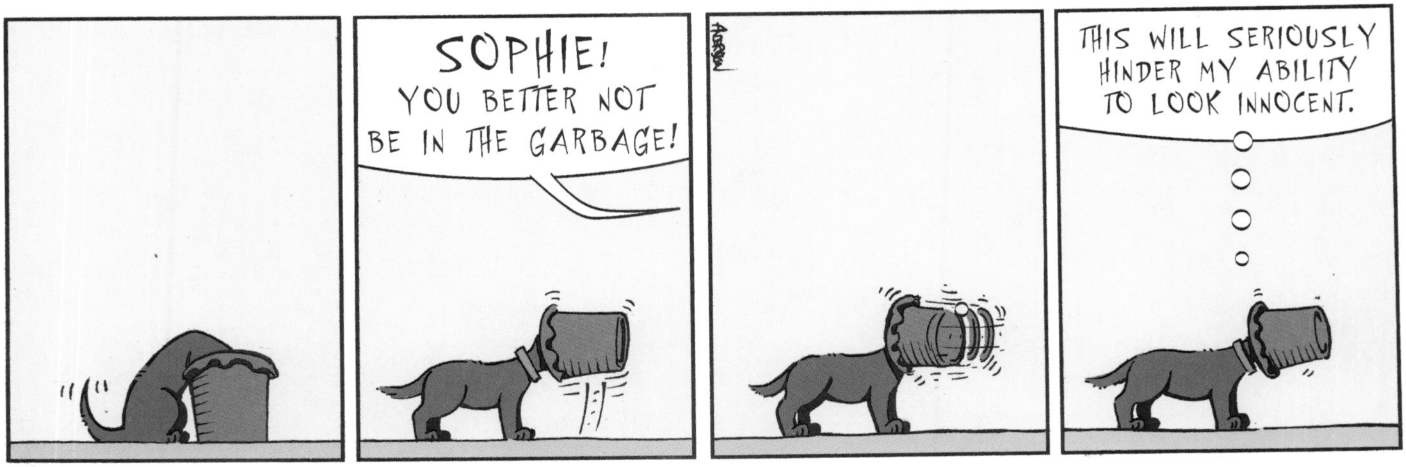
SOPHIE! YOU BETTER NOT BE IN THE GARBAGE!
THIS WILL SERIOUSLY HINDER MY ABILITY TO LOOK INNOCENT.

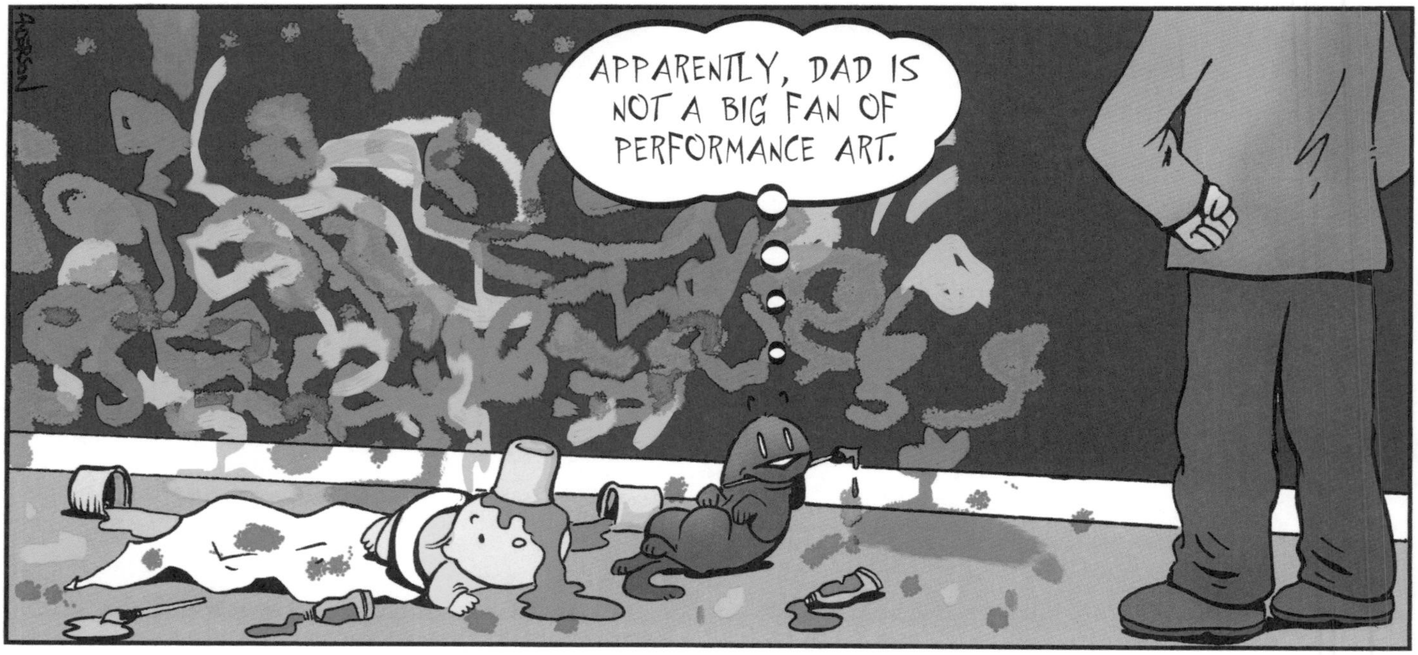
APPARENTLY, DAD IS NOT A BIG FAN OF PERFORMANCE ART.

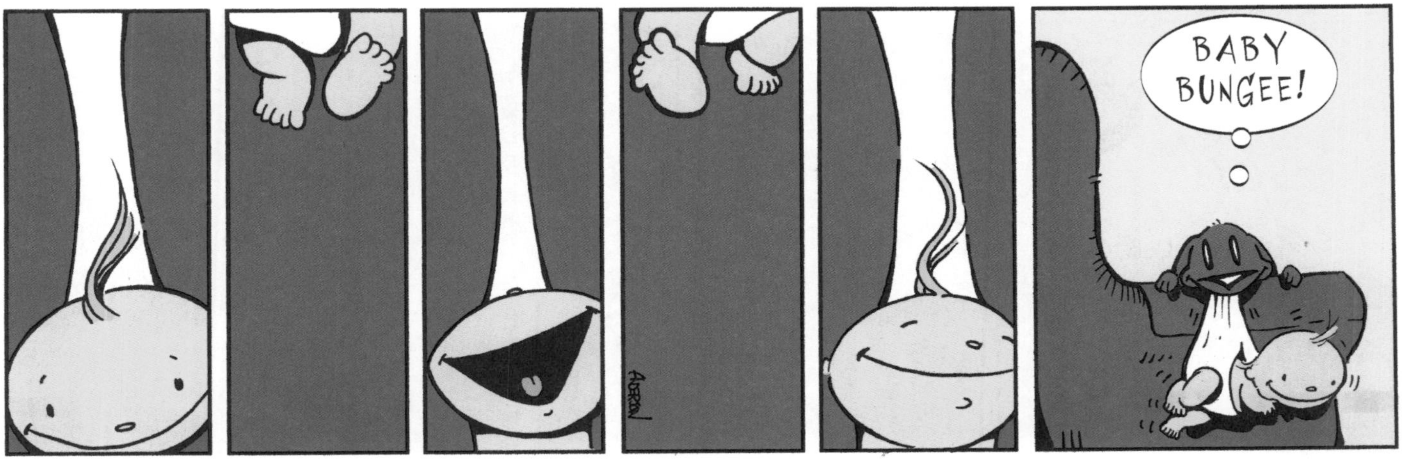
BABY BUNGEE!

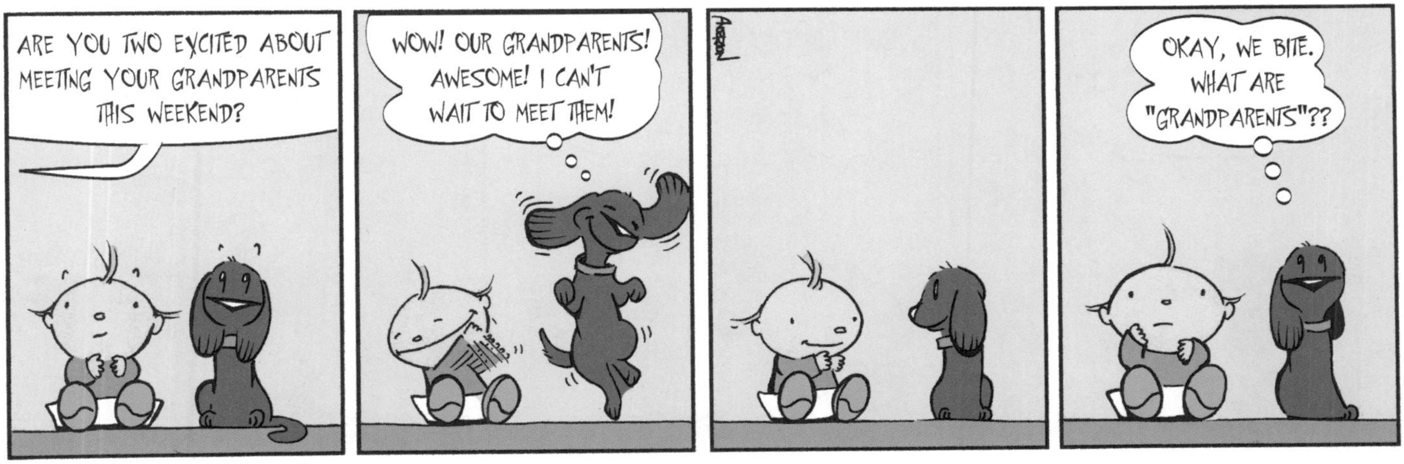
ARE YOU TWO EXCITED ABOUT MEETING YOUR GRANDPARENTS THIS WEEKEND?
WOW! OUR GRANDPARENTS! AWESOME! I CAN'T WAIT TO MEET THEM!
OKAY, WE BITE. WHAT ARE "GRANDPARENTS"??

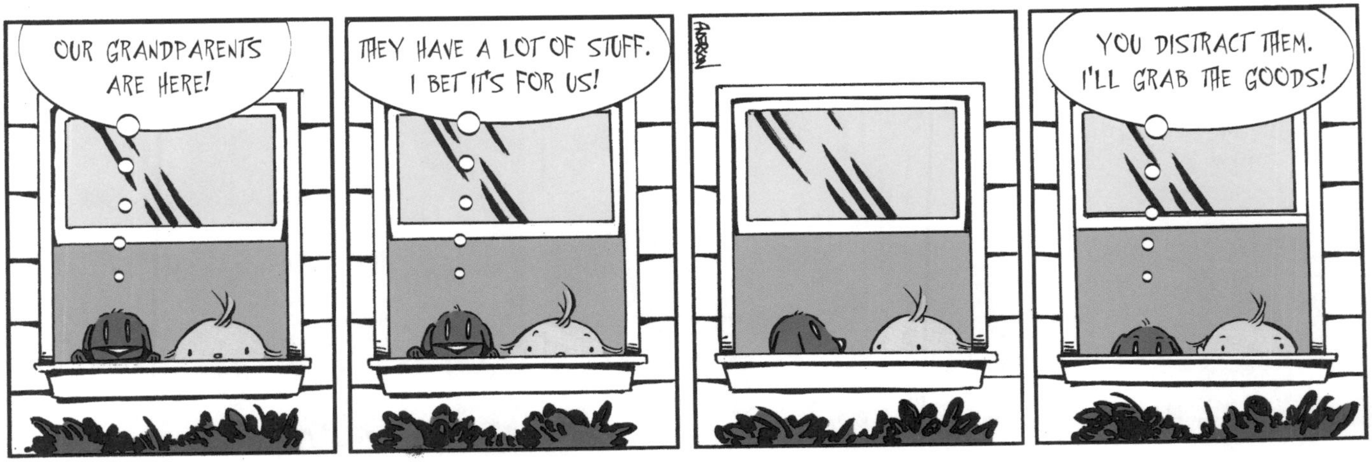
OUR GRANDPARENTS ARE HERE!
THEY HAVE A LOT OF STUFF. I BET IT'S FOR US!
YOU DISTRACT THEM. I'LL GRAB THE GOODS!

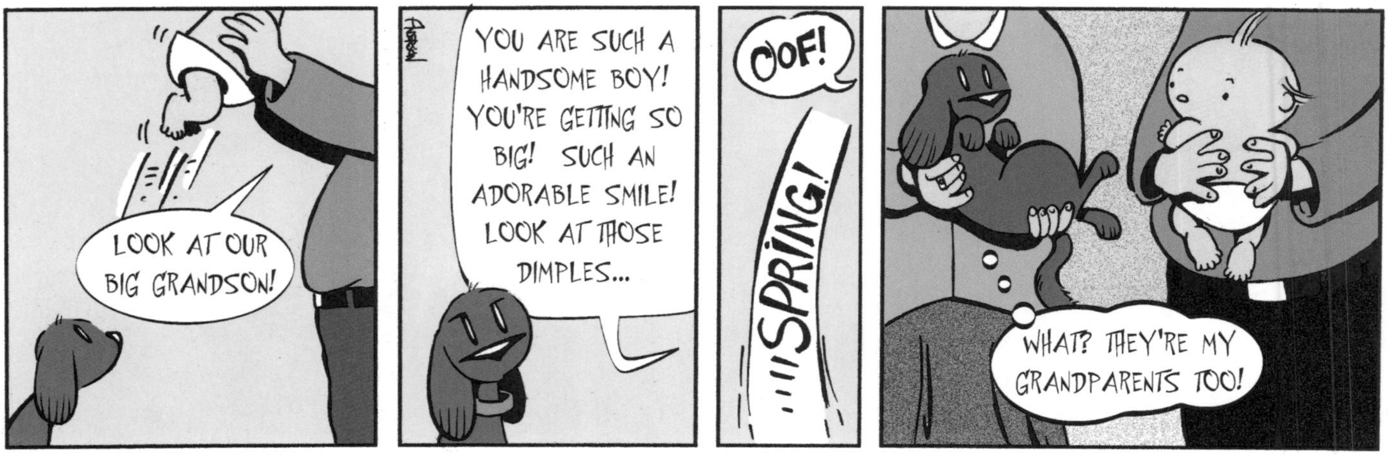
LOOK AT OUR BIG GRANDSON!
YOU ARE SUCH A HANDSOME BOY! YOU'RE GETTING SO BIG! SUCH AN ADORABLE SMILE! LOOK AT THOSE DIMPLES...
OOF!
SPRING!
WHAT? THEY'RE MY GRANDPARENTS TOO!

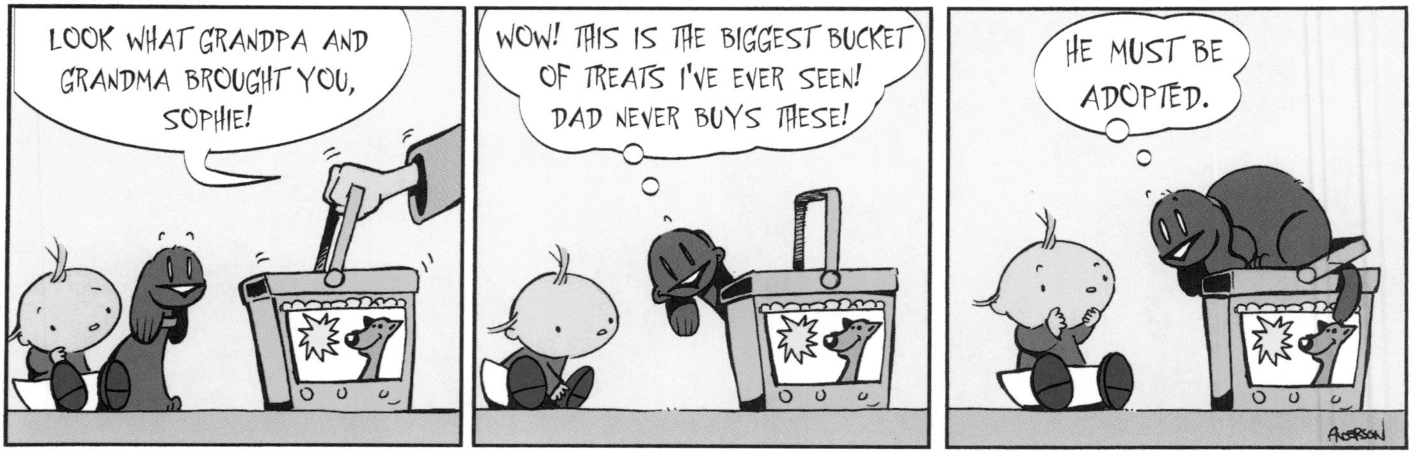
LOOK WHAT GRANDPA AND GRANDMA BROUGHT YOU, SOPHIE!
WOW! THIS IS THE BIGGEST BUCKET OF TREATS I'VE EVER SEEN! DAD NEVER BUYS THESE!
HE MUST BE ADOPTED.

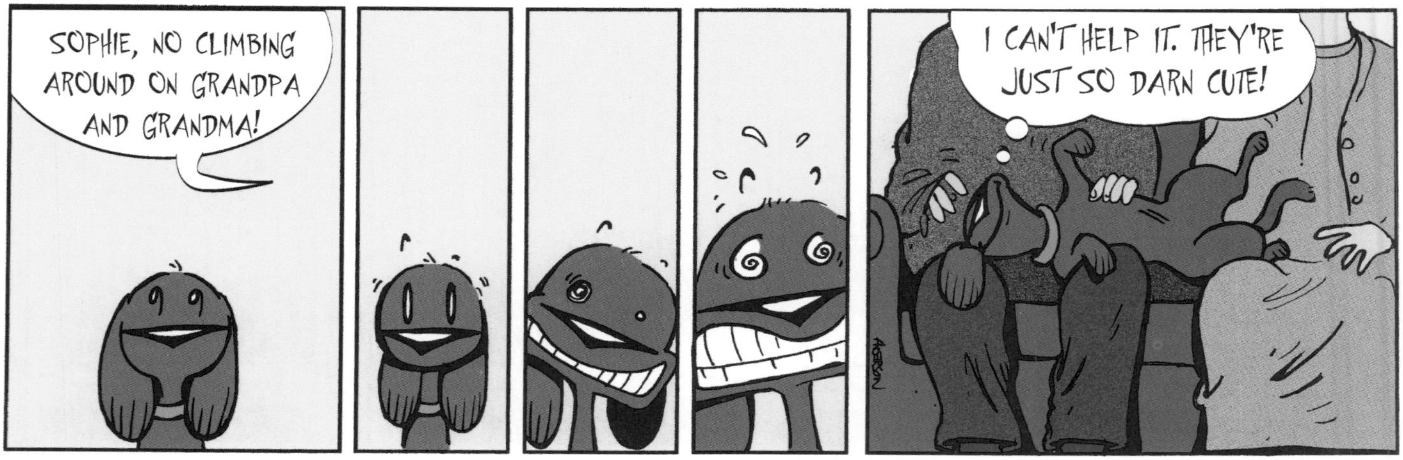
SOPHIE, NO CLIMBING AROUND ON GRANDPA AND GRANDMA!
I CAN'T HELP IT. THEY'RE JUST SO DARN CUTE!

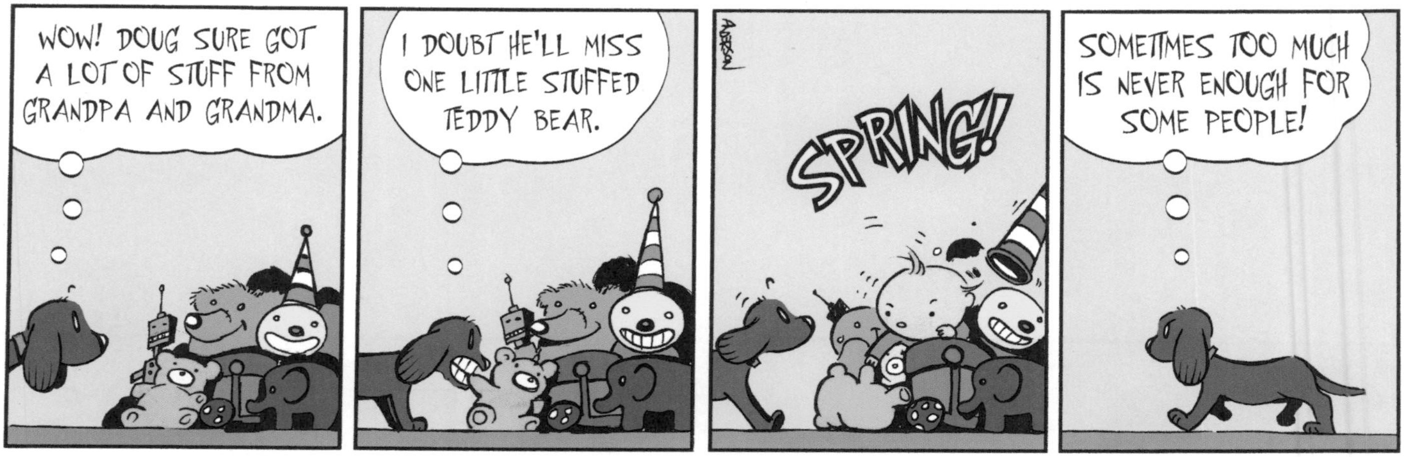
WOW! DOUG SURE GOT A LOT OF STUFF FROM GRANDPA AND GRANDMA.
I DOUBT HE'LL MISS ONE LITTLE STUFFED TEDDY BEAR.
SPRING!
SOMETIMES TOO MUCH IS NEVER ENOUGH FOR SOME PEOPLE!

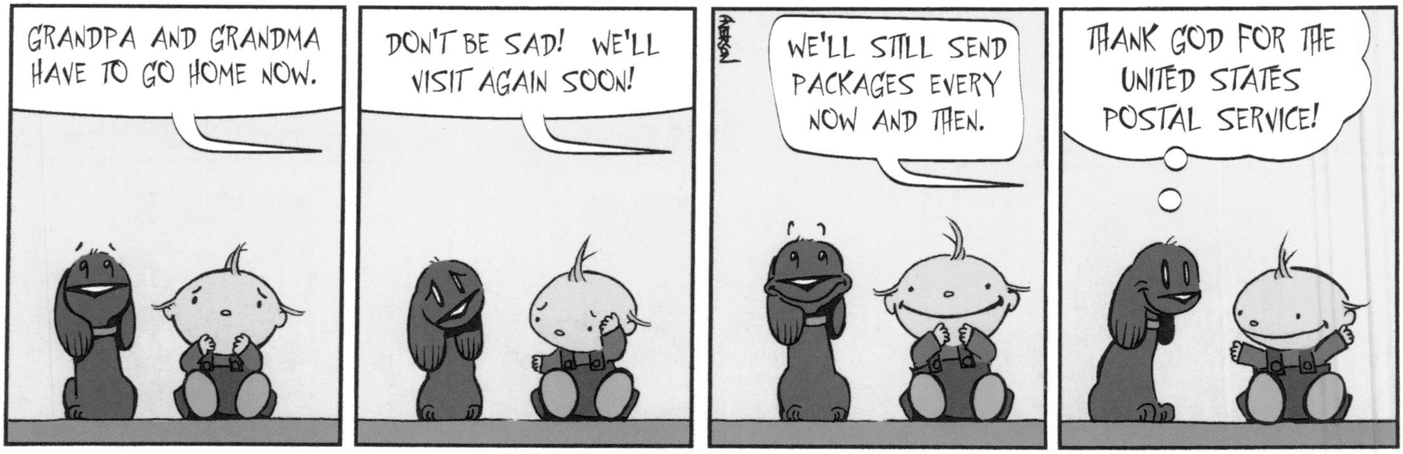
GRANDPA AND GRANDMA HAVE TO GO HOME NOW.
DON'T BE SAD! WE'LL VISIT AGAIN SOON!
WE'LL STILL SEND PACKAGES EVERY NOW AND THEN.
THANK GOD FOR THE UNITED STATES POSTAL SERVICE!

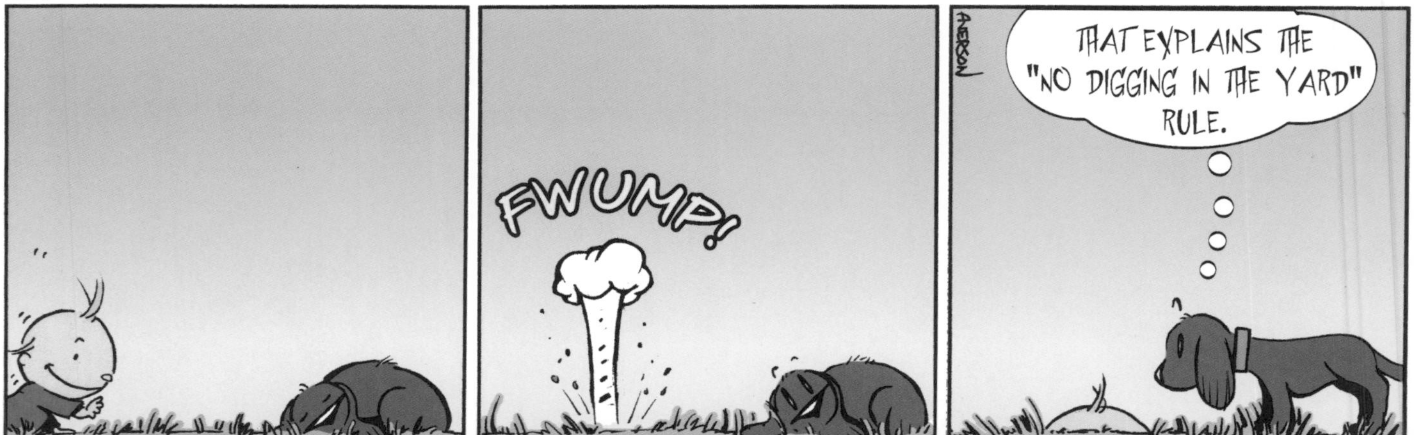
FWUMP!
THAT EXPLAINS THE "NO DIGGING IN THE YARD" RULE.

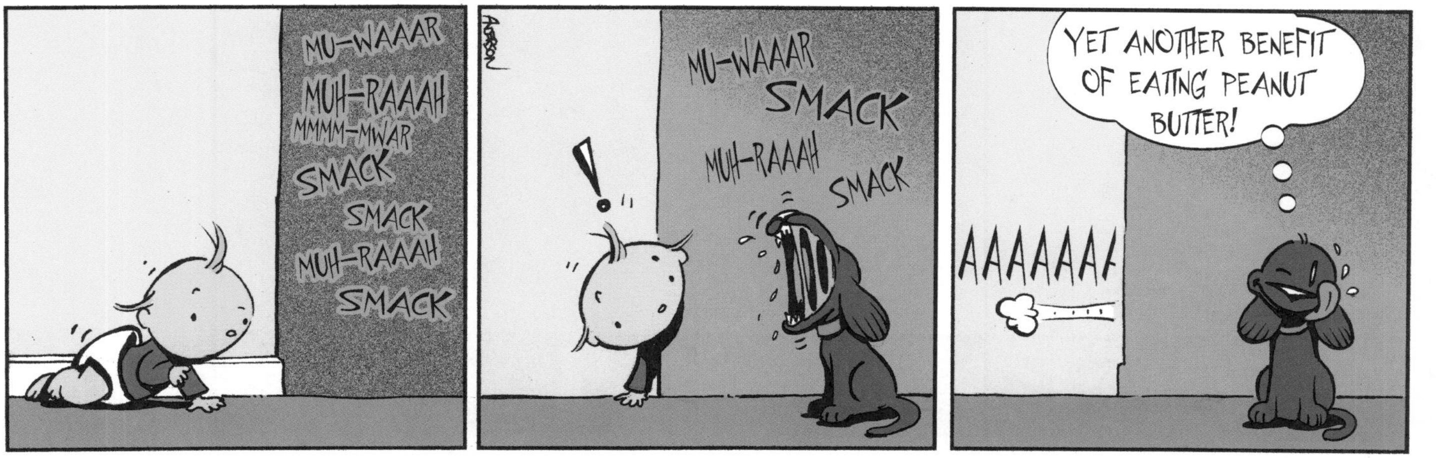
MU-WAAAR
MUH-RAAAH
MMMM-MWAR
SMACK
SMACK
MUH-RAAAH
SMACK
!
MU-WAAAR
SMACK
MUH-RAAAH
SMACK
AAAAAA!
YET ANOTHER BENEFIT OF EATING PEANUT BUTTER!

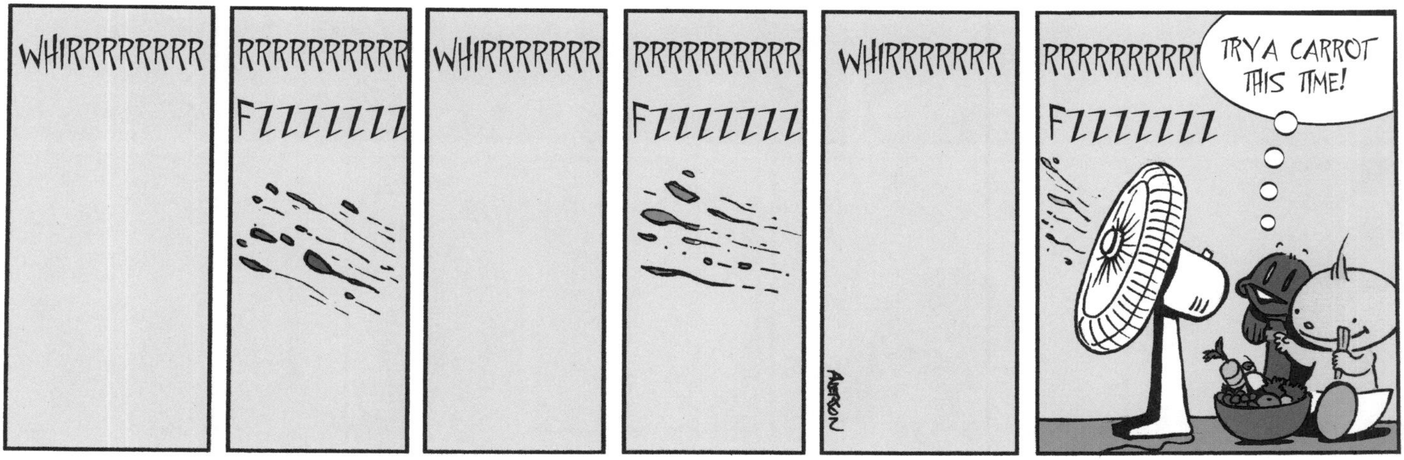
WHIRRRRRRRR
RRRRRRRRRR
FZZZZZZZ
WHIRRRRRRR
RRRRRRRRRR
FZZZZZZZ
WHIRRRRRRR
RRRRRRRRRR
FZZZZZZZ
TRY A CARROT THIS TIME!

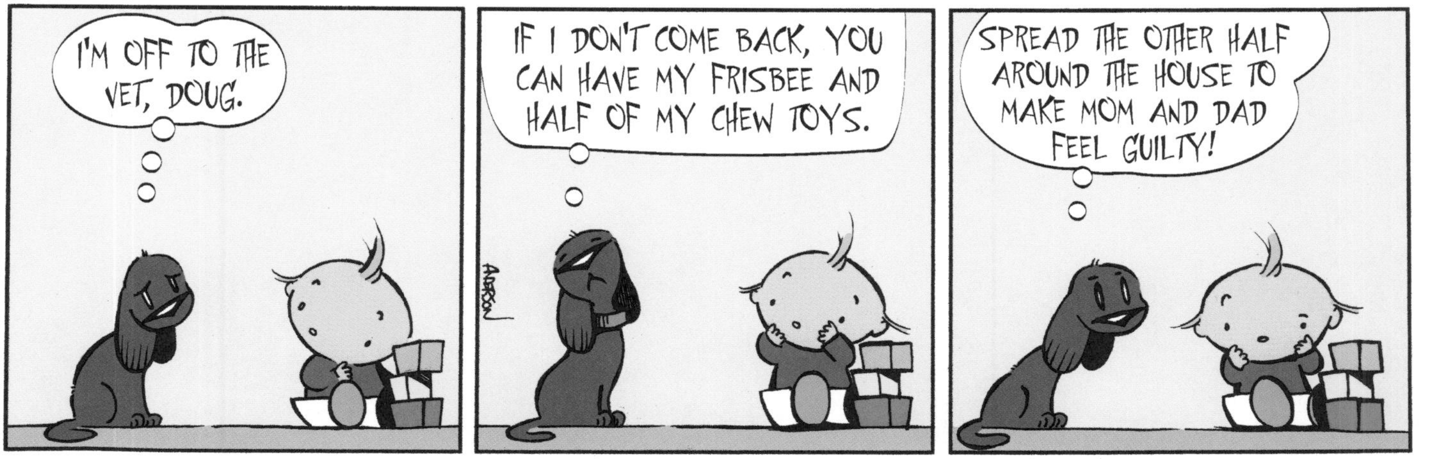
I'M OFF TO THE VET, DOUG.
IF I DON'T COME BACK, YOU CAN HAVE MY FRISBEE AND HALF OF MY CHEW TOYS.
SPREAD THE OTHER HALF AROUND THE HOUSE TO MAKE MOM AND DAD FEEL GUILTY!

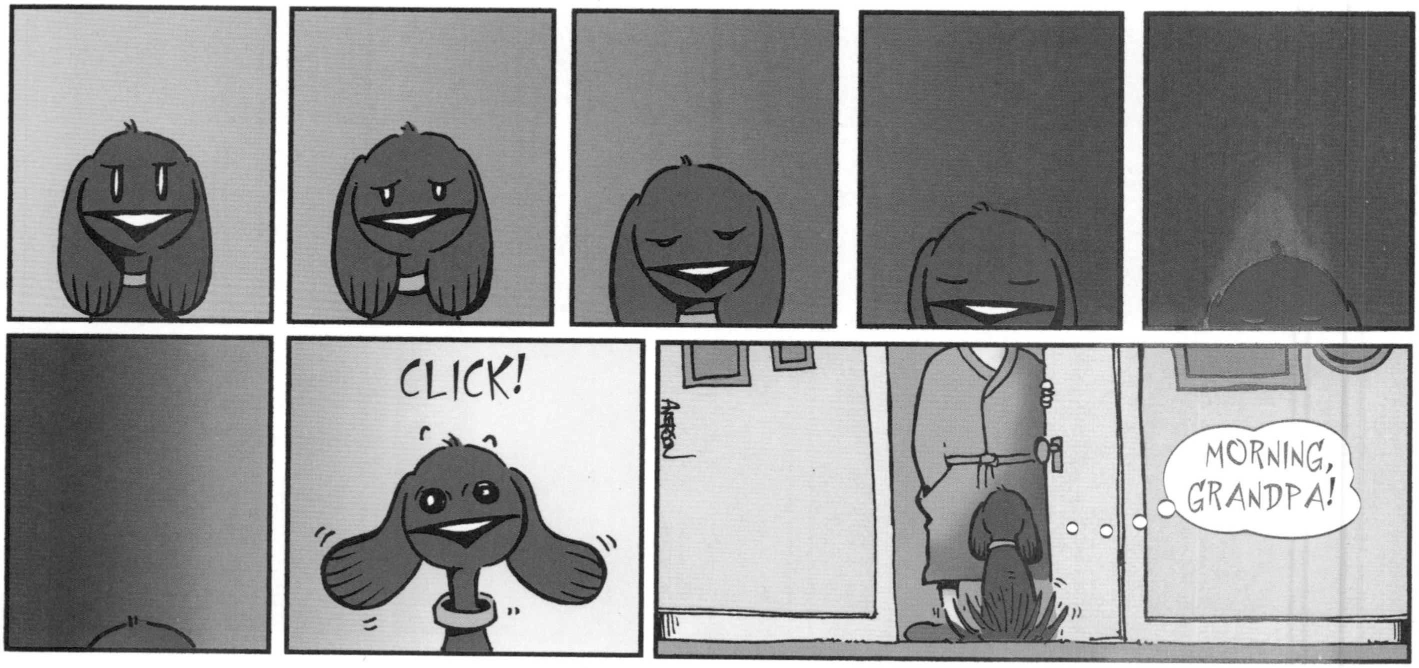
CLICK!
MORNING, GRANDPA!

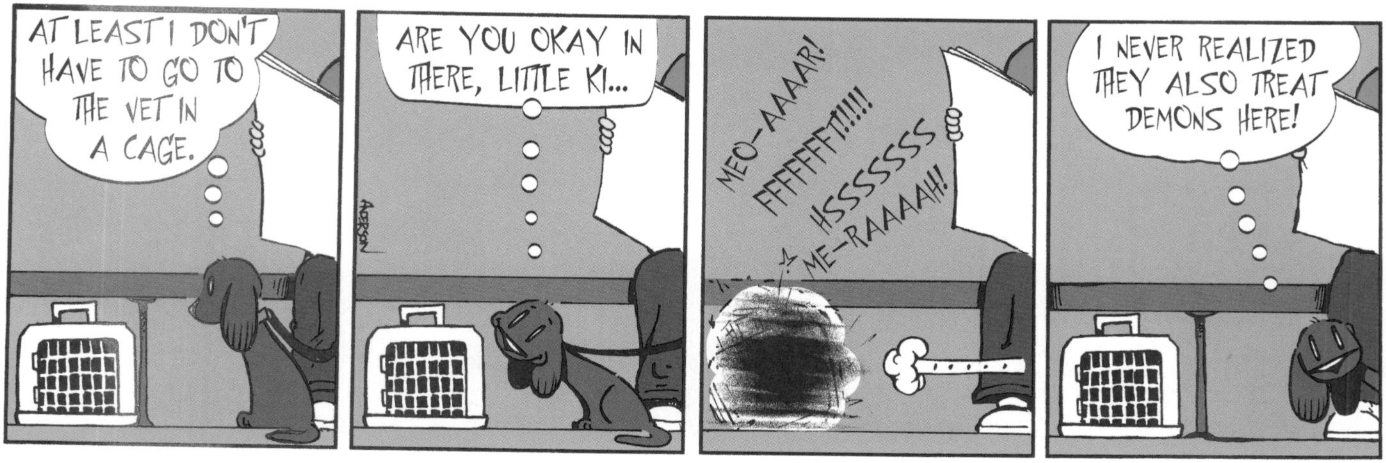
AT LEAST I DON'T HAVE TO GO TO THE VET IN A CAGE.
ARE YOU OKAY IN THERE, LITTLE KI...
MEO-AAAAR!
FFFFFFFT!!!!!
HSSSSSSS
ME-RAAAAH!
I NEVER REALIZED THEY ALSO TREAT DEMONS HERE!

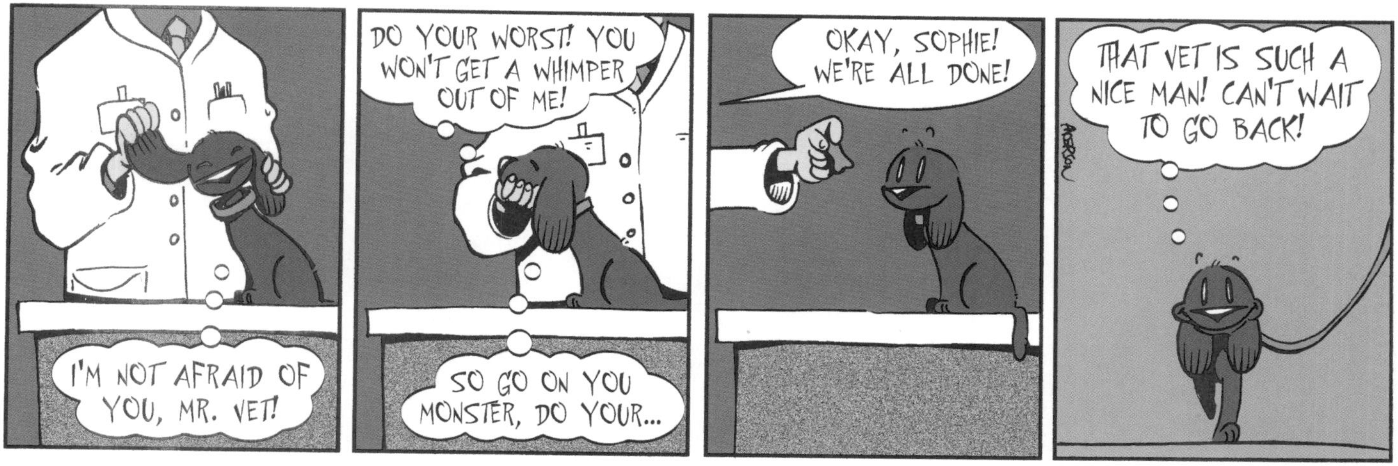
I'M NOT AFRAID OF YOU, MR. VET!
DO YOUR WORST! YOU WON'T GET A WHIMPER OUT OF ME!
SO GO ON YOU MONSTER, DO YOUR...
OKAY, SOPHIE! WE'RE ALL DONE!
THAT VET IS SUCH A NICE MAN! CAN'T WAIT TO GO BACK!

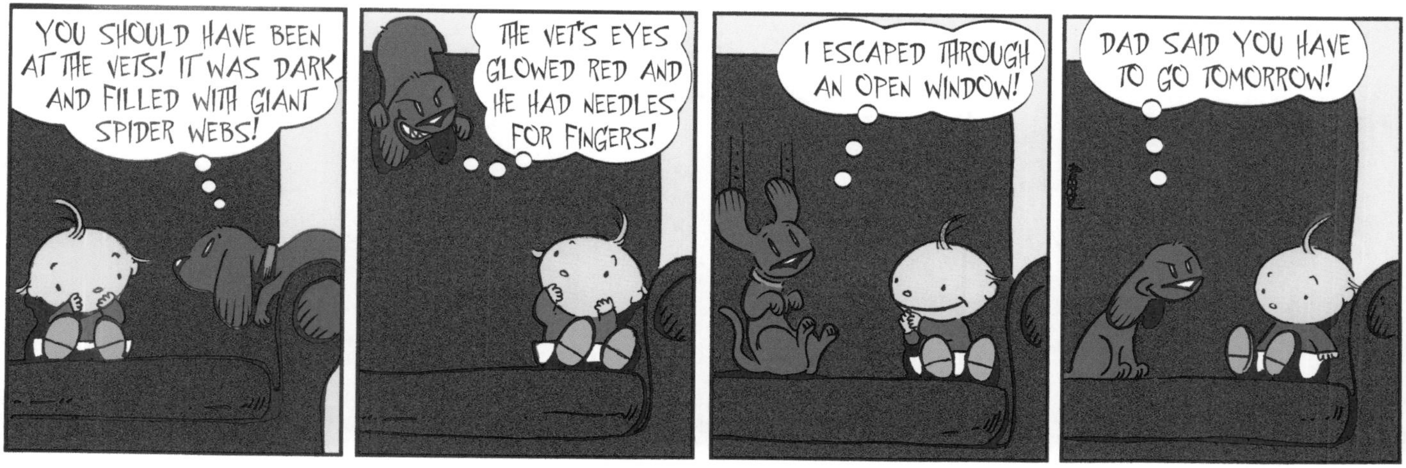
YOU SHOULD HAVE BEEN AT THE VETS! IT WAS DARK AND FILLED WITH GIANT SPIDER WEBS!
THE VET'S EYES GLOWED RED AND HE HAD NEEDLES FOR FINGERS!
I ESCAPED THROUGH AN OPEN WINDOW!
DAD SAID YOU HAVE TO GO TOMORROW!

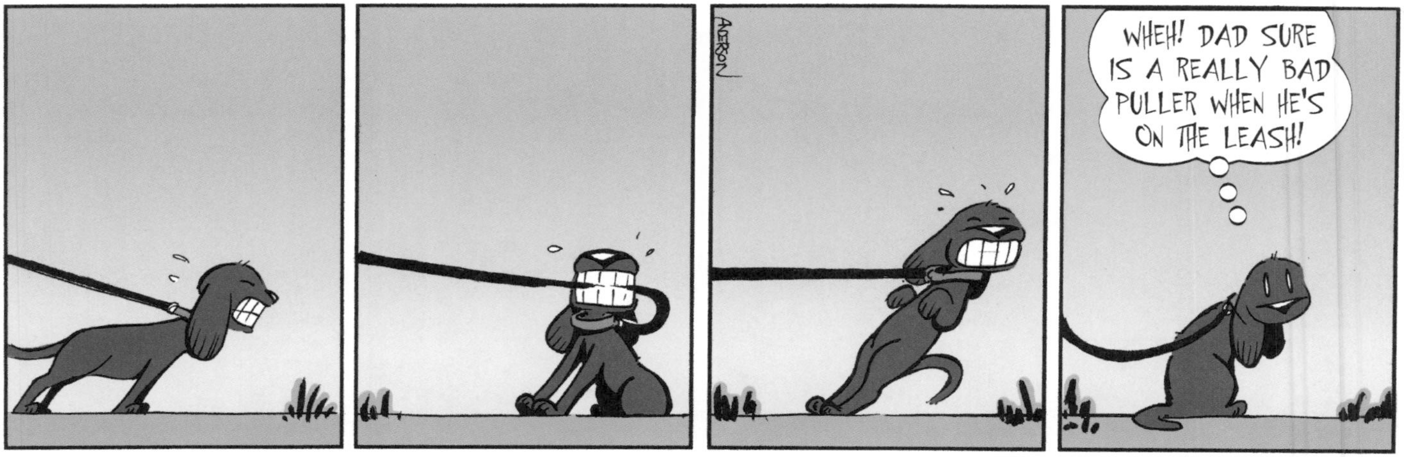
WHEH! DAD SURE IS A REALLY BAD PULLER WHEN HE'S ON THE LEASH!

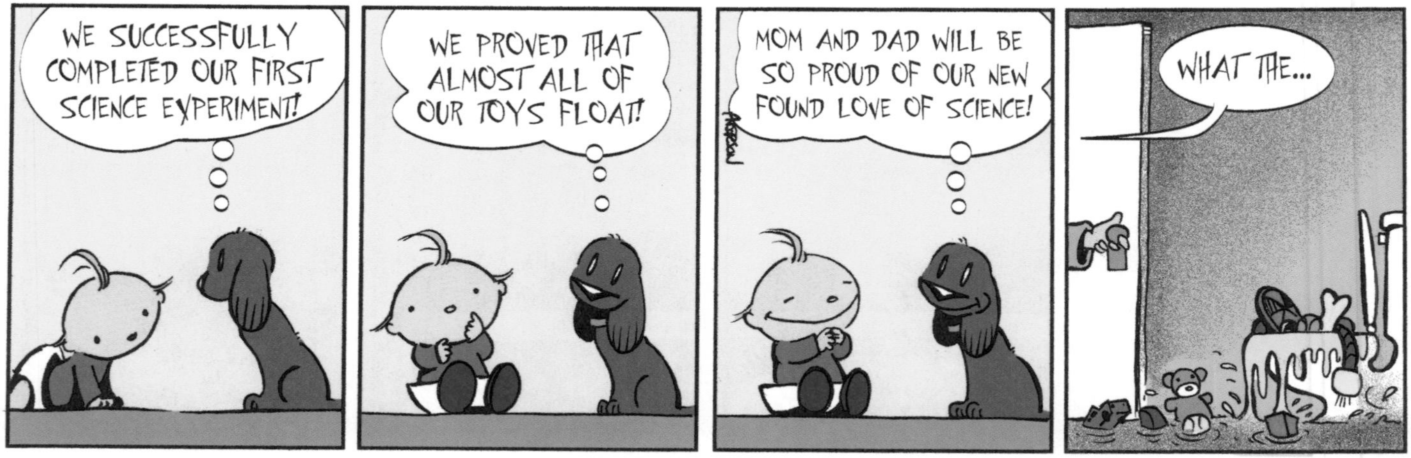
WE SUCCESSFULLY COMPLETED OUR FIRST SCIENCE EXPERIMENT!
WE PROVED THAT ALMOST ALL OF OUR TOYS FLOAT!
MOM AND DAD WILL BE SO PROUD OF OUR NEW FOUND LOVE OF SCIENCE!
WHAT THE...

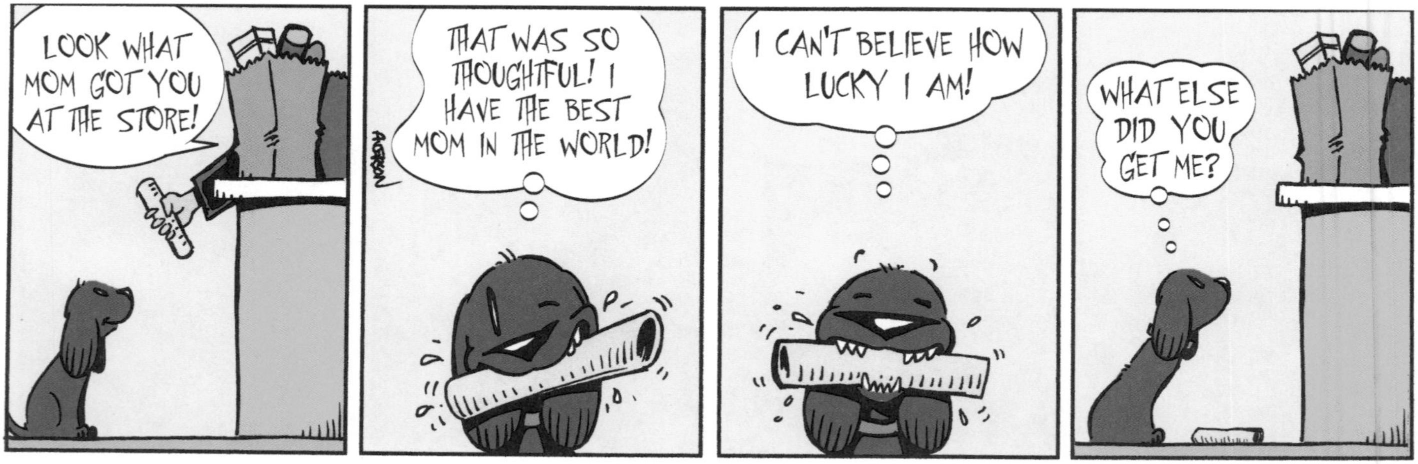
LOOK WHAT MOM GOT YOU AT THE STORE!
THAT WAS SO THOUGHTFUL! I HAVE THE BEST MOM IN THE WORLD!
I CAN'T BELIEVE HOW LUCKY I AM!
WHAT ELSE DID YOU GET ME?

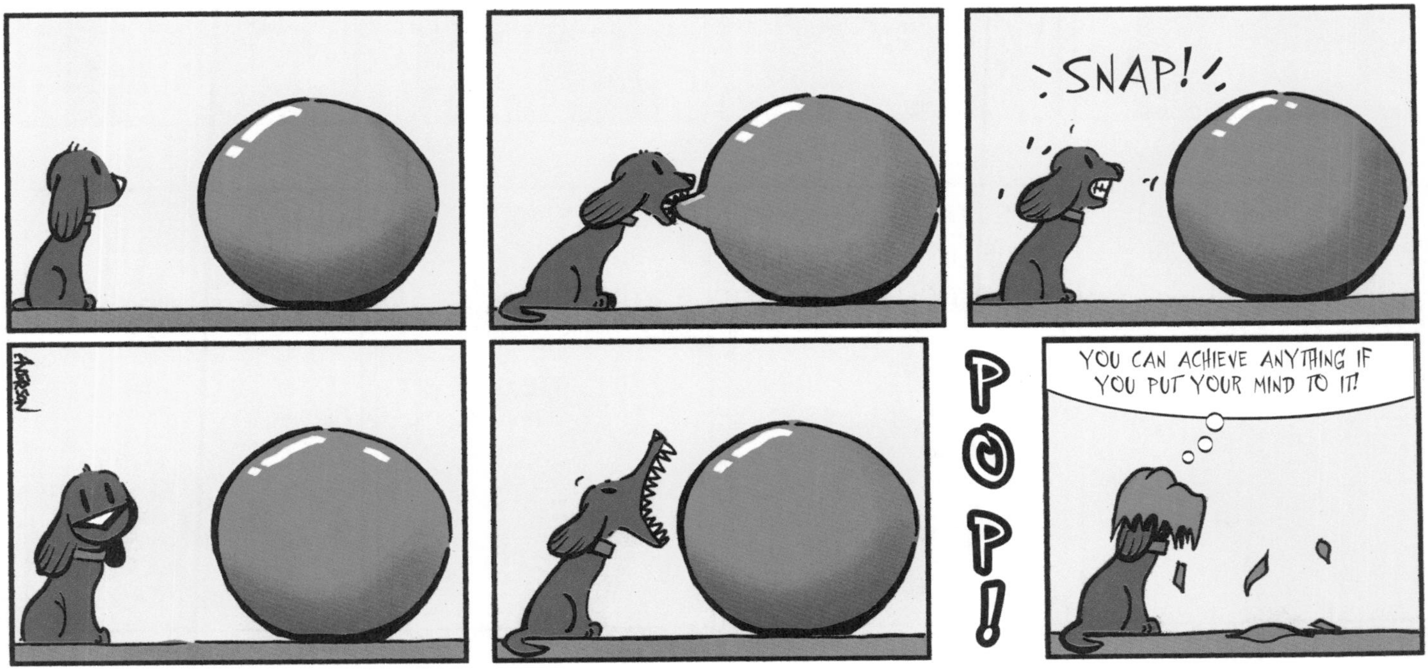
SNAP!
ANDERSON
POP!
YOU CAN ACHIEVE ANYTHING IF YOU PUT YOUR MIND TO IT!

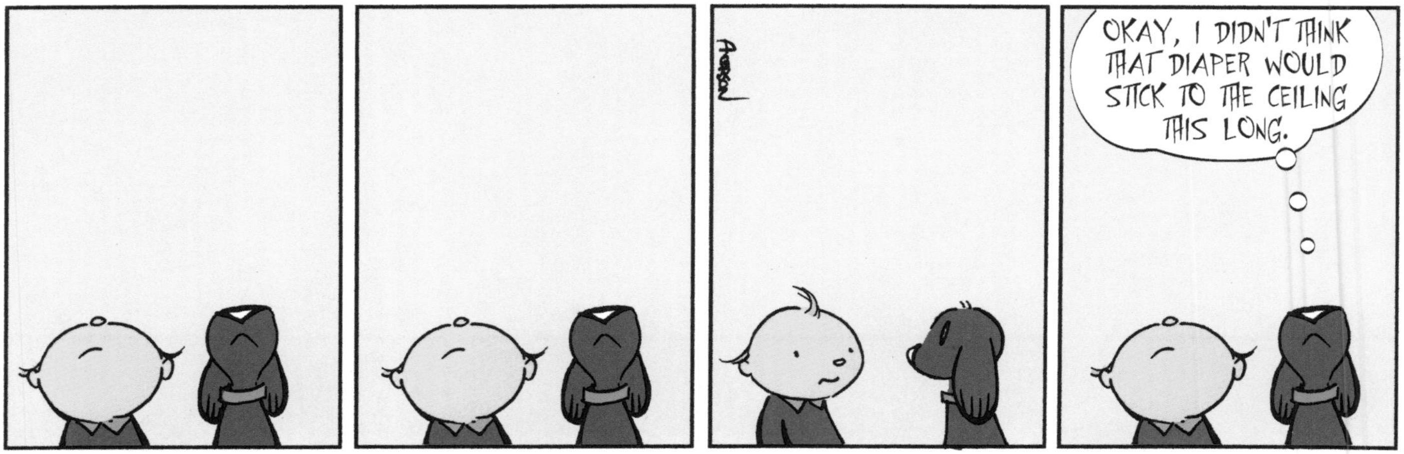
OKAY, I DIDN'T THINK THAT DIAPER WOULD STICK TO THE CEILING THIS LONG.

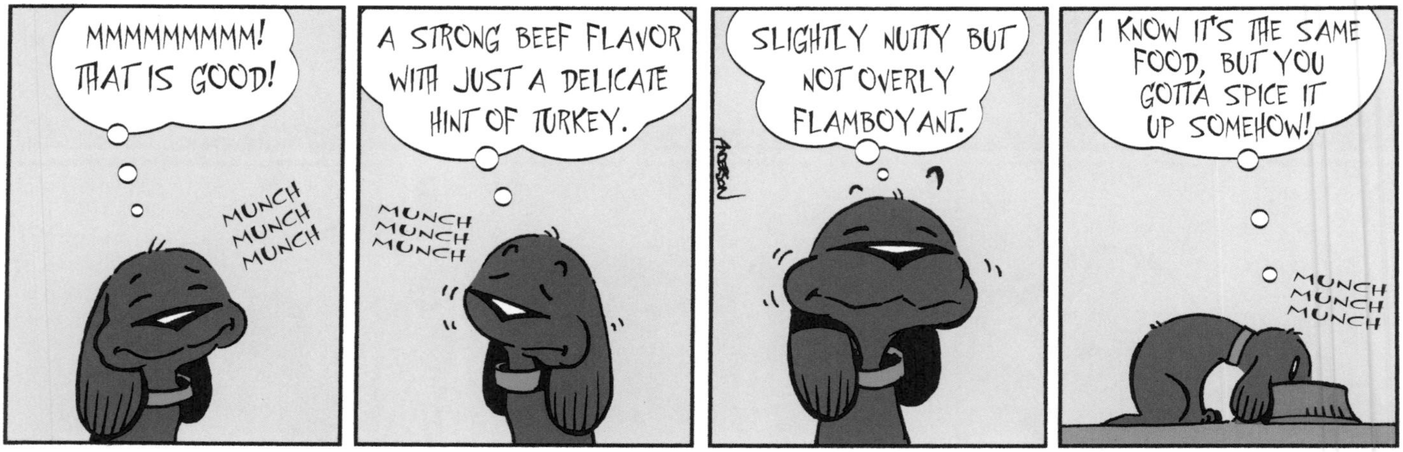
MMMMMMMMM! THAT IS GOOD!
MUNCH MUNCH MUNCH
A STRONG BEEF FLAVOR WITH JUST A DELICATE HINT OF TURKEY.
MUNCH MUNCH MUNCH
SLIGHTLY NUTTY BUT NOT OVERLY FLAMBOYANT.
I KNOW IT'S THE SAME FOOD, BUT YOU GOTTA SPICE IT UP SOMEHOW!
MUNCH MUNCH MUNCH

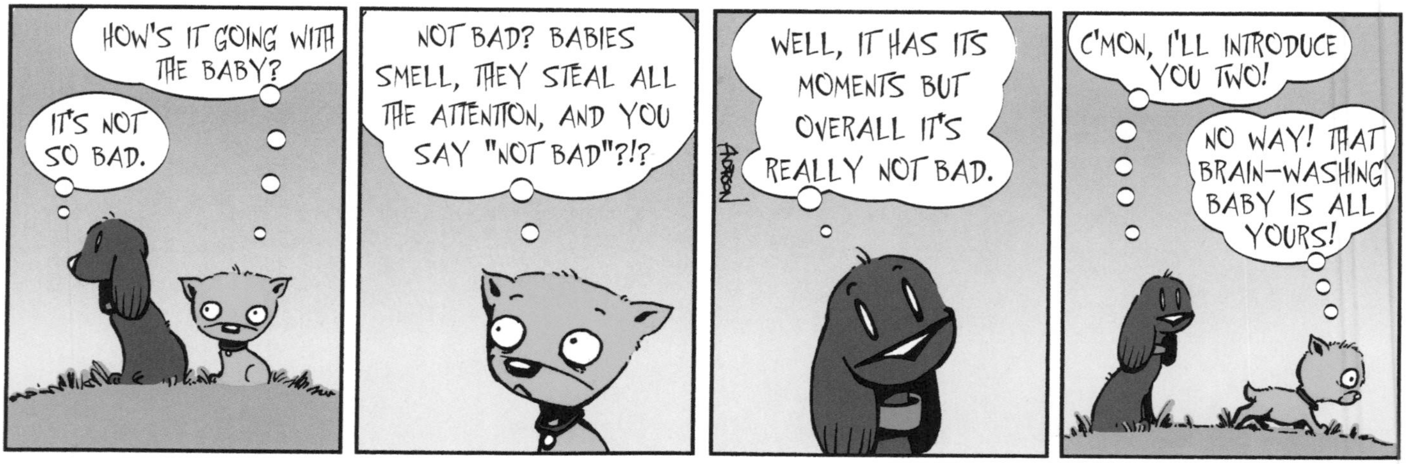
HOW'S IT GOING WITH THE BABY?
IT'S NOT SO BAD.
NOT BAD? BABIES SMELL, THEY STEAL ALL THE ATTENTION, AND YOU SAY "NOT BAD"?!?
WELL, IT HAS ITS MOMENTS BUT OVERALL IT'S REALLY NOT BAD.
C'MON, I'LL INTRODUCE YOU TWO!
NO WAY! THAT BRAIN-WASHING BABY IS ALL YOURS!

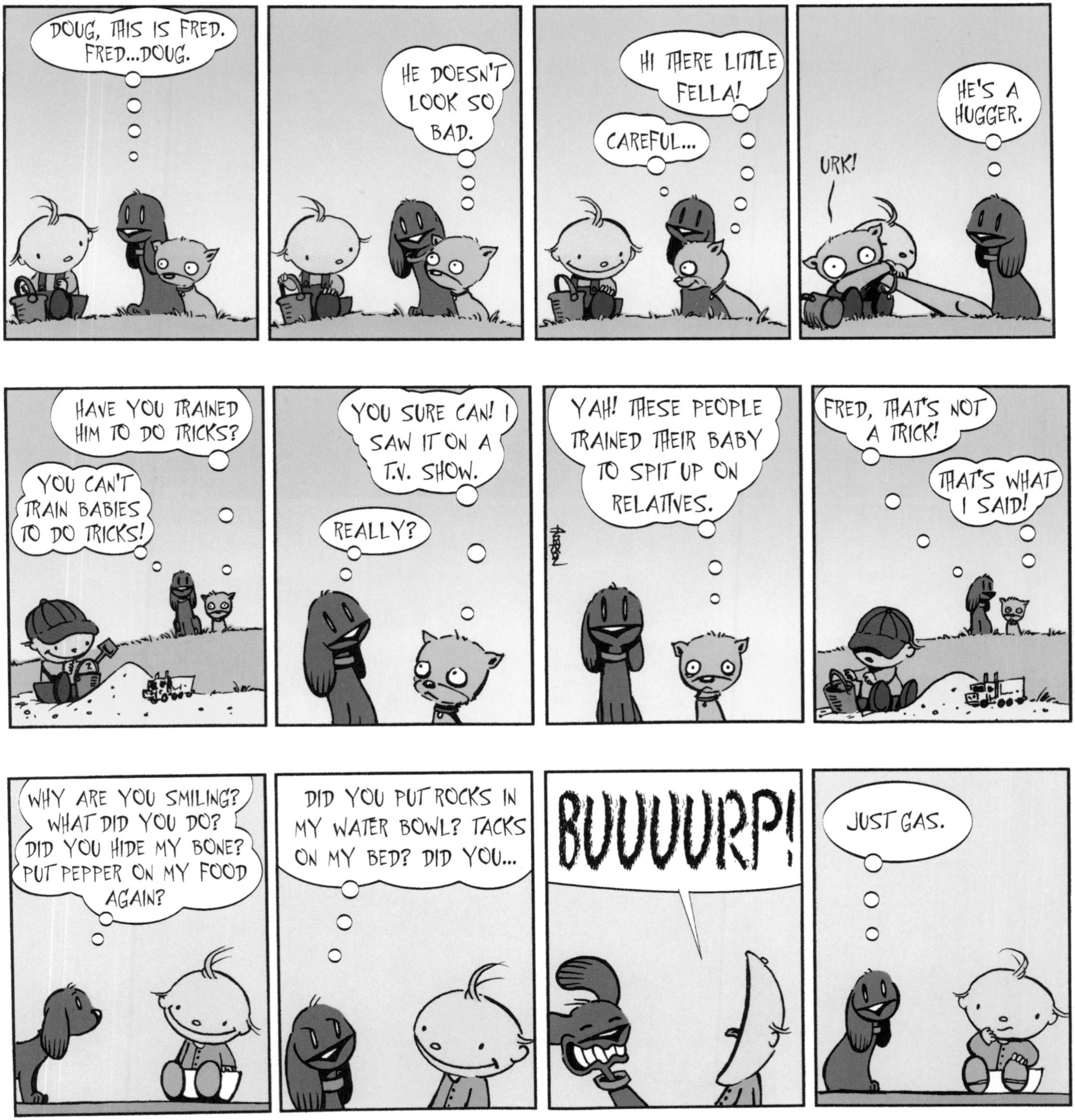
DOUG, THIS IS FRED. FRED...DOUG.
HE DOESN'T LOOK SO BAD.
HI THERE LITTLE FELLA!
CAREFUL...
URK!
HE'S A HUGGER.
HAVE YOU TRAINED HIM TO DO TRICKS?
YOU CAN'T TRAIN BABIES TO DO TRICKS!
YOU SURE CAN! I SAW IT ON A T.V. SHOW.
REALLY?
YAH! THESE PEOPLE TRAINED THEIR BABY TO SPIT UP ON RELATIVES.
FRED, THAT'S NOT A TRICK!
THAT'S WHAT I SAID!
WHY ARE YOU SMILING? WHAT DID YOU DO? DID YOU HIDE MY BONE? PUT PEPPER ON MY FOOD AGAIN?
DID YOU PUT ROCKS IN MY WATER BOWL? TACKS ON MY BED? DID YOU...
BUUUURP!
JUST GAS.

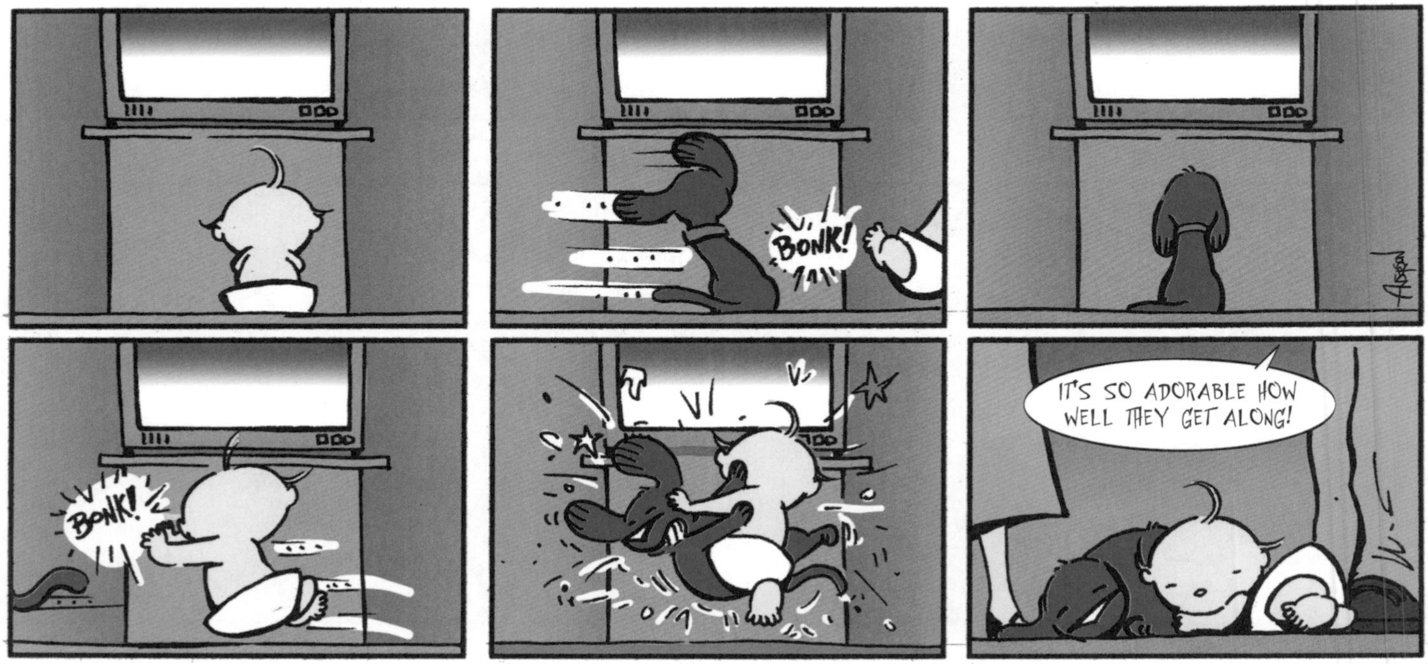
BONK!
BONK!
IT'S SO ADORABLE HOW WELL THEY GET ALONG!

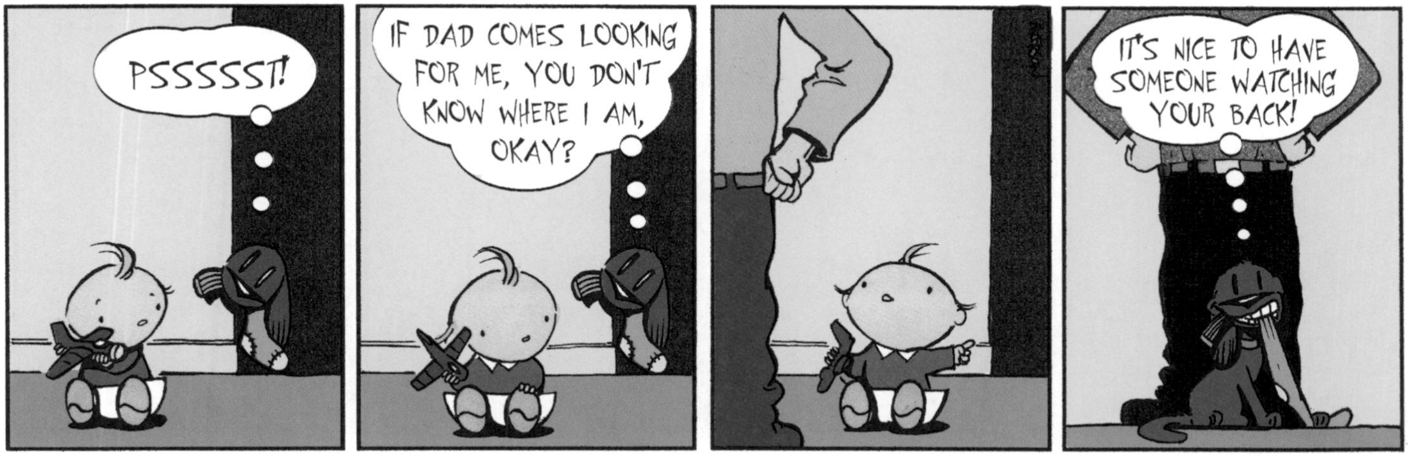
PSSSSST!
IF DAD COMES LOOKING FOR ME, YOU DON'T KNOW WHERE I AM, OKAY?
IT'S NICE TO HAVE SOMEONE WATCHING YOUR BACK!

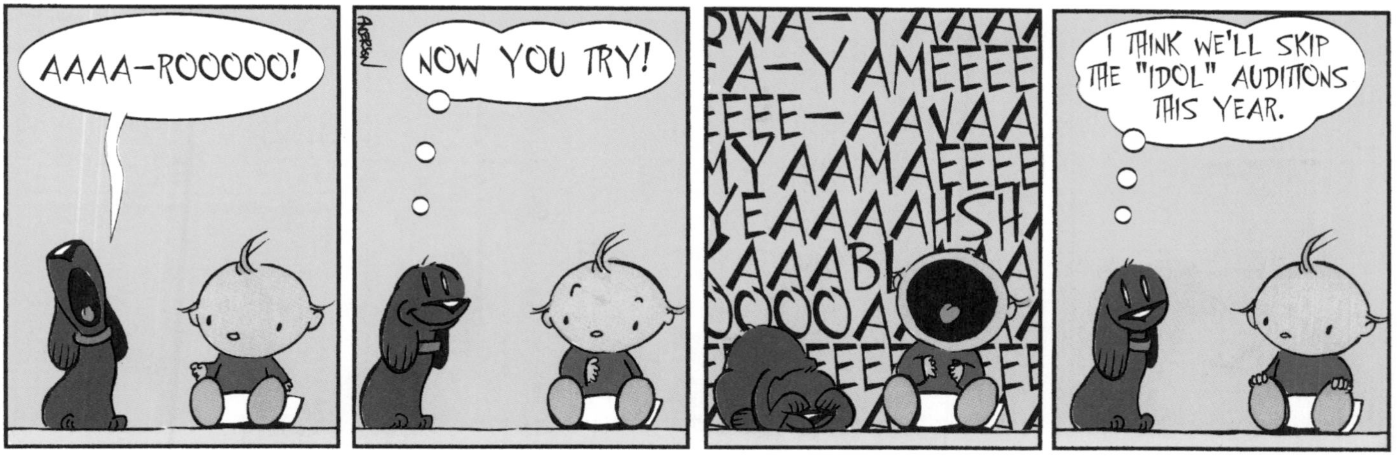
AAAA-ROOOOO!
NOW YOU TRY!
I THINK WE'LL SKIP THE "IDOL" AUDITIONS THIS YEAR.

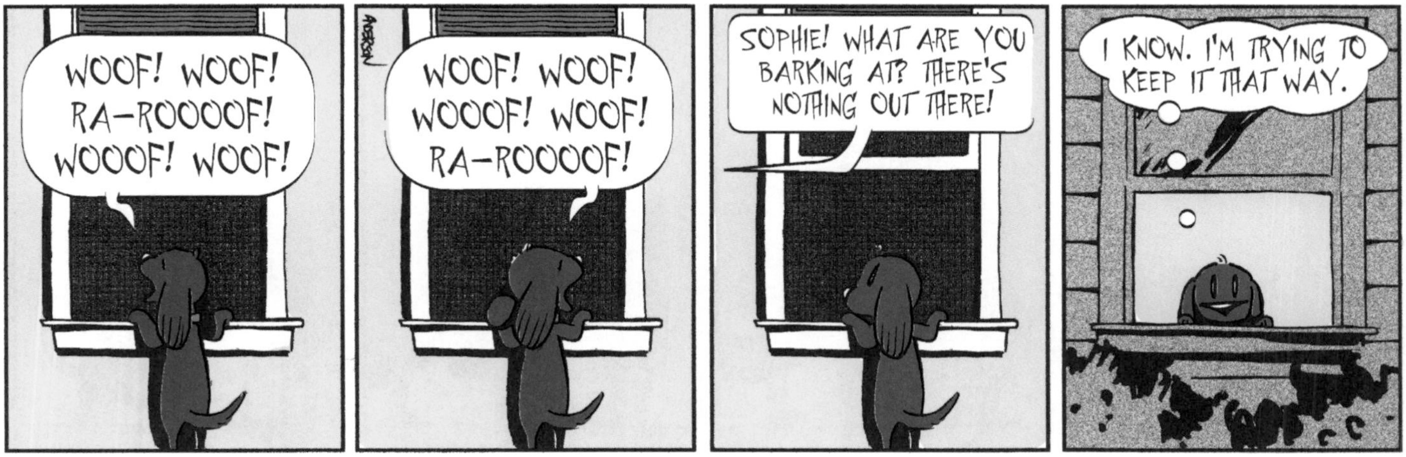
WOOF! WOOF! RA-ROOOOF! WOOOF! WOOF!
WOOF! WOOF! WOOOF! WOOF! RA-ROOOOF!
SOPHIE! WHAT ARE YOU BARKING AT? THERE'S NOTHING OUT THERE!
I KNOW. I'M TRYING TO KEEP IT THAT WAY.

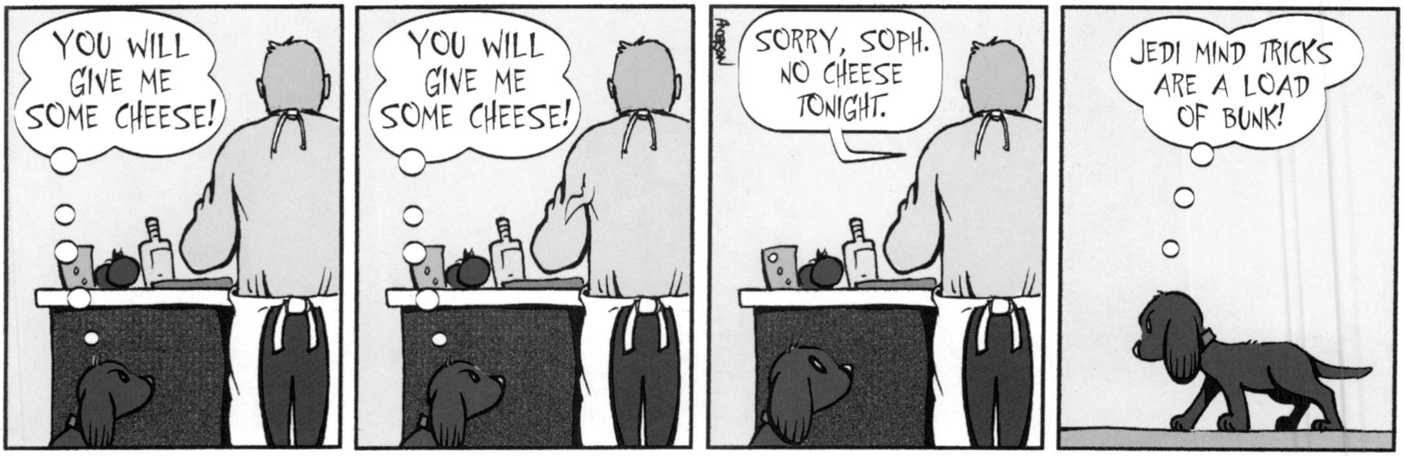
YOU WILL GIVE ME SOME CHEESE!
YOU WILL GIVE ME SOME CHEESE!
SORRY, SOPH. NO CHEESE TONIGHT.
JEDI MIND TRICKS ARE A LOAD OF BUNK!

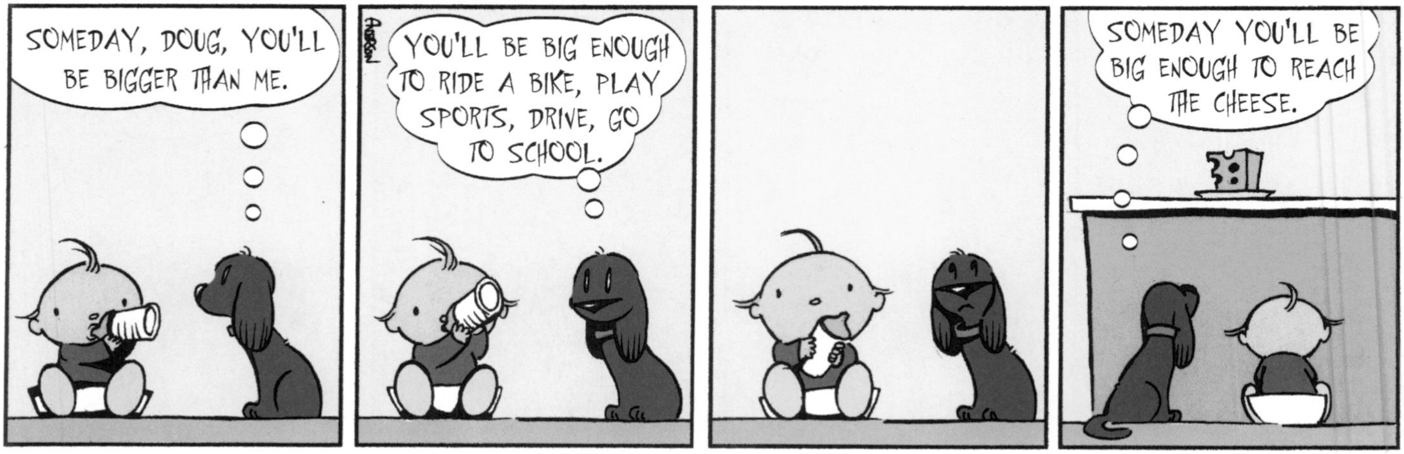
SOMEDAY, DOUG, YOU'LL BE BIGGER THAN ME.
YOU'LL BE BIG ENOUGH TO RIDE A BIKE, PLAY SPORTS, DRIVE, GO TO SCHOOL.
SOMEDAY YOU'LL BE BIG ENOUGH TO REACH THE CHEESE.

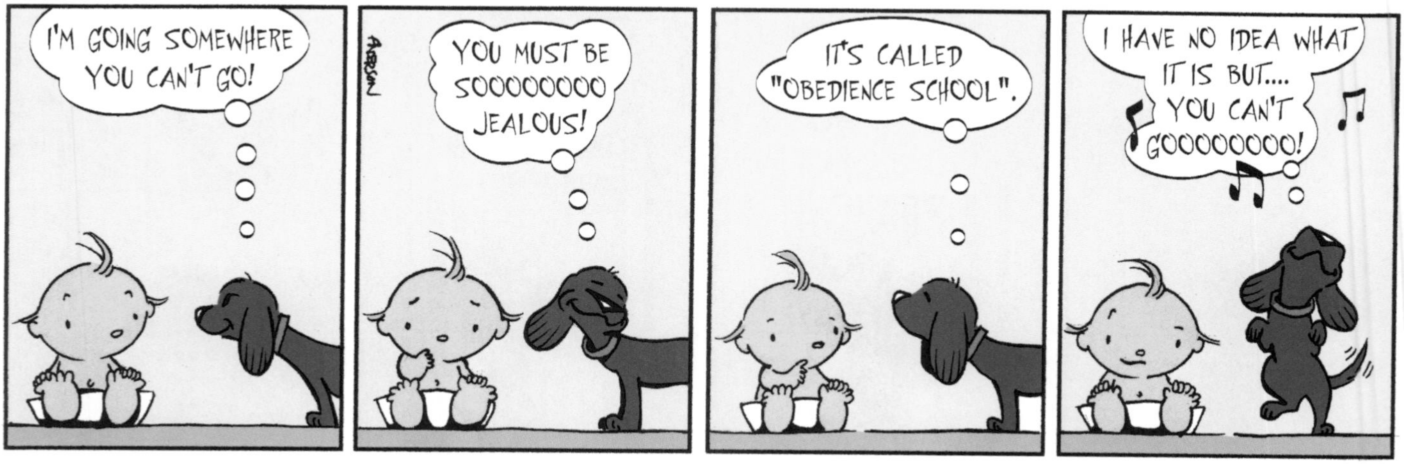
I'M GOING SOMEWHERE YOU CAN'T GO!
YOU MUST BE SOOOOOOOO JEALOUS!
IT'S CALLED "OBEDIENCE SCHOOL".
I HAVE NO IDEA WHAT IT IS BUT.... YOU CAN'T GOOOOOOOO!

DAD! I REALLY NEED TO GO POTTY!
UNG..ZZNORT!
HOLD ON, SOPHIE! LET ME GET DRESSED!
NO TIME TO WASTE!
IT'S POURING OUT! LET ME GET MY RAINCOAT.
UUGH!
SHOOT! FORGOT THE UMBRELLA. HOLD ON!
EASE UP, SOPHIE!
NOT...GOING... TO...MAKE IT!
OOPS. FALSE ALARM.

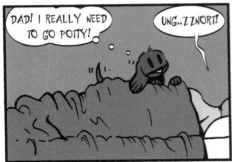

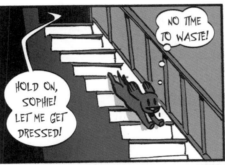

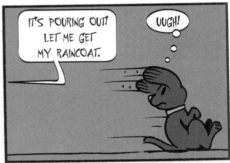

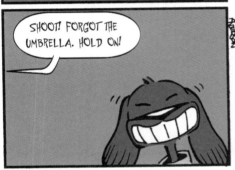

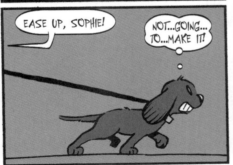

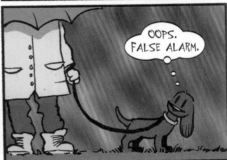

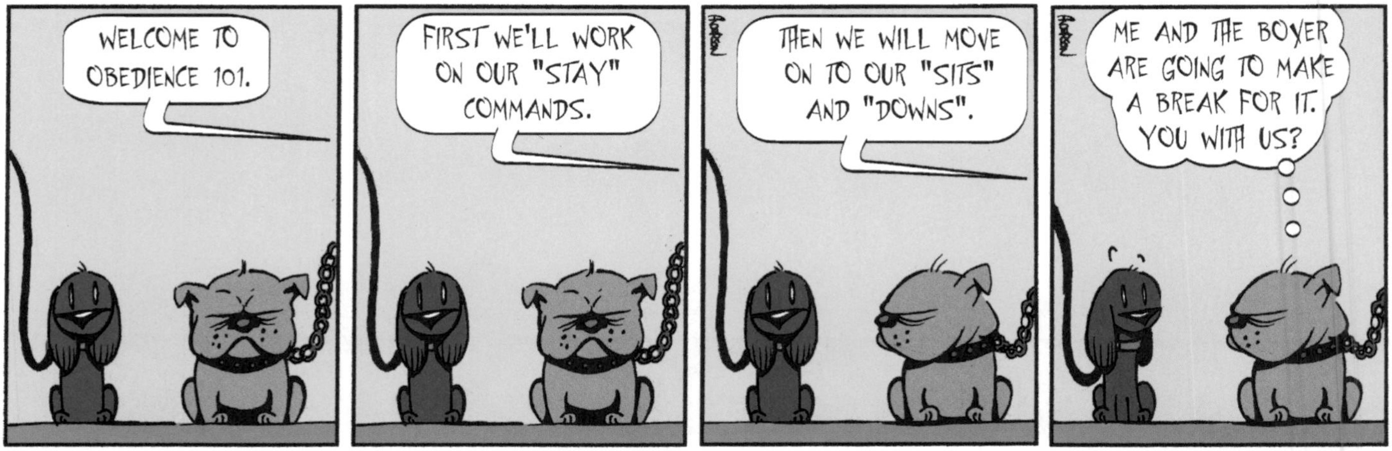
WELCOME TO OBEDIENCE 101.
FIRST WE'LL WORK ON OUR "STAY" COMMANDS.
THEN WE WILL MOVE ON TO OUR "SITS" AND "DOWNS".
ME AND THE BOXER ARE GOING TO MAKE A BREAK FOR IT. YOU WITH US?

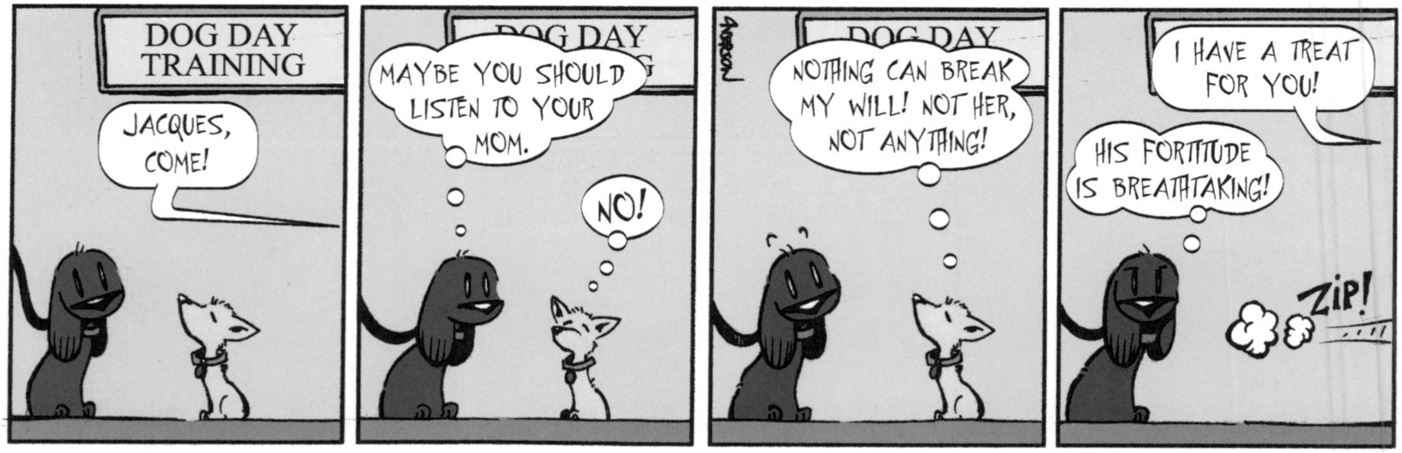
DOG DAY TRAINING
JACQUES, COME!
MAYBE YOU SHOULD LISTEN TO YOUR MOM.
NO!
NOTHING CAN BREAK MY WILL! NOT HER, NOT ANYTHING!
I HAVE A TREAT FOR YOU!
HIS FORTITUDE IS BREATHTAKING!
ZIP!

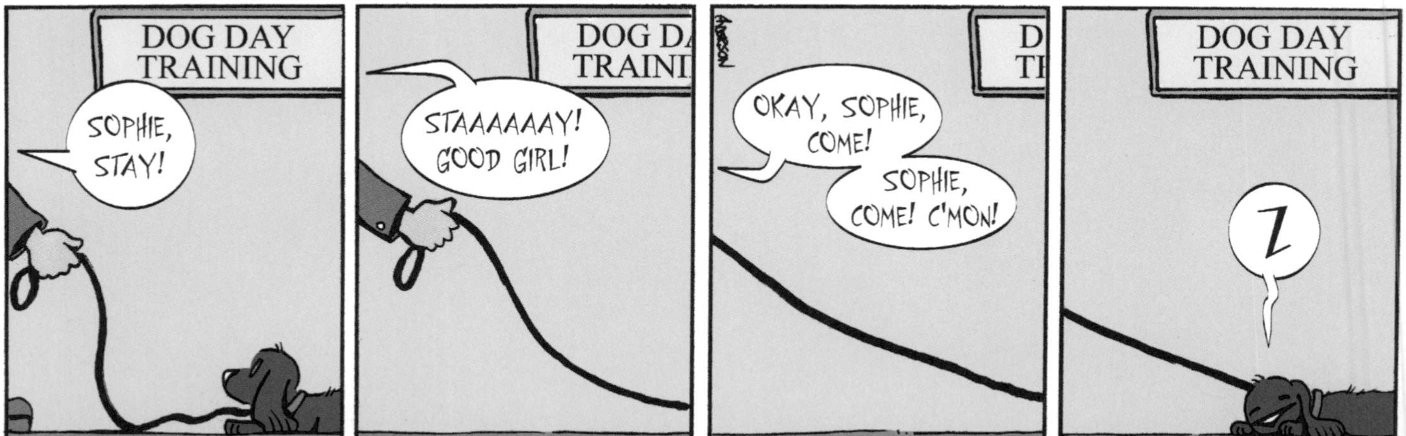
DOG DAY TRAINING
SOPHIE, STAY!
STAAAAAAY! GOOD GIRL!
OKAY, SOPHIE, COME!
SOPHIE, COME! C'MON!
DOG DAY TRAINING
Z

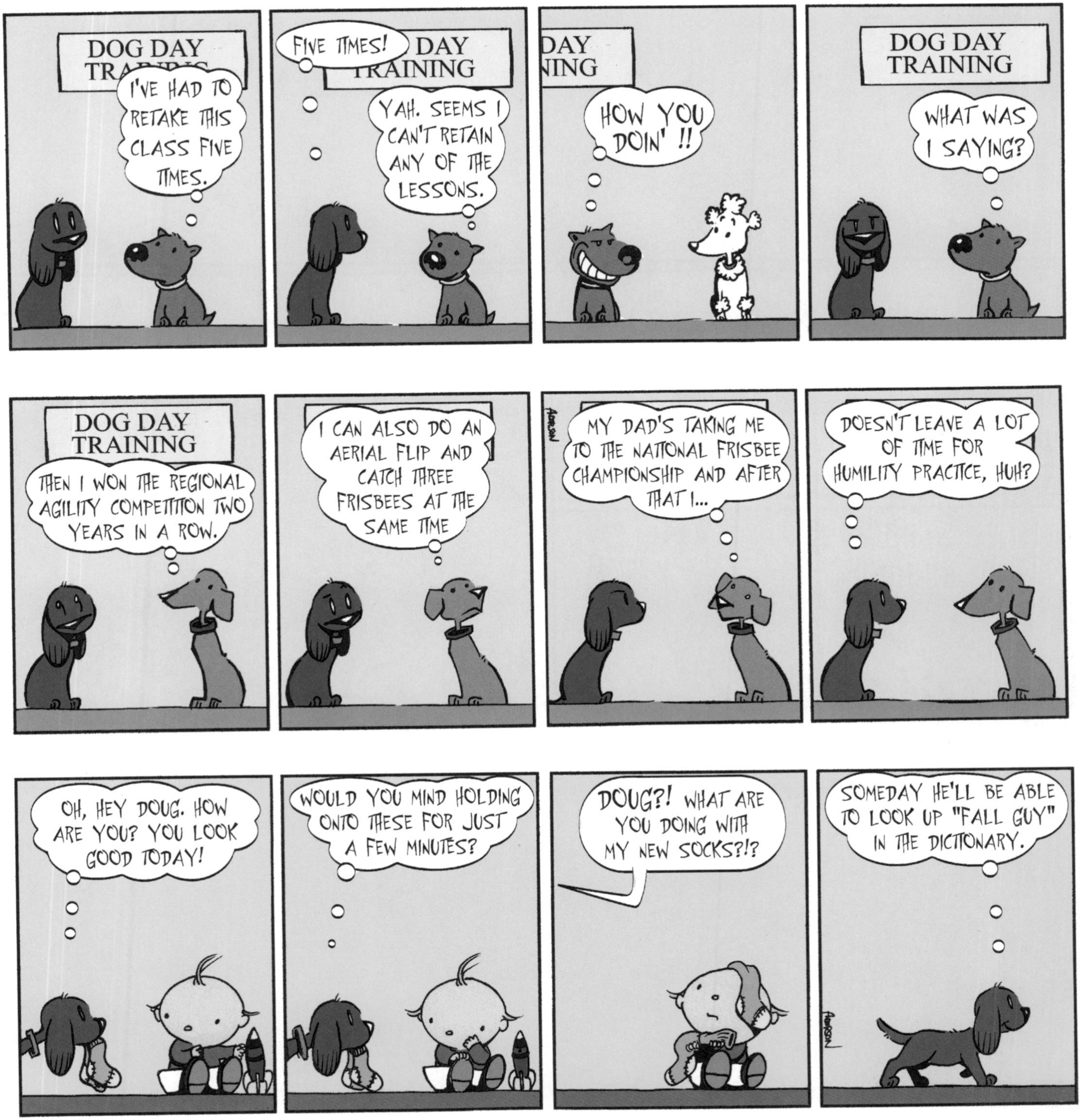
DOG DAY
I'VE HAD TO RETAKE THIS CLASS FIVE TIMES.
FIVE TIMES!
DAY TRAINING
YAH. SEEMS I CAN'T RETAIN ANY OF THE LESSONS.
HOW YOU DOIN' !!
DOG DAY TRAINING
WHAT WAS I SAYING?
DOG DAY TRAINING
THEN I WON THE REGIONAL AGILITY COMPETITION TWO YEARS IN A ROW.
I CAN ALSO DO AN AERIAL FLIP AND CATCH THREE FRISBEES AT THE SAME TIME
MY DAD'S TAKING ME TO THE NATIONAL FRISBEE CHAMPIONSHIP AND AFTER THAT I...
DOESN'T LEAVE A LOT OF TIME FOR HUMILITY PRACTICE, HUH?
OH, HEY DOUG. HOW ARE YOU? YOU LOOK GOOD TODAY!
WOULD YOU MIND HOLDING ONTO THESE FOR JUST A FEW MINUTES?
DOUG?! WHAT ARE YOU DOING WITH MY NEW SOCKS?!?
SOMEDAY HE'LL BE ABLE TO LOOK UP "FALL GUY" IN THE DICTIONARY.

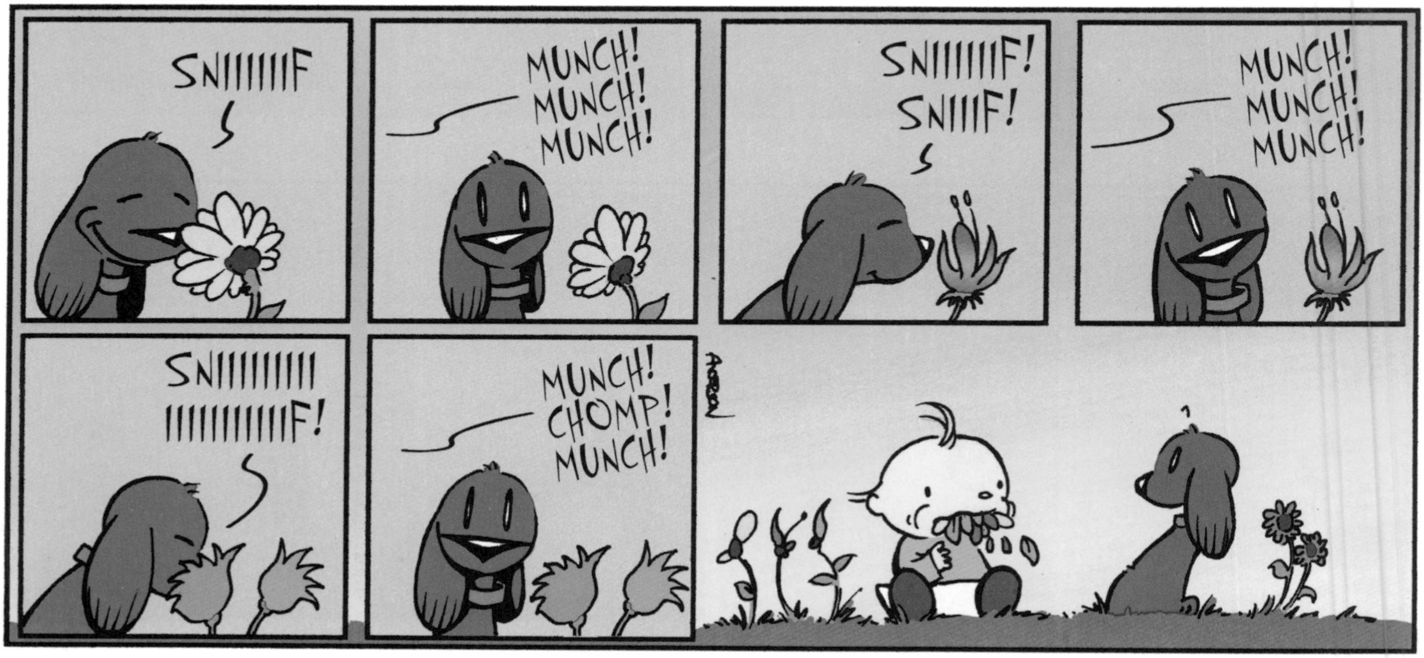
SNIIIIIIIF
MUNCH! MUNCH! MUNCH!
SNIIIIIIIF! SNIIIF!
MUNCH! MUNCH! MUNCH!
SNIIIIIIIII IIIIIIIIIIIF!
MUNCH! CHOMP! MUNCH!

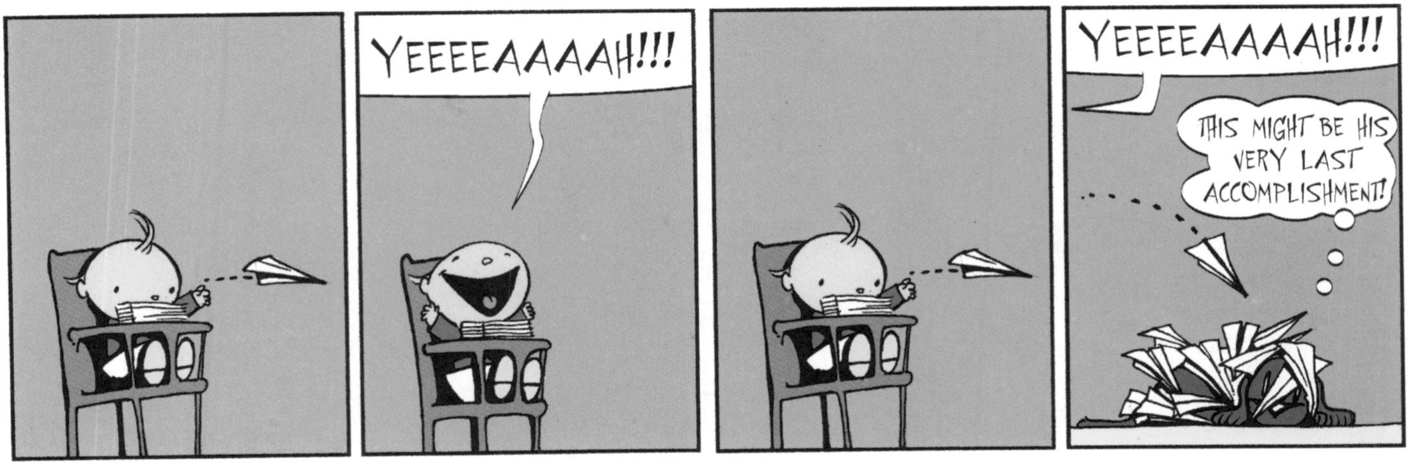
YEEEEAAAAH!!!
YEEEEAAAAH!!!
THIS MIGHT BE HIS VERY LAST ACCOMPLISHMENT!

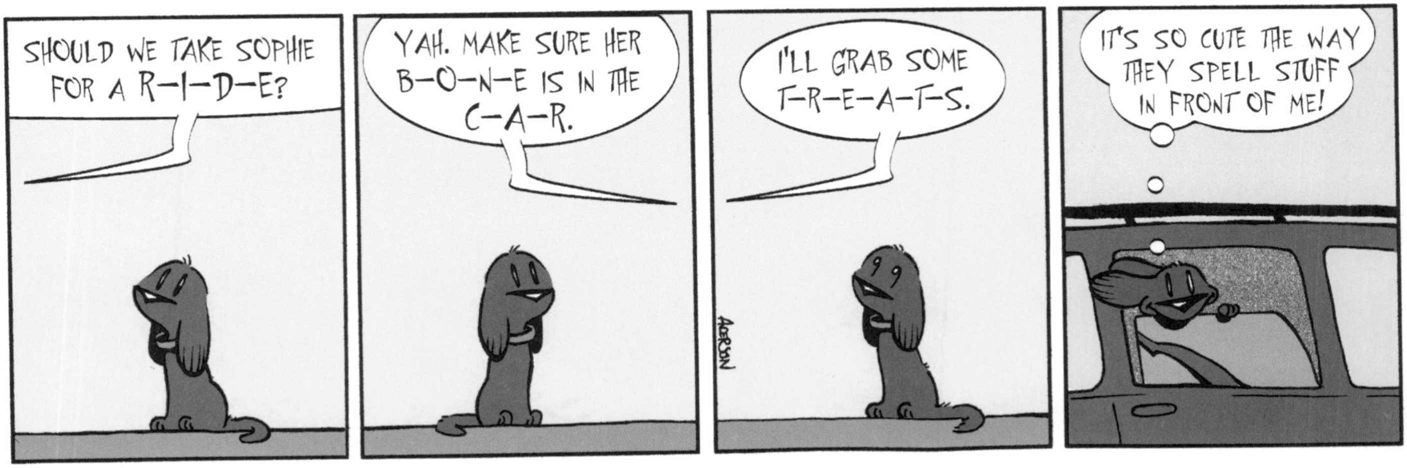
SHOULD WE TAKE SOPHIE FOR A R—I—D—E?
YAH. MAKE SURE HER B—O—N—E IS IN THE C—A—R.
I'LL GRAB SOME T—R—E—A—T—S.
IT'S SO CUTE THE WAY THEY SPELL STUFF IN FRONT OF ME!

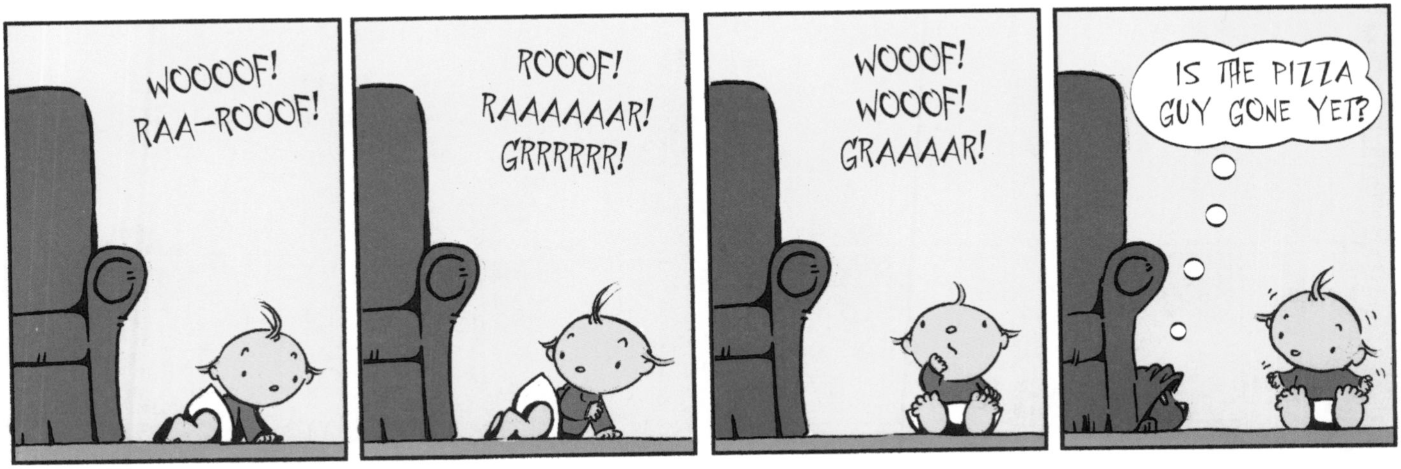
WOOOOF! RAA—ROOOF!
ROOOF! RAAAAAAR! GRRRRRR!
WOOOF! WOOOF! GRAAAAR!
IS THE PIZZA GUY GONE YET?

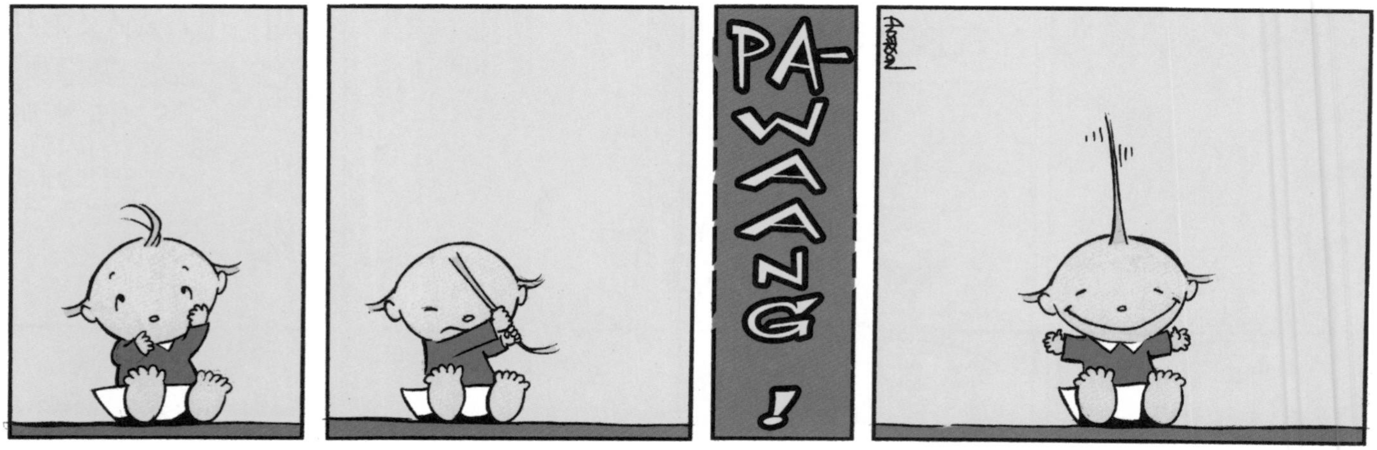
PA-WAANG!

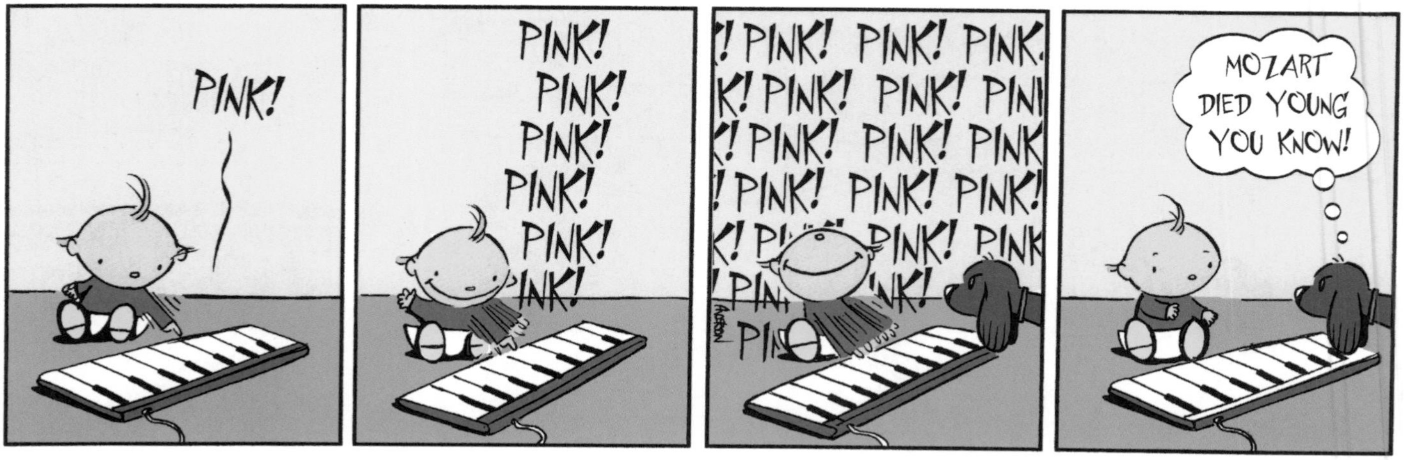
PINK!
PINK!
PINK!
PINK!
PINK!
PINK!
PINK! PINK! PINK!
PINK! PINK!
PINK! PINK! PINK!
PINK! PINK! PINK!
MOZART DIED YOUNG YOU KNOW!

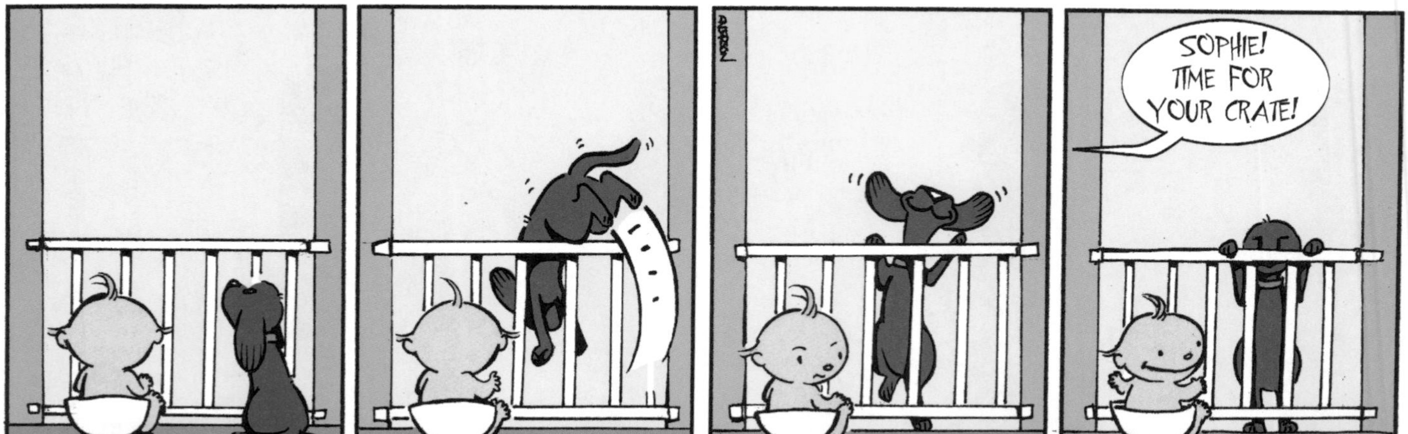
SOPHIE! TIME FOR YOUR CRATE!

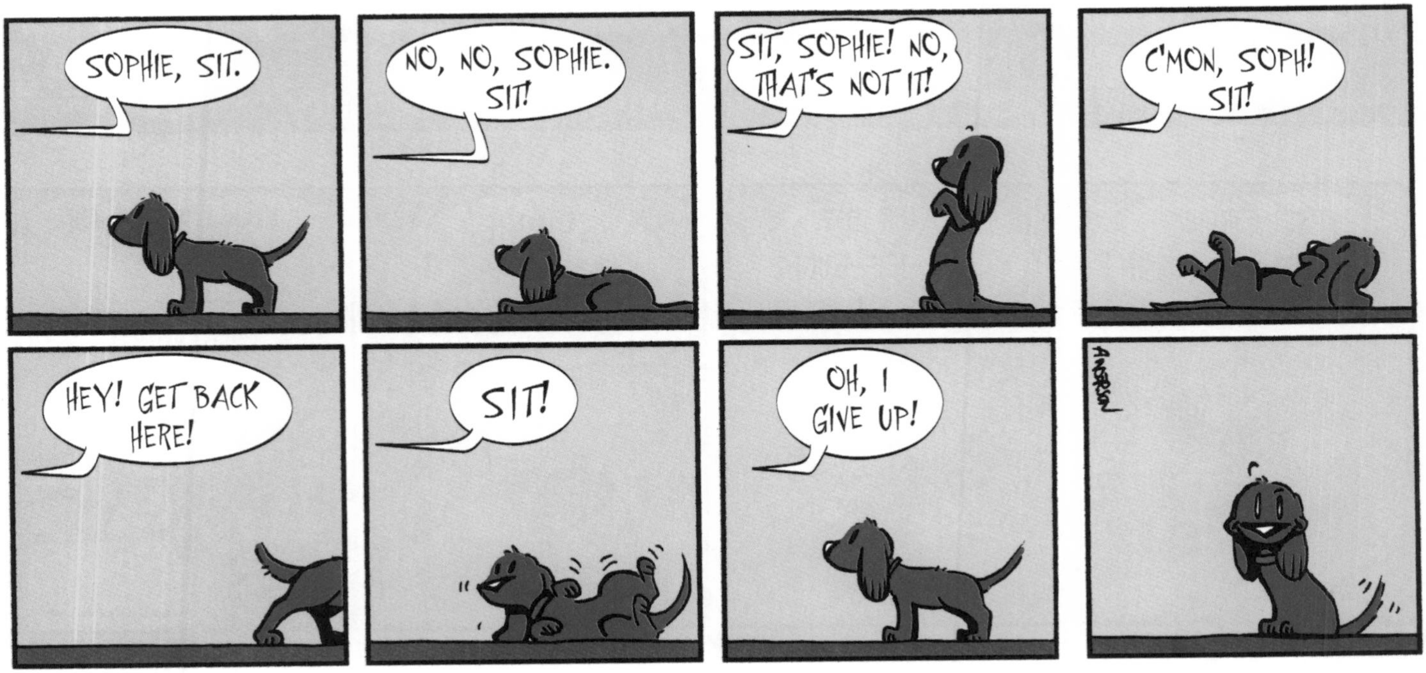
SOPHIE, SIT.
NO, NO, SOPHIE. SIT!
SIT, SOPHIE! NO, THAT'S NOT IT!
C'MON, SOPH! SIT!
HEY! GET BACK HERE!
SIT!
OH, I GIVE UP!
ANDERSON

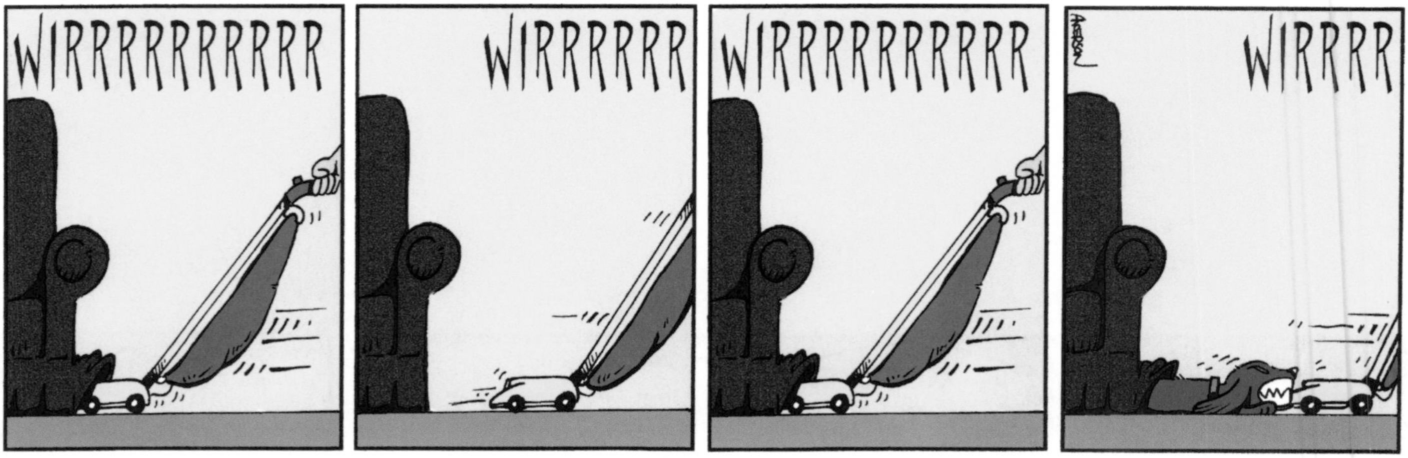
WIRRRRRRRRRR
WIRRRRRR
WIRRRRRRRRRR
WIRRRR

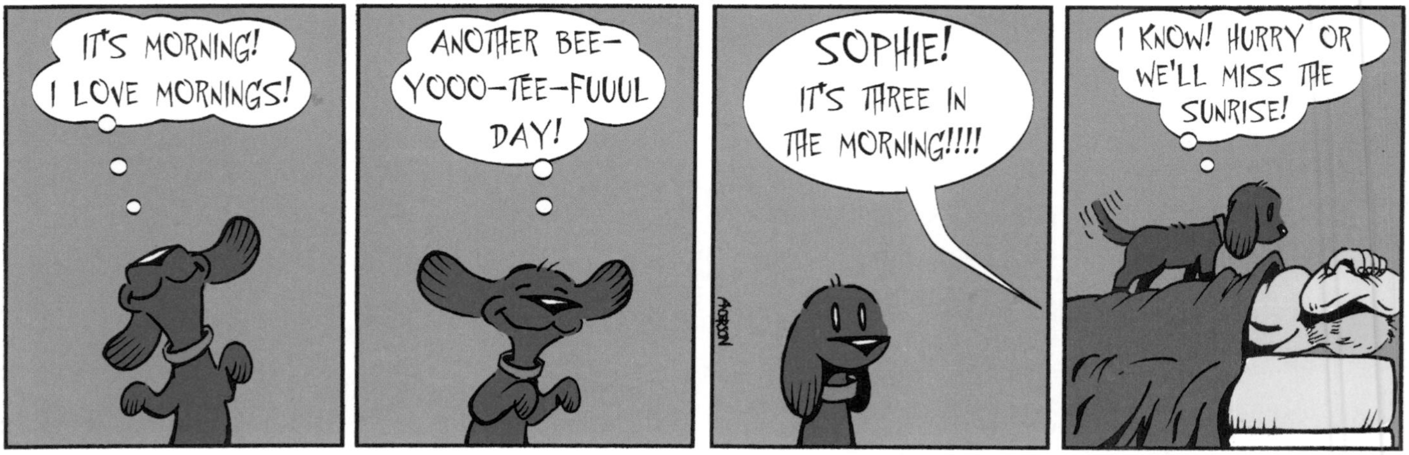
IT'S MORNING! I LOVE MORNINGS!
ANOTHER BEE-YOOO-TEE-FUUUL DAY!
SOPHIE! IT'S THREE IN THE MORNING!!!!
I KNOW! HURRY OR WE'LL MISS THE SUNRISE!

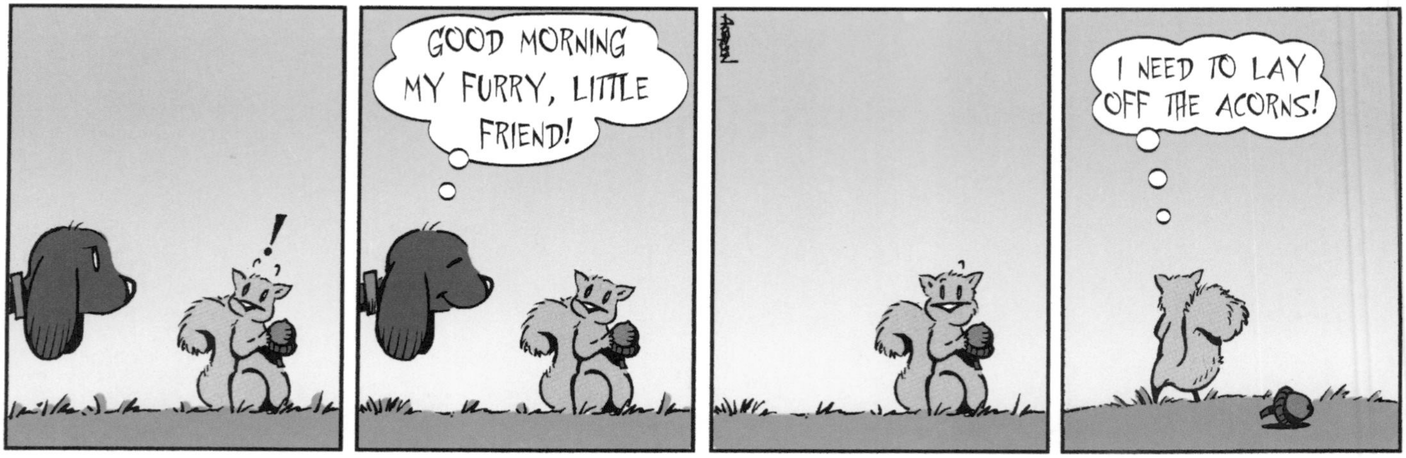
!
GOOD MORNING MY FURRY, LITTLE FRIEND!
I NEED TO LAY OFF THE ACORNS!

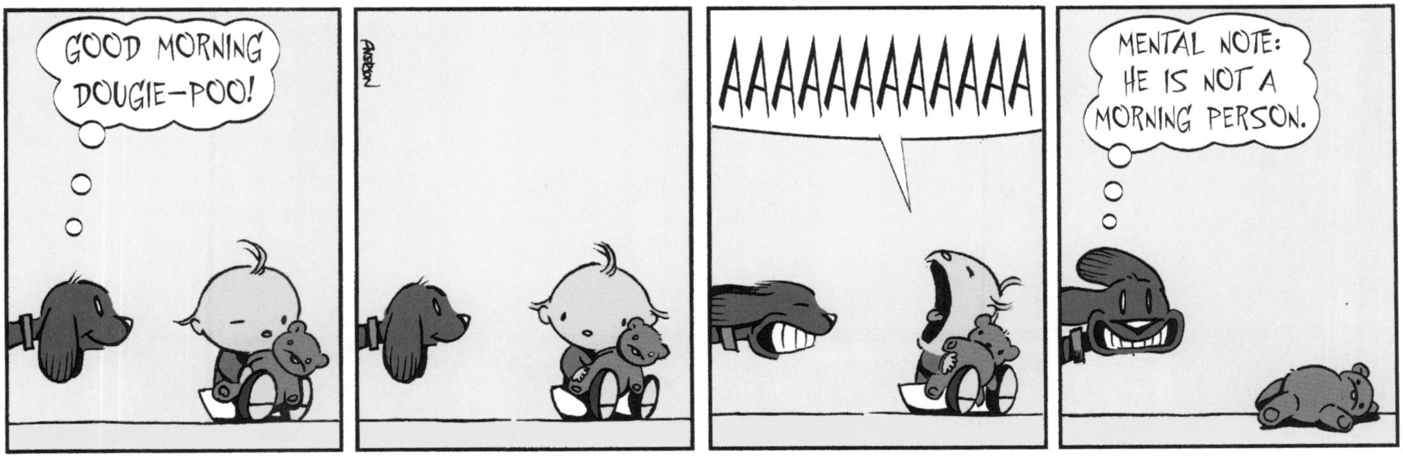
GOOD MORNING DOUGIE-POO!
AAAAAAAAAAAA
MENTAL NOTE: HE IS NOT A MORNING PERSON.

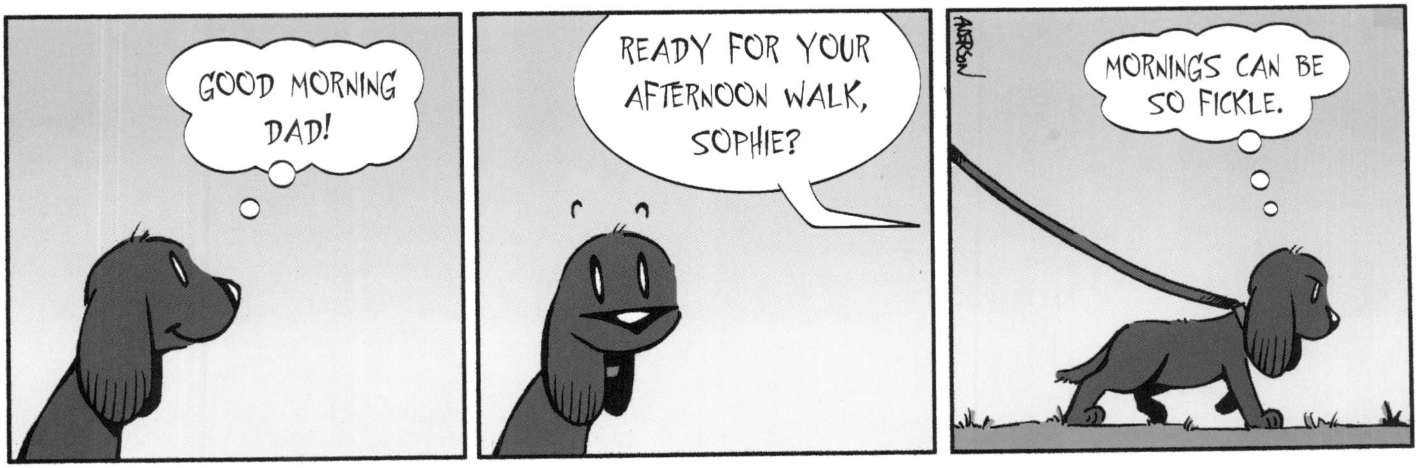
GOOD MORNING DAD!
READY FOR YOUR AFTERNOON WALK, SOPHIE?
MORNINGS CAN BE SO FICKLE.

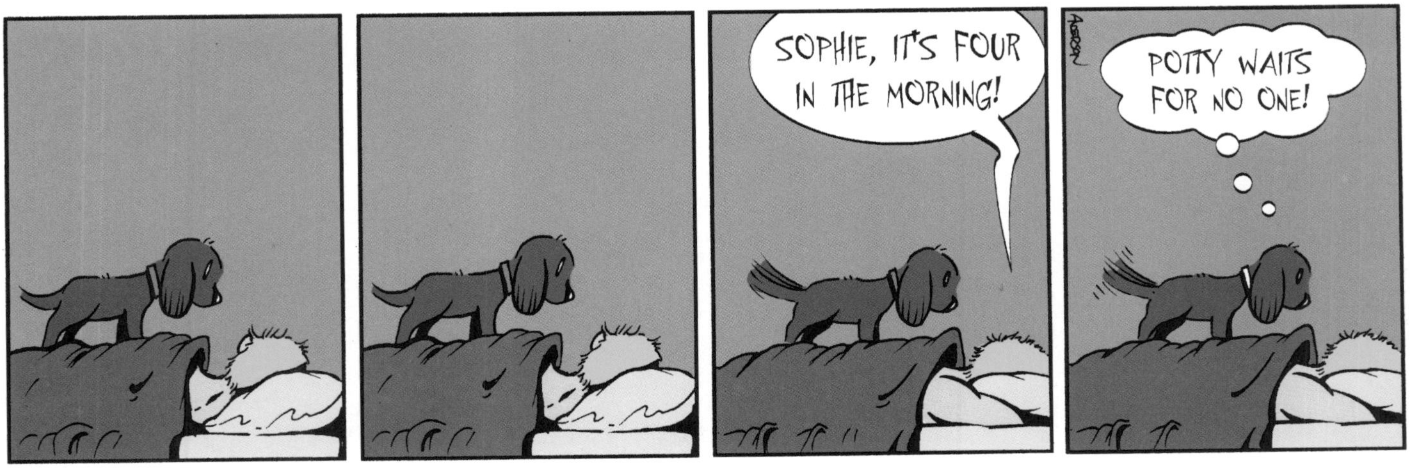
SOPHIE, IT'S FOUR IN THE MORNING!
POTTY WAITS FOR NO ONE!

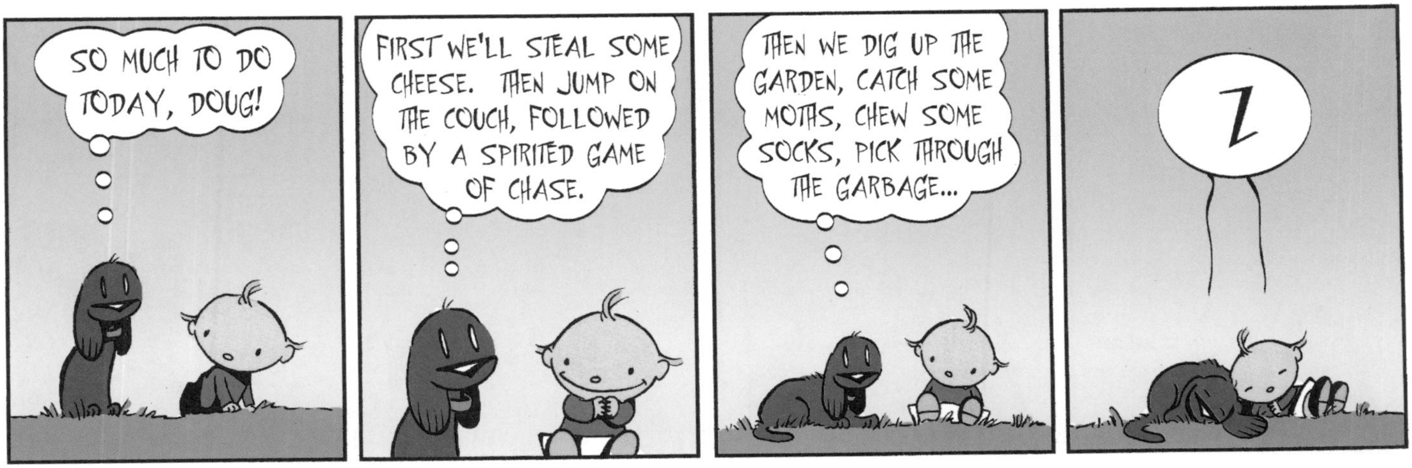
SO MUCH TO DO TODAY, DOUG!
FIRST WE'LL STEAL SOME CHEESE. THEN JUMP ON THE COUCH, FOLLOWED BY A SPIRITED GAME OF CHASE.
THEN WE DIG UP THE GARDEN, CATCH SOME MOTHS, CHEW SOME SOCKS, PICK THROUGH THE GARBAGE...
Z

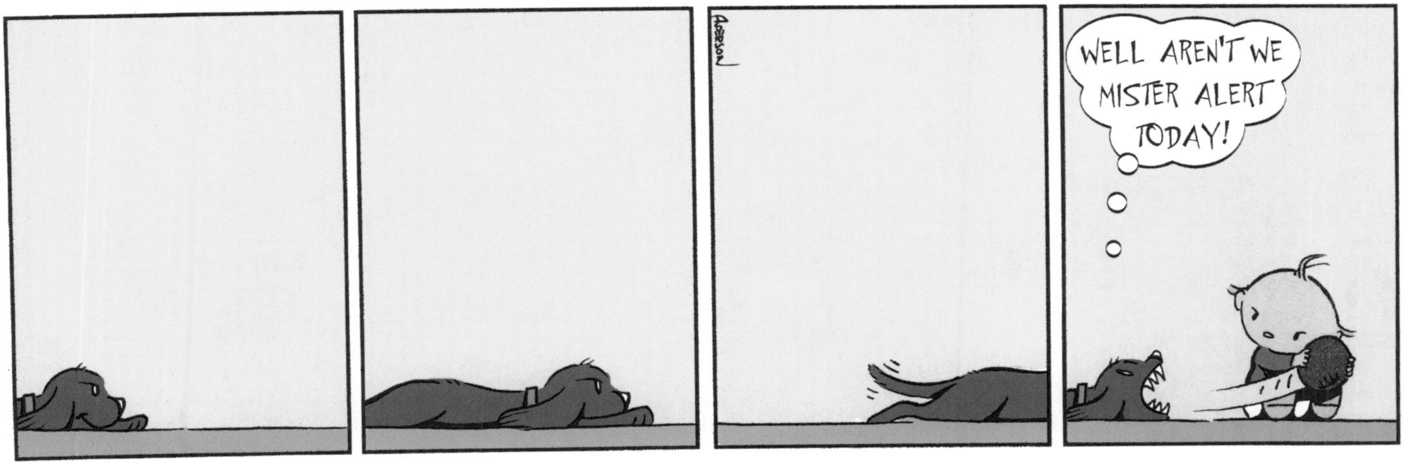
WELL AREN'T WE MISTER ALERT TODAY!

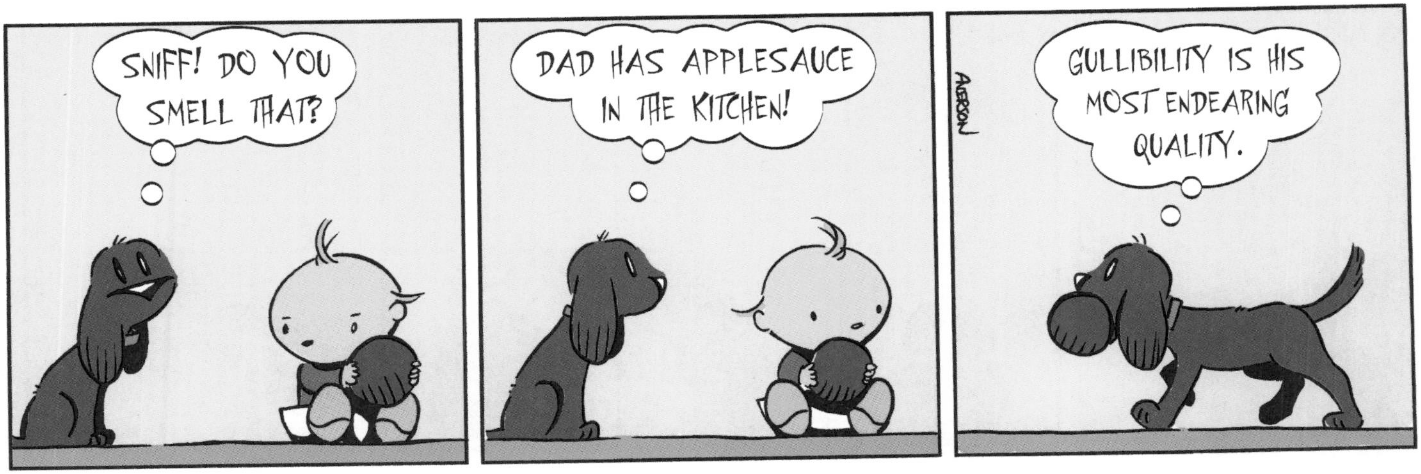
SNIFF! DO YOU SMELL THAT?
DAD HAS APPLESAUCE IN THE KITCHEN!
GULLIBILITY IS HIS MOST ENDEARING QUALITY.

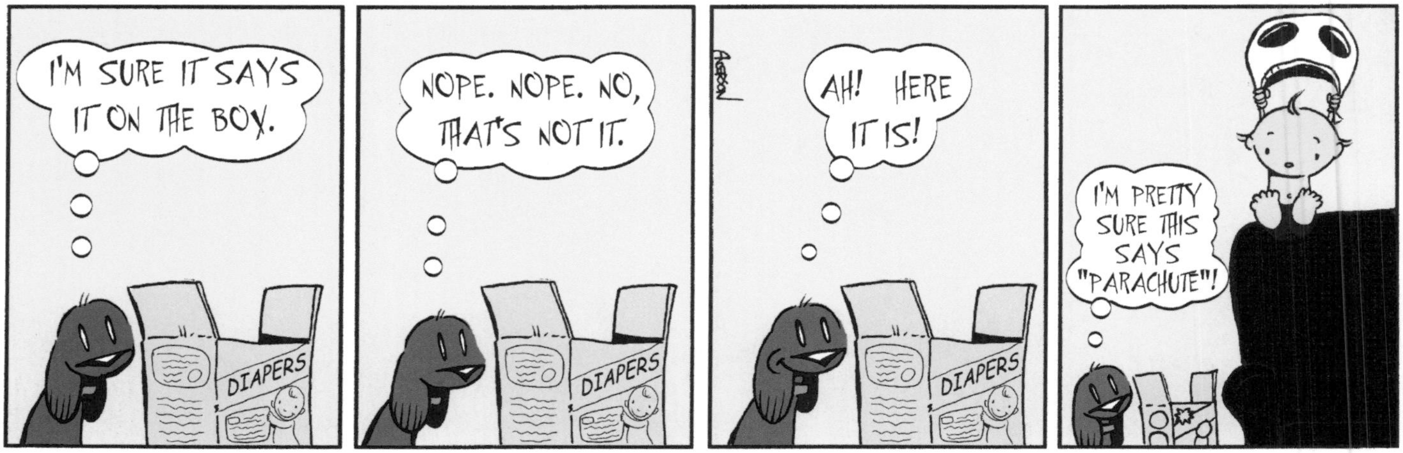
I'M SURE IT SAYS IT ON THE BOX.
NOPE. NOPE. NO, THAT'S NOT IT.
AH! HERE IT IS!
DIAPERS
I'M PRETTY SURE THIS SAYS "PARACHUTE"!

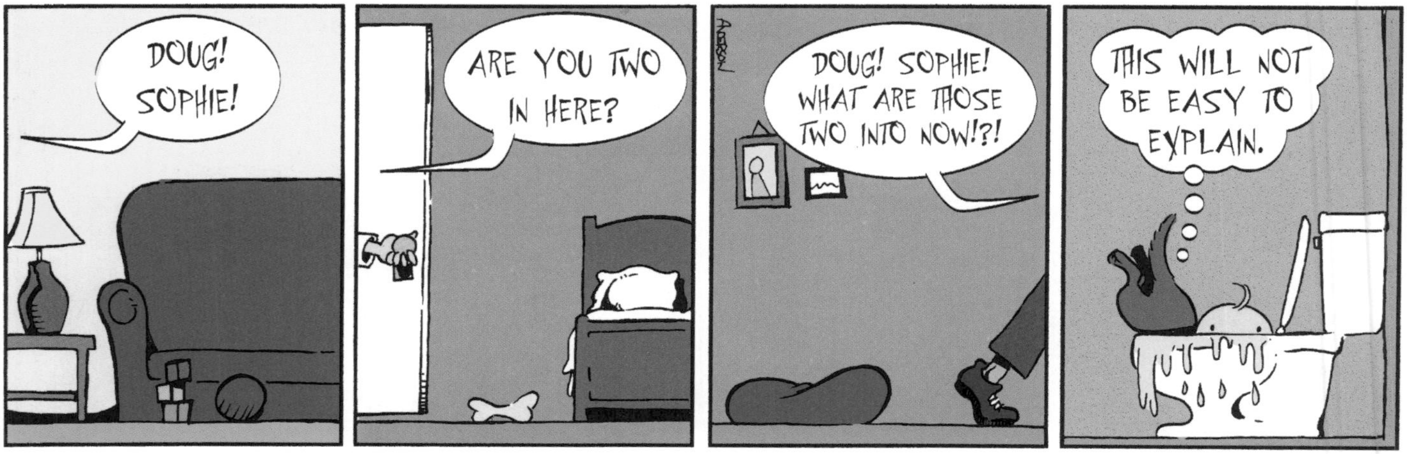
DOUG! SOPHIE!
ARE YOU TWO IN HERE?
DOUG! SOPHIE! WHAT ARE THOSE TWO INTO NOW!?!
THIS WILL NOT BE EASY TO EXPLAIN.

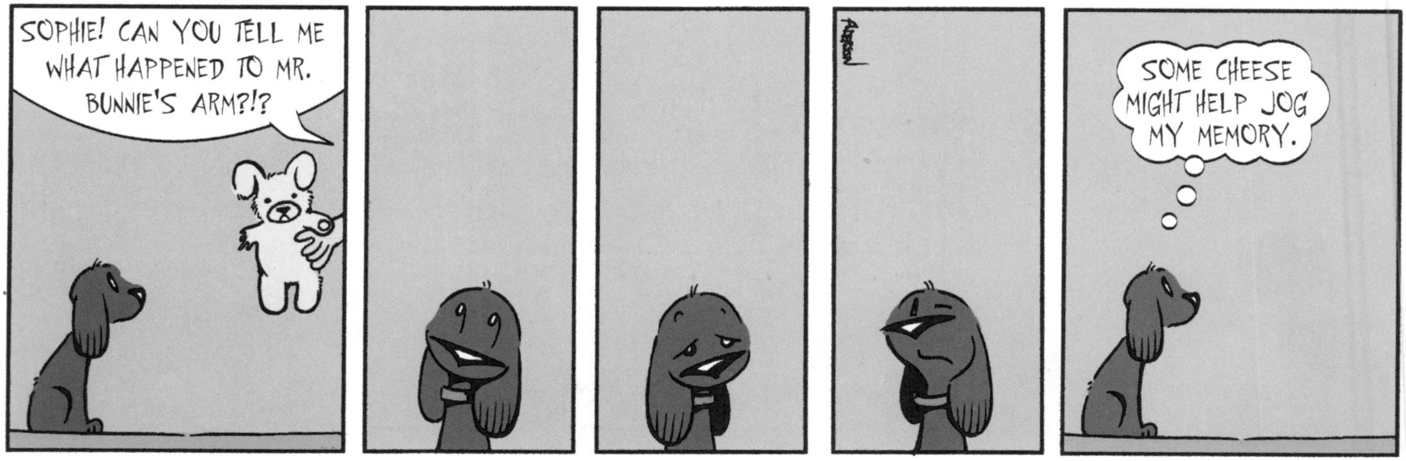
SOPHIE! CAN YOU TELL ME WHAT HAPPENED TO MR. BUNNIE'S ARM?!?
SOME CHEESE MIGHT HELP JOG MY MEMORY.

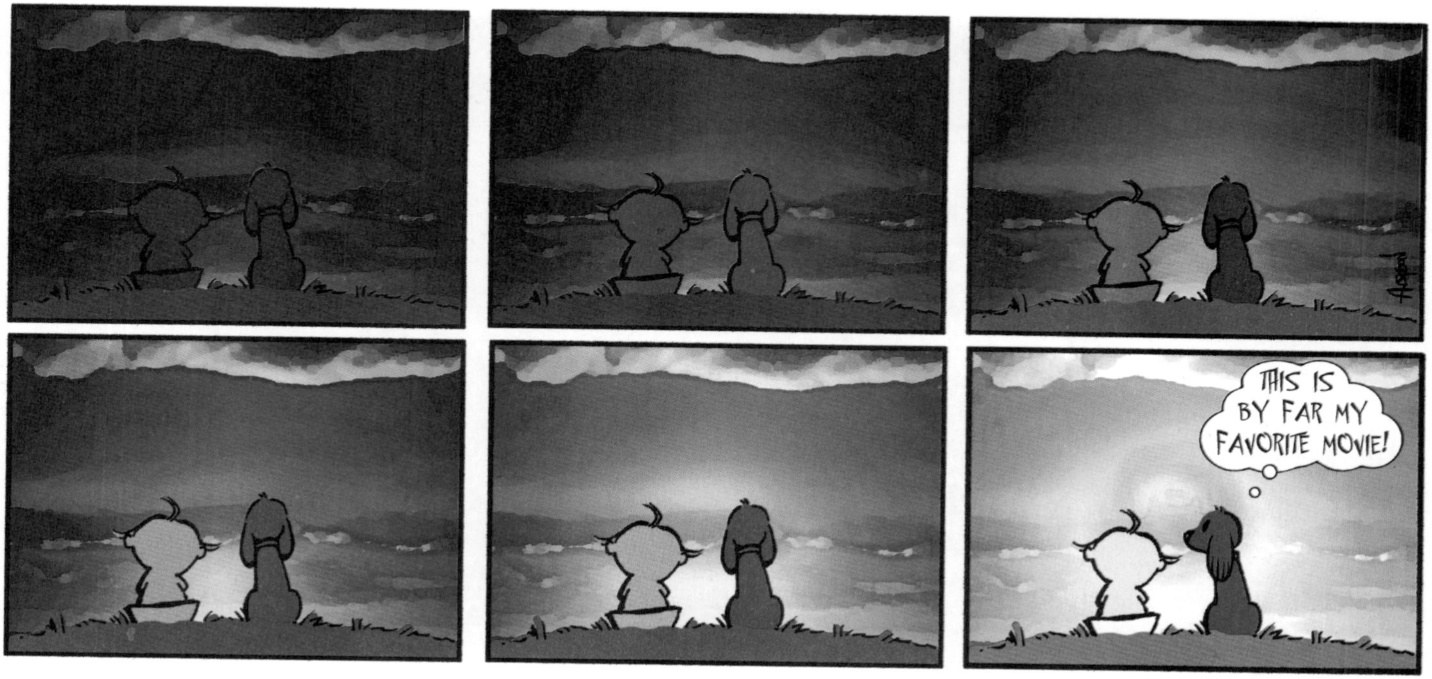
THIS IS BY FAR MY FAVORITE MOVIE!

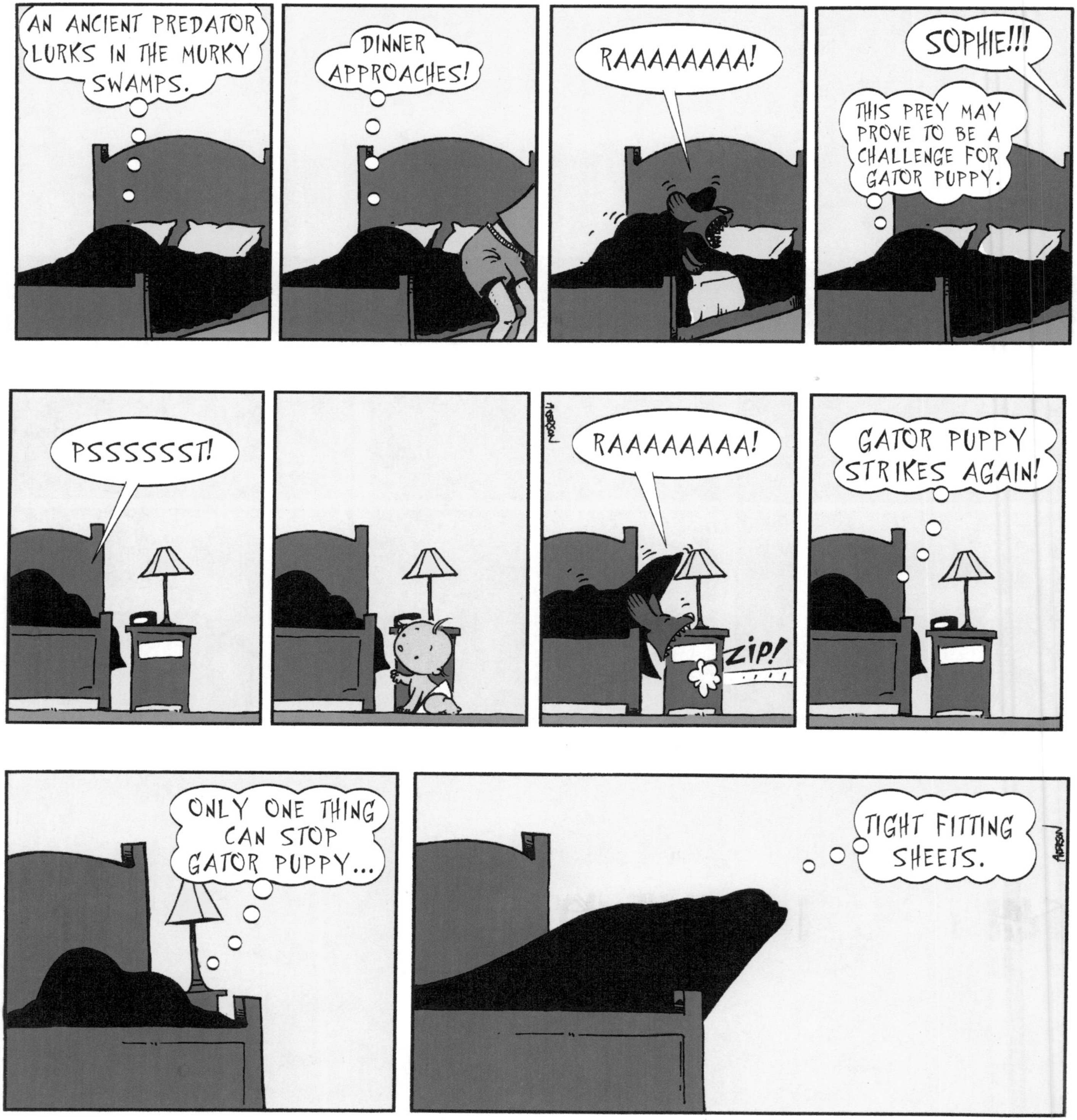
AN ANCIENT PREDATOR LURKS IN THE MURKY SWAMPS.
DINNER APPROACHES!
RAAAAAAAA!
SOPHIE!!!
THIS PREY MAY PROVE TO BE A CHALLENGE FOR GATOR PUPPY.
PSSSSSST!
RAAAAAAAA!
ZIP!
GATOR PUPPY STRIKES AGAIN!
ONLY ONE THING CAN STOP GATOR PUPPY...
TIGHT FITTING SHEETS.

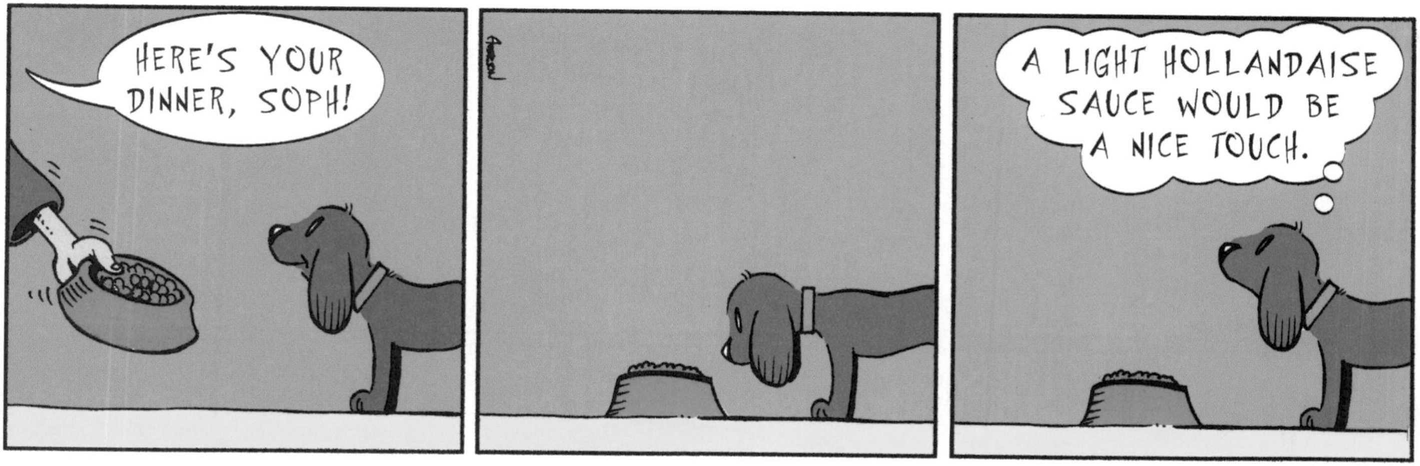
HERE'S YOUR DINNER, SOPH!
A LIGHT HOLLANDAISE SAUCE WOULD BE A NICE TOUCH.

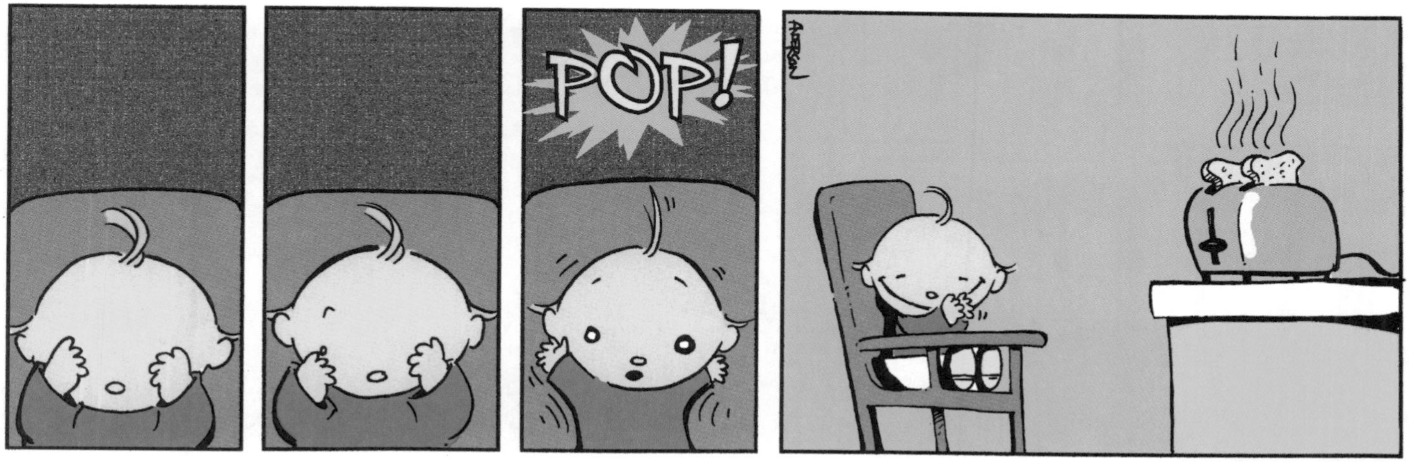
POP!

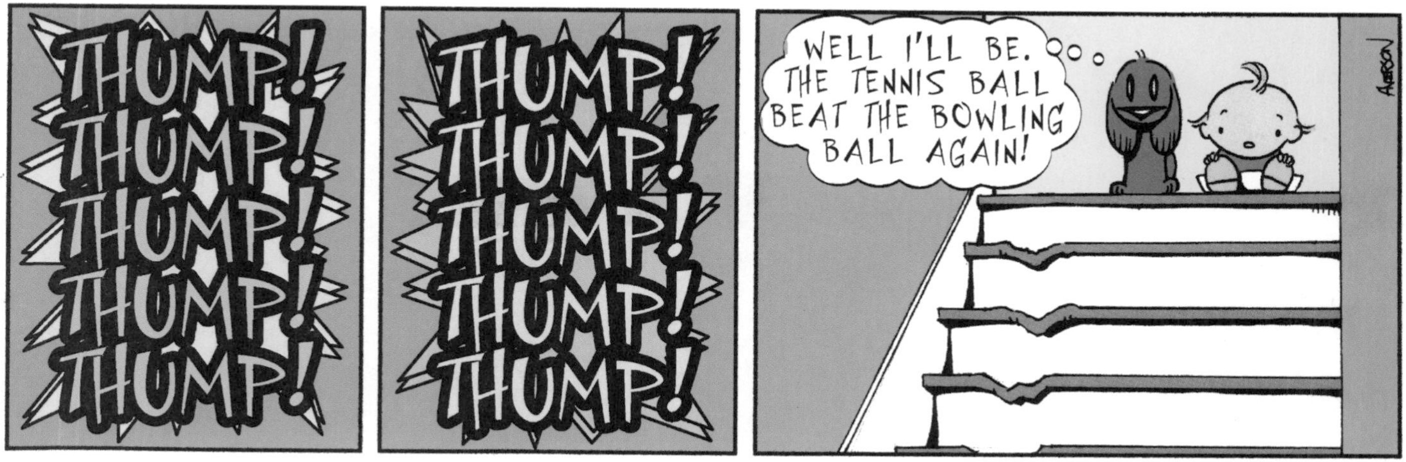
THUMP! THUMP! THUMP! THUMP! THUMP!
THUMP! THUMP! THUMP! THUMP! THUMP!
WELL I'LL BE. THE TENNIS BALL BEAT THE BOWLING BALL AGAIN!

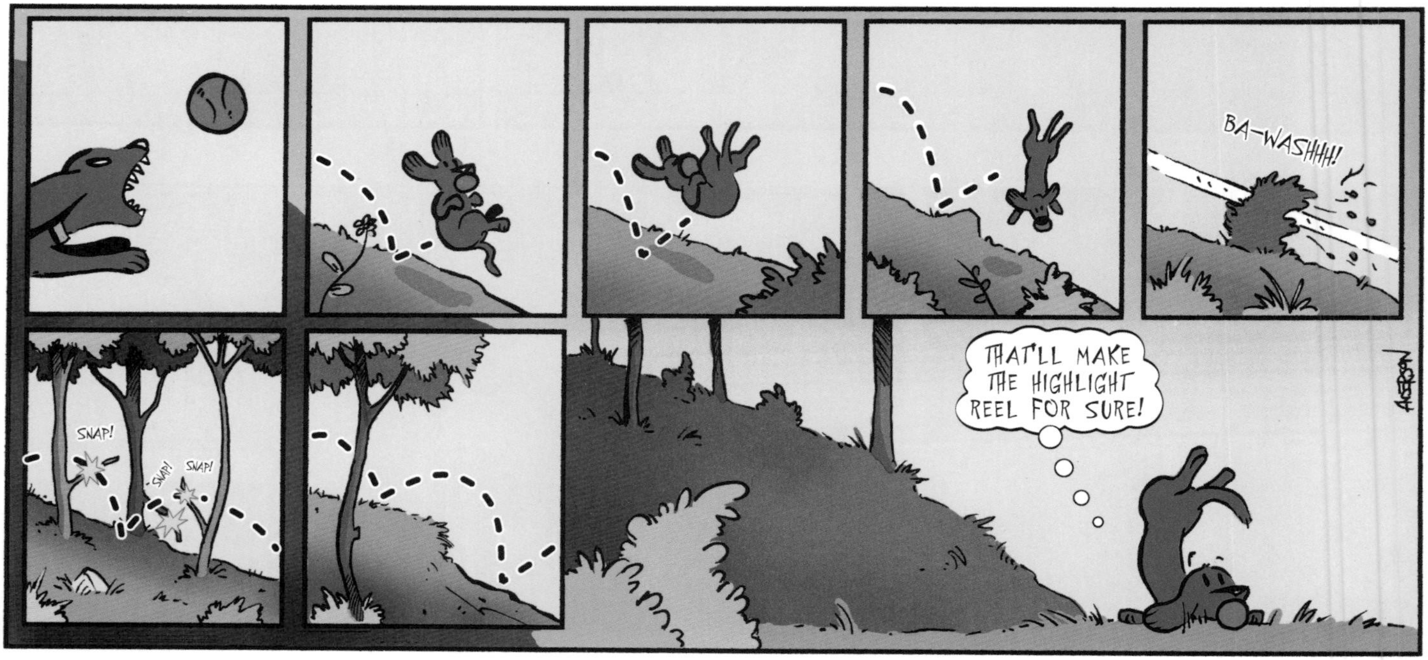
BA-WASHHH!
SNAP!
SNAP!
SNAP!
THAT'LL MAKE THE HIGHLIGHT REEL FOR SURE!

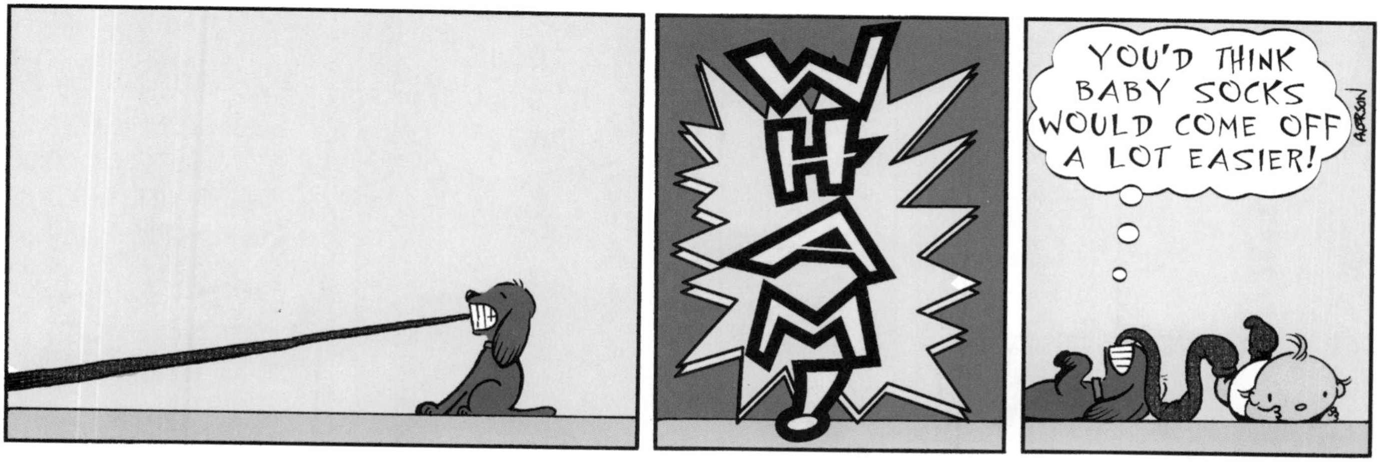
WHAM!
YOU'D THINK BABY SOCKS WOULD COME OFF A LOT EASIER!

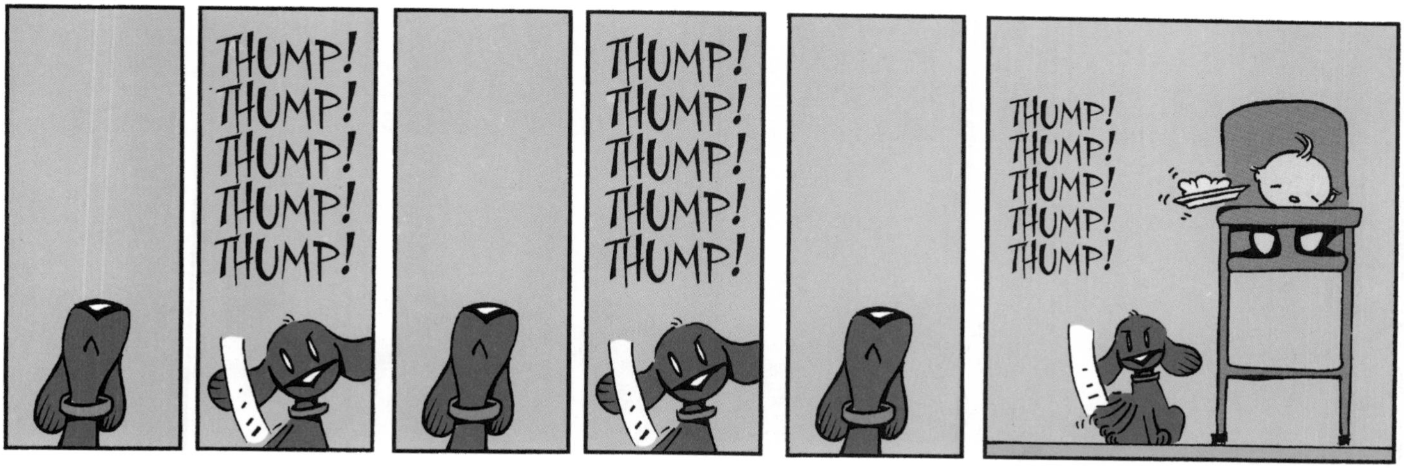
THUMP! THUMP! THUMP! THUMP! THUMP!
THUMP! THUMP! THUMP! THUMP! THUMP!
THUMP! THUMP! THUMP! THUMP! THUMP!

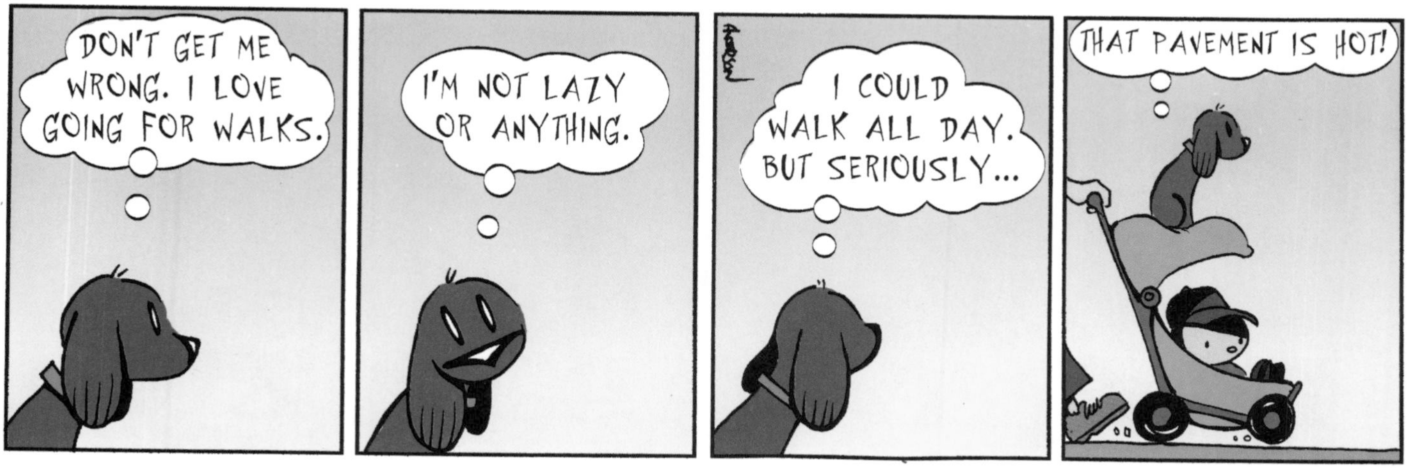
DON'T GET ME WRONG. I LOVE GOING FOR WALKS.
I'M NOT LAZY OR ANYTHING.
I COULD WALK ALL DAY. BUT SERIOUSLY...
THAT PAVEMENT IS HOT!

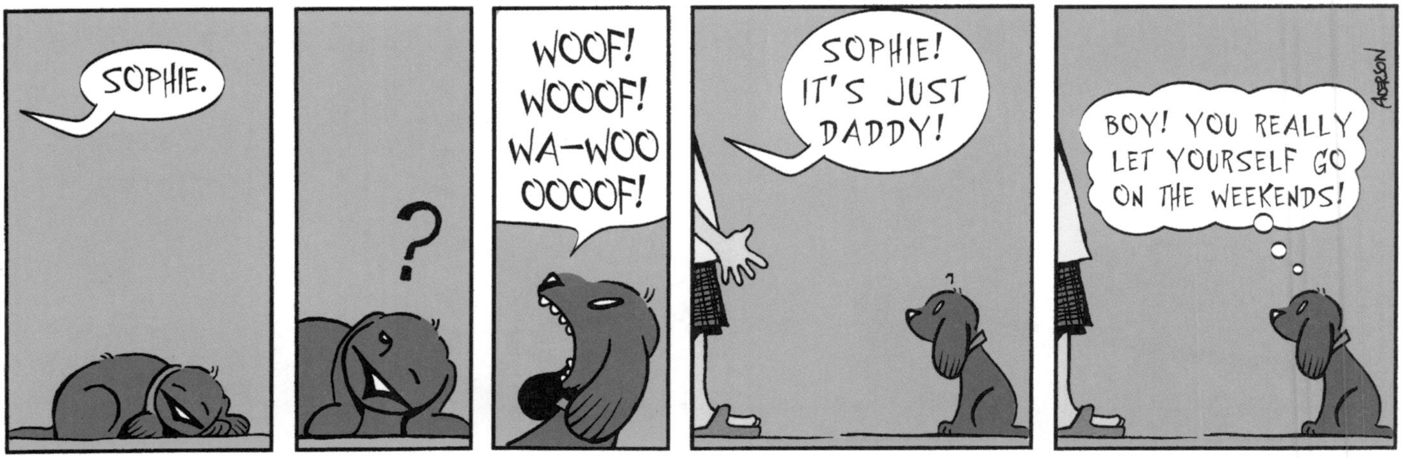
SOPHIE.
?
WOOF! WOOOF! WA-WOO OOOOF!
SOPHIE! IT'S JUST DADDY!
BOY! YOU REALLY LET YOURSELF GO ON THE WEEKENDS!

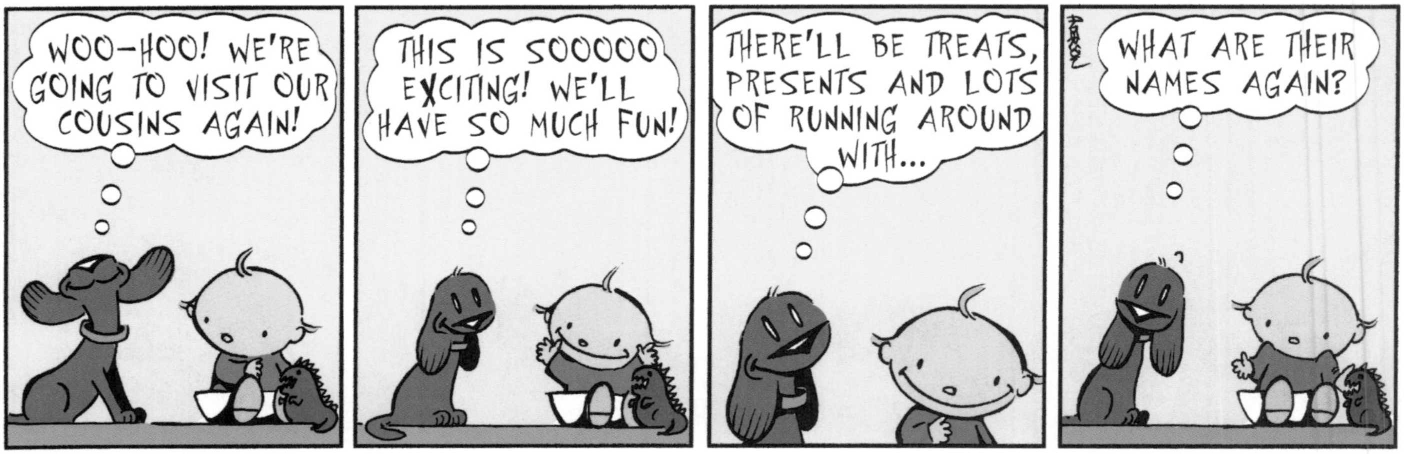
WOO-HOO! WE'RE GOING TO VISIT OUR COUSINS AGAIN!
THIS IS SOOOOO EXCITING! WE'LL HAVE SO MUCH FUN!
THERE'LL BE TREATS, PRESENTS AND LOTS OF RUNNING AROUND WITH...
WHAT ARE THEIR NAMES AGAIN?

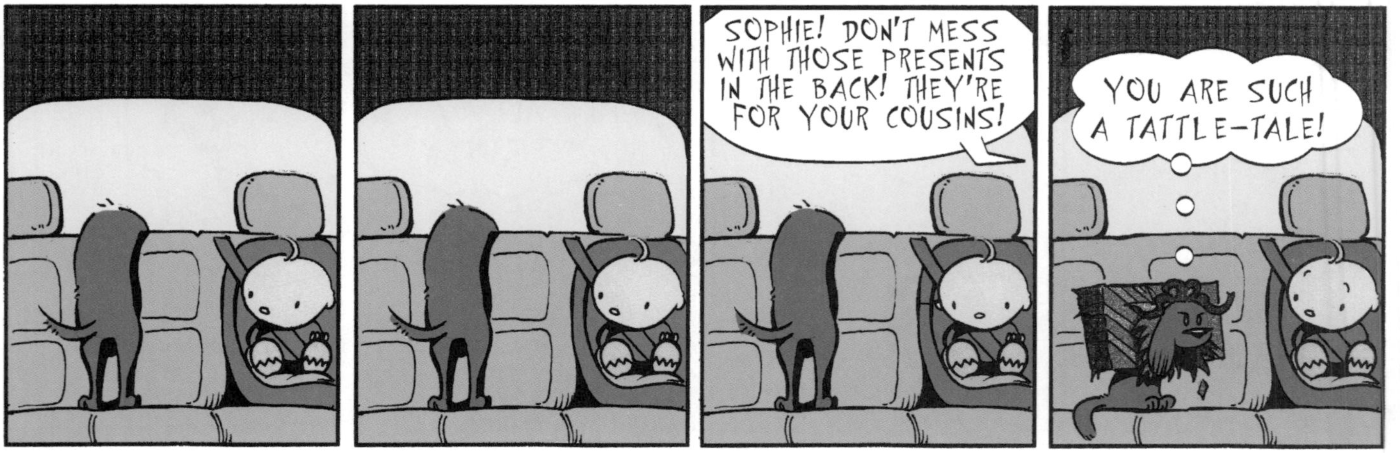
SOPHIE! DON'T MESS WITH THOSE PRESENTS IN THE BACK! THEY'RE FOR YOUR COUSINS!
YOU ARE SUCH A TATTLE-TALE!

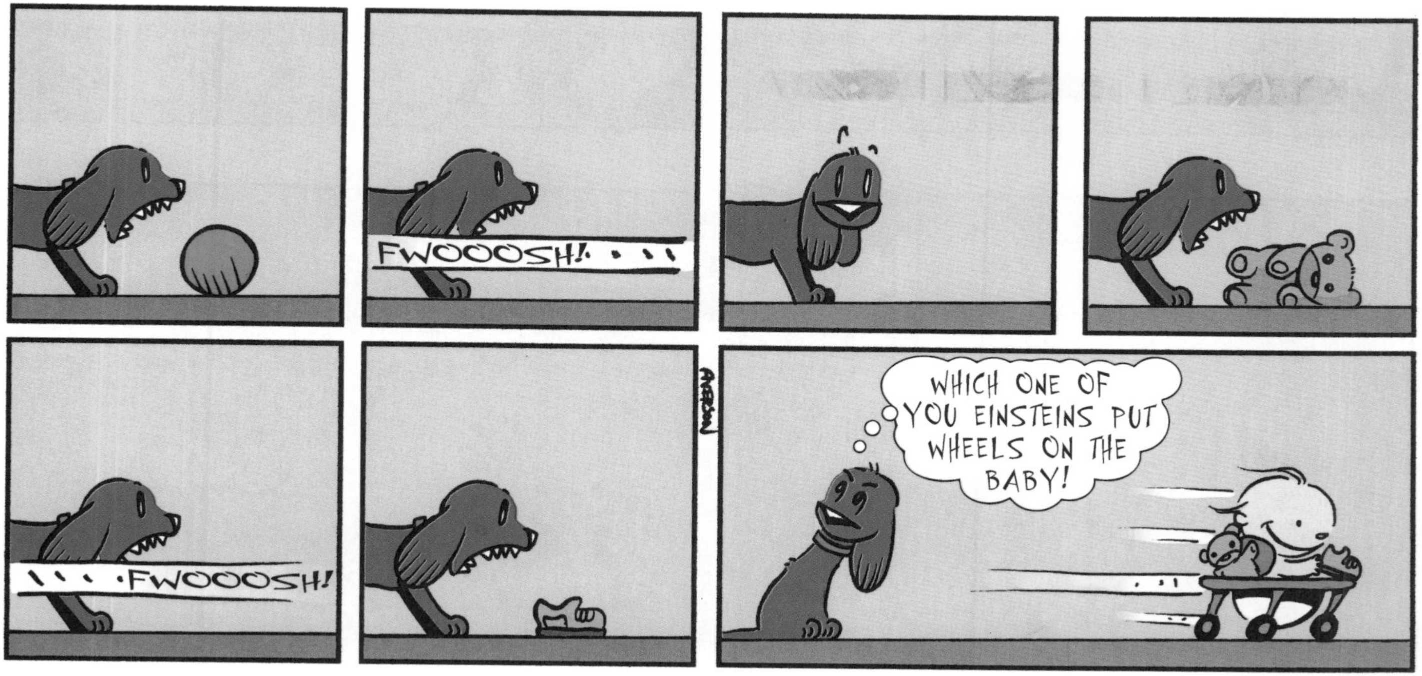
FWOOOSH!
FWOOOSH!
ANDERSON
WHICH ONE OF YOU EINSTEINS PUT WHEELS ON THE BABY!

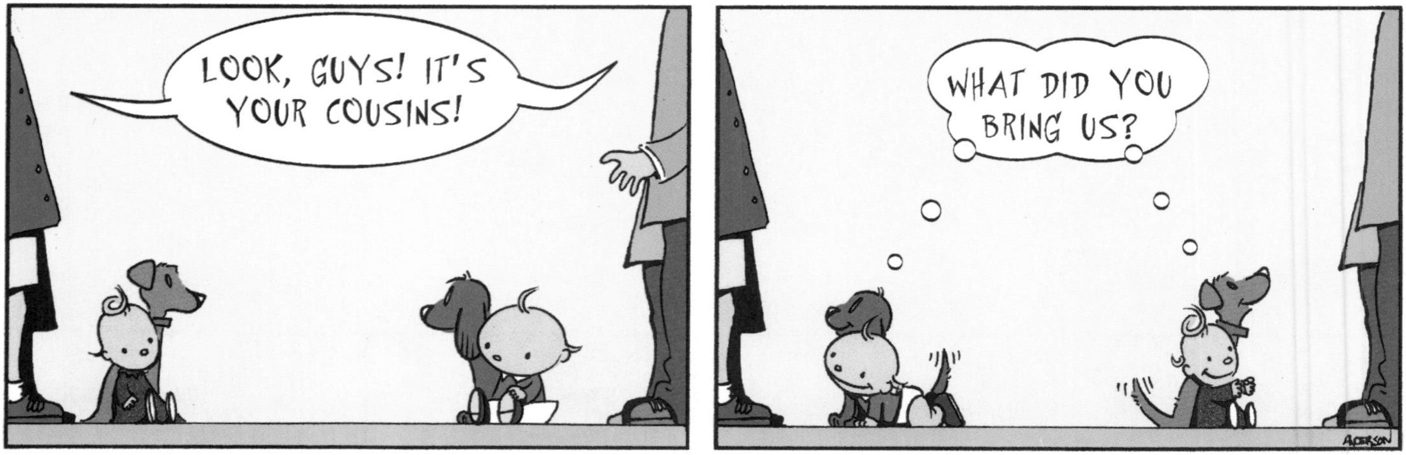
LOOK, GUYS! IT'S YOUR COUSINS!
WHAT DID YOU BRING US?

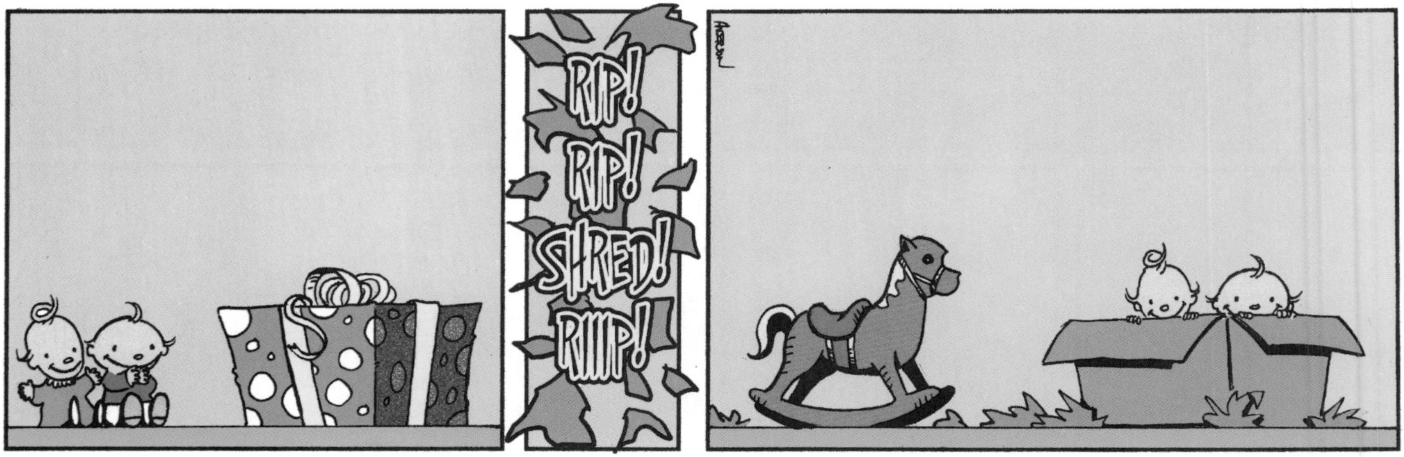
RIP!
RIP!
SHRED!
RIIIP!

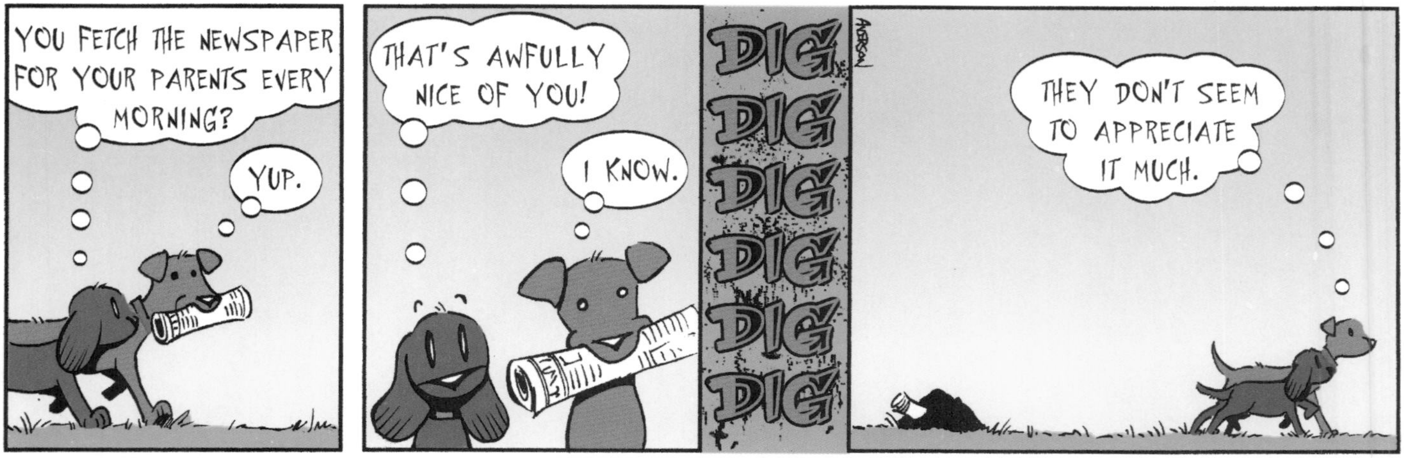
YOU FETCH THE NEWSPAPER FOR YOUR PARENTS EVERY MORNING?
YUP.
THAT'S AWFULLY NICE OF YOU!
I KNOW.
DIG
DIG
DIG
DIG
DIG
DIG
THEY DON'T SEEM TO APPRECIATE IT MUCH.

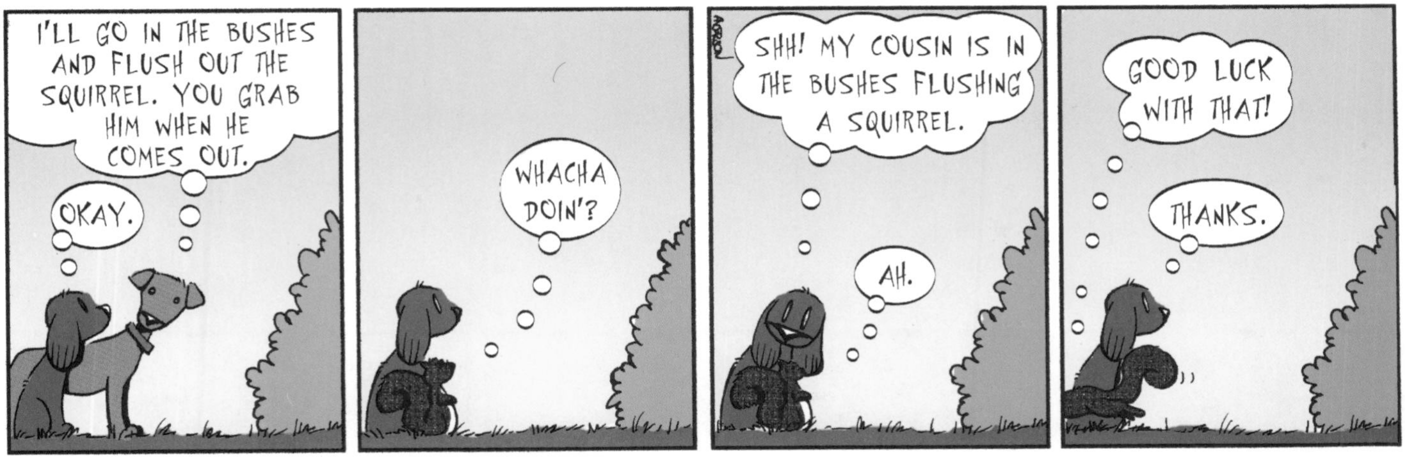
I'LL GO IN THE BUSHES AND FLUSH OUT THE SQUIRREL. YOU GRAB HIM WHEN HE COMES OUT.
OKAY.
WHACHA DOIN'?
SHH! MY COUSIN IS IN THE BUSHES FLUSHING A SQUIRREL.
AH.
GOOD LUCK WITH THAT!
THANKS.

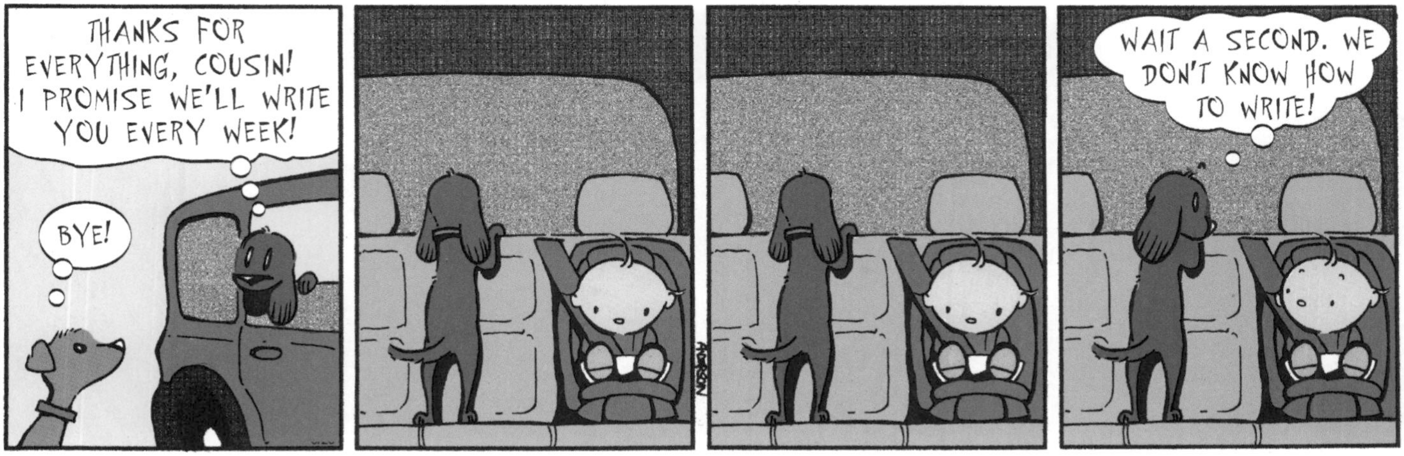
THANKS FOR EVERYTHING, COUSIN! I PROMISE WE'LL WRITE YOU EVERY WEEK!
BYE!
WAIT A SECOND. WE DON'T KNOW HOW TO WRITE!

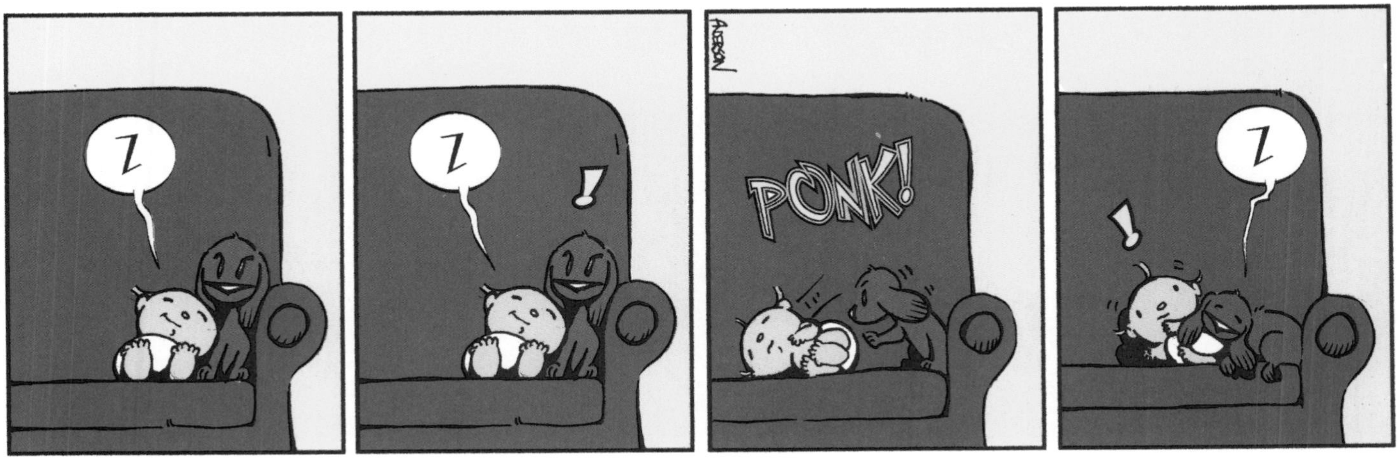
Z
Z
!
PONK!
!
Z

CRASH!
OW!
ANDERSON
QUICK! EAT A MINT! YOUR BREATH SMELLS LIKE FORMULA!

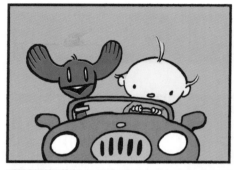

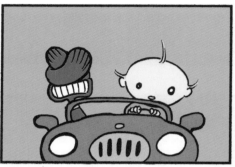

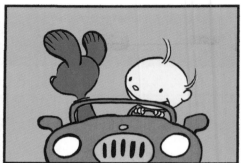

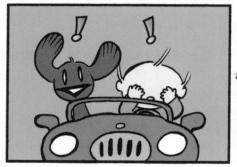

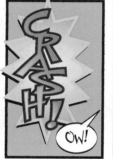

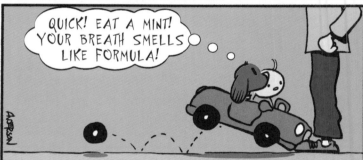

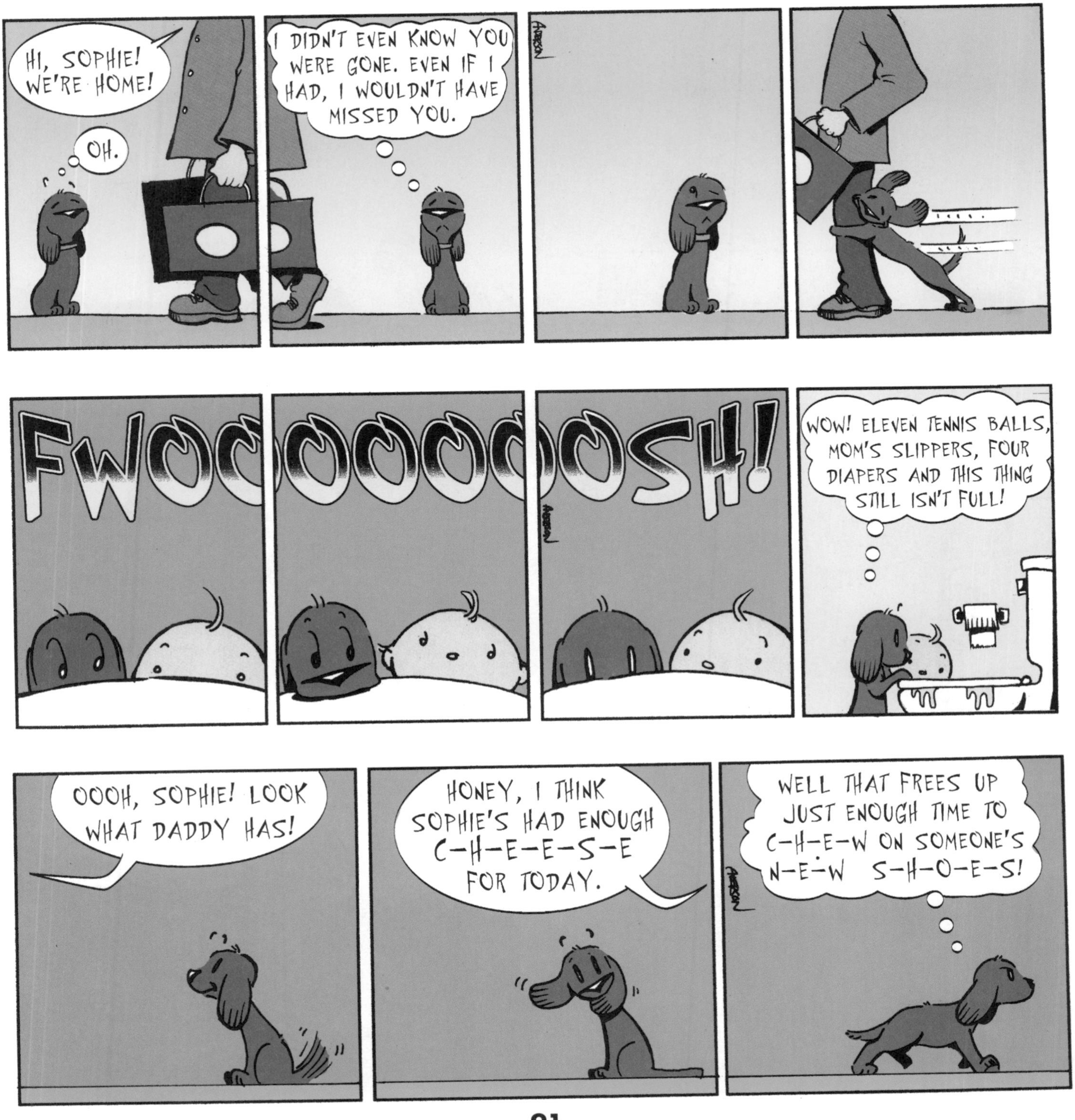

HI, SOPHIE! WE'RE HOME!
OH.
I DIDN'T EVEN KNOW YOU WERE GONE. EVEN IF I HAD, I WOULDN'T HAVE MISSED YOU.
FWOOOOOOOOOSH!
WOW! ELEVEN TENNIS BALLS, MOM'S SLIPPERS, FOUR DIAPERS AND THIS THING STILL ISN'T FULL!
OOOH, SOPHIE! LOOK WHAT DADDY HAS!
HONEY, I THINK SOPHIE'S HAD ENOUGH C-H-E-E-S-E FOR TODAY.
WELL THAT FREES UP JUST ENOUGH TIME TO C-H-E-W ON SOMEONE'S N-E-W S-H-O-E-S!

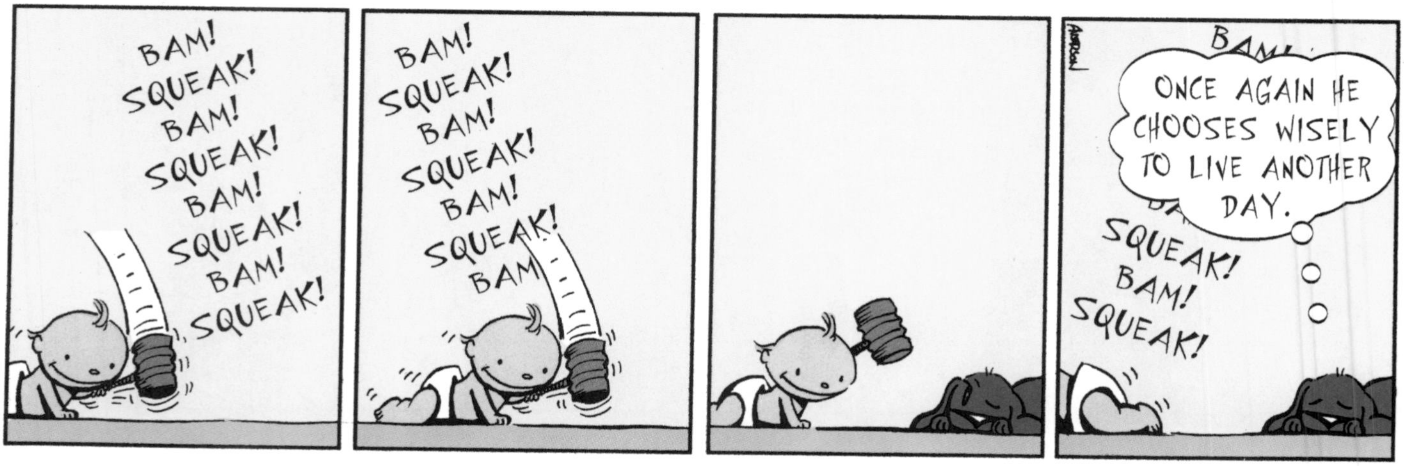
BAM!
SQUEAK!
BAM!
SQUEAK!
SQUEAK!
BAM!
SQUEAK!
BAM!
SQUEAK!
BAM!
SQUEAK!
BAM!
SQUEAK!
BAM!
SQUEAK!
BAM
ONCE AGAIN HE CHOOSES WISELY TO LIVE ANOTHER DAY.
SQUEAK!
BAM!
SQUEAK!

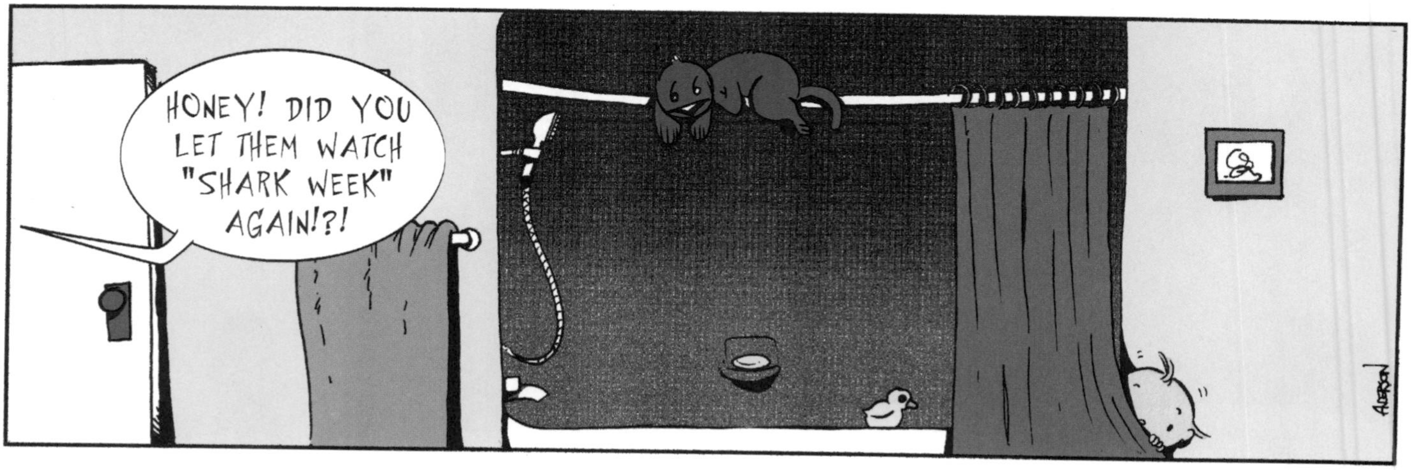
HONEY! DID YOU LET THEM WATCH "SHARK WEEK" AGAIN!?!

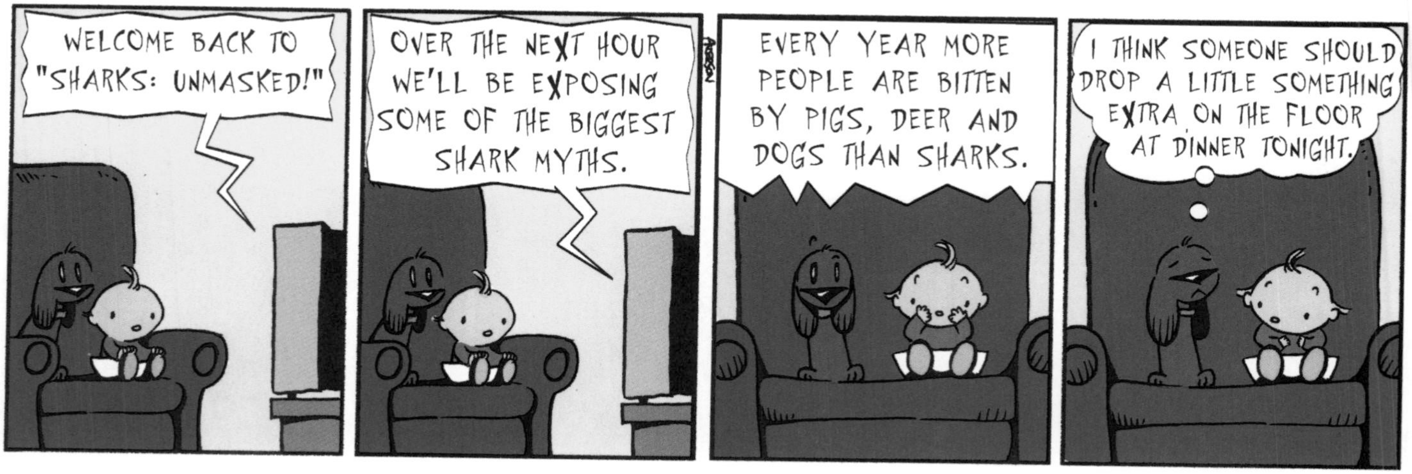
WELCOME BACK TO "SHARKS: UNMASKED!"
OVER THE NEXT HOUR WE'LL BE EXPOSING SOME OF THE BIGGEST SHARK MYTHS.
EVERY YEAR MORE PEOPLE ARE BITTEN BY PIGS, DEER AND DOGS THAN SHARKS.
I THINK SOMEONE SHOULD DROP A LITTLE SOMETHING EXTRA ON THE FLOOR AT DINNER TONIGHT.

LICK LICK LICK LICK LICK LICK LICK LICK LICK
LICK LICK LICK LICK LICK LICK LICK LICK LICK
LICK LICK LICK LICK LICK LICK LICK LICK LICK
OOOOH! A TELYTUBBY!
SLURP!
NOPE. IT'S JUST DAD.

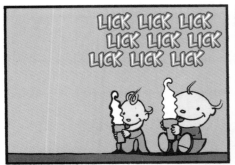

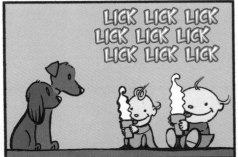

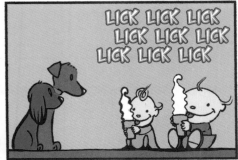

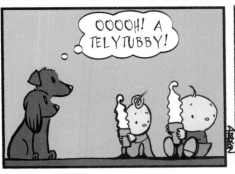

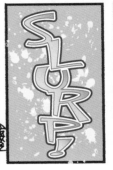

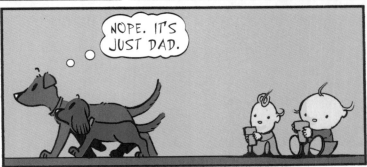

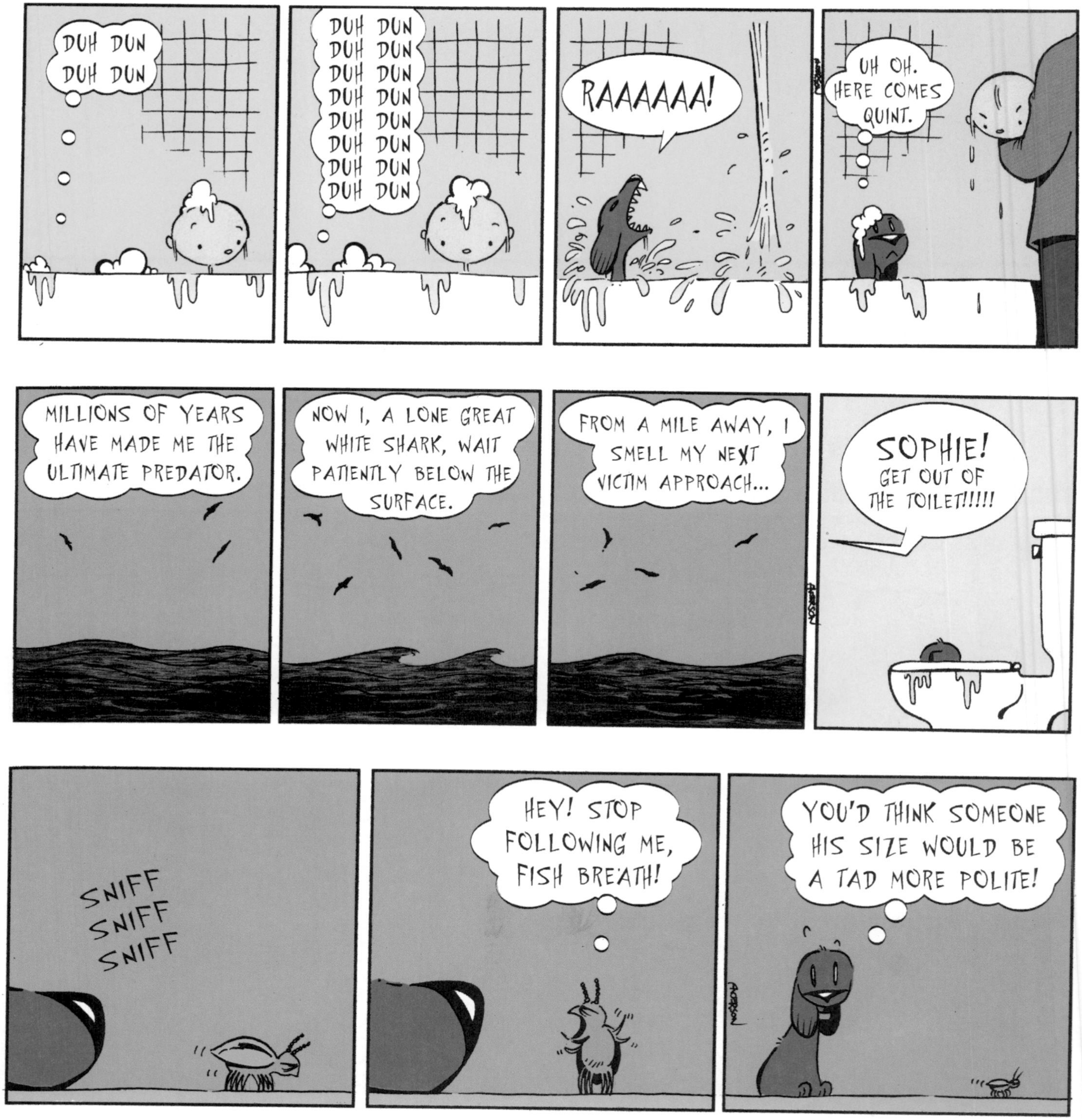
DUH DUN
DUH DUN
DUH DUN
DUH DUN
DUH DUN
DUH DUN
DUH DUN
DUH DUN
DUH DUN
DUH DUN
RAAAAAA!
UH OH.
HERE COMES
QUINT.
MILLIONS OF YEARS HAVE MADE ME THE ULTIMATE PREDATOR.
NOW I, A LONE GREAT WHITE SHARK, WAIT PATIENTLY BELOW THE SURFACE.
FROM A MILE AWAY, I SMELL MY NEXT VICTIM APPROACH...
SOPHIE! GET OUT OF THE TOILET!!!!!
SNIFF
SNIFF
SNIFF
HEY! STOP FOLLOWING ME, FISH BREATH!
YOU'D THINK SOMEONE HIS SIZE WOULD BE A TAD MORE POLITE!

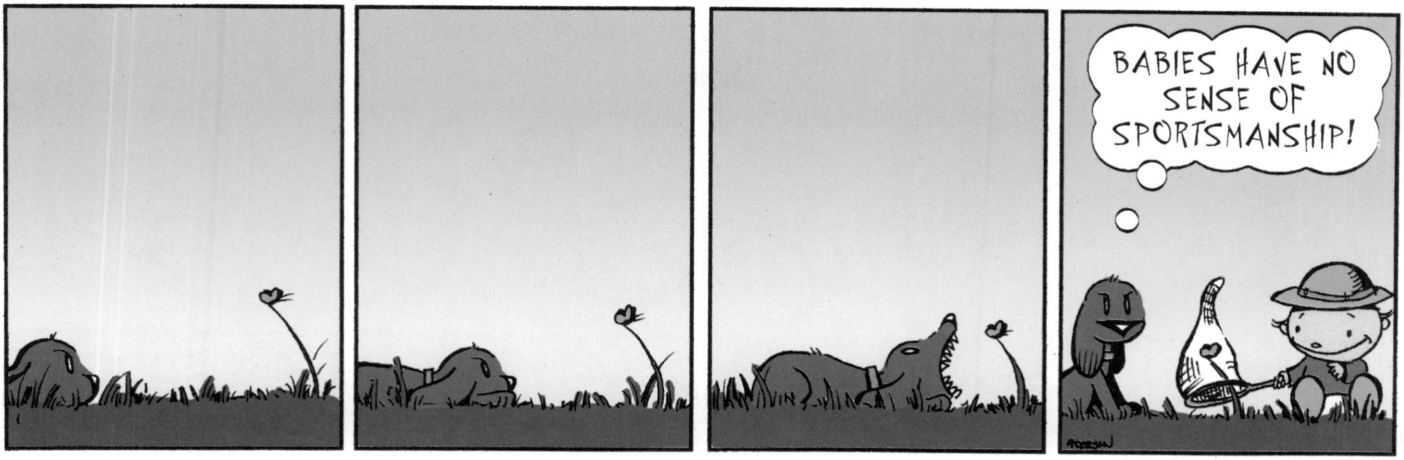
BABIES HAVE NO SENSE OF SPORTSMANSHIP!

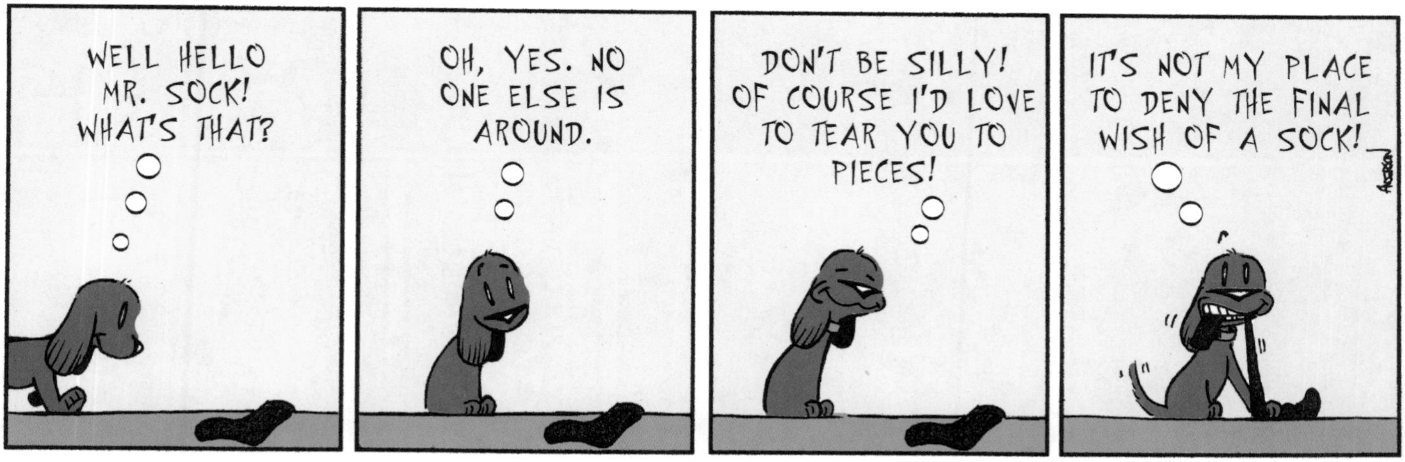
WELL HELLO MR. SOCK! WHAT'S THAT?
OH, YES. NO ONE ELSE IS AROUND.
DON'T BE SILLY! OF COURSE I'D LOVE TO TEAR YOU TO PIECES!
IT'S NOT MY PLACE TO DENY THE FINAL WISH OF A SOCK!

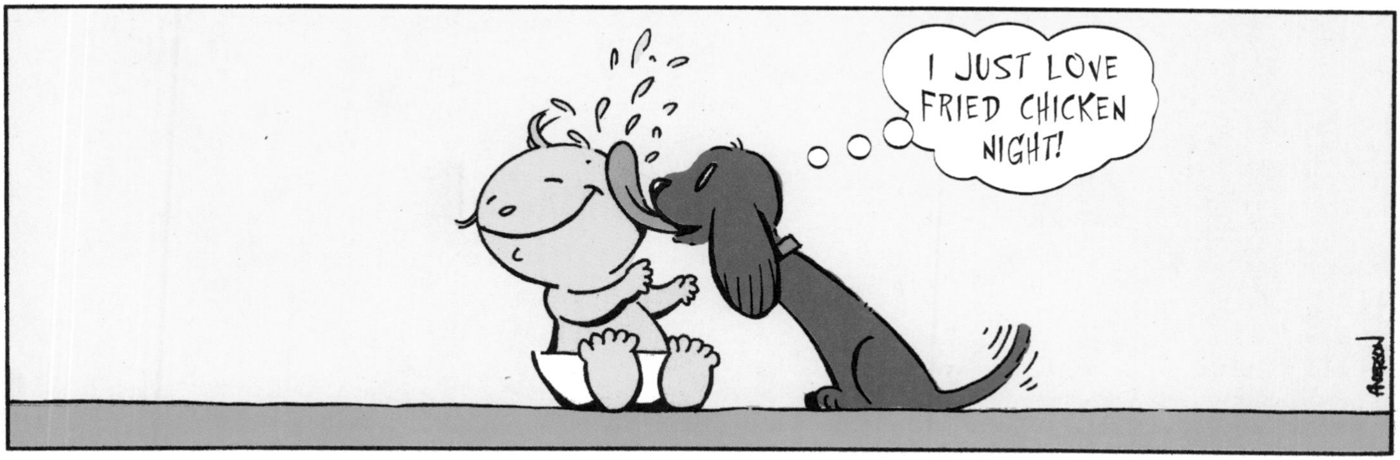
I JUST LOVE FRIED CHICKEN NIGHT!

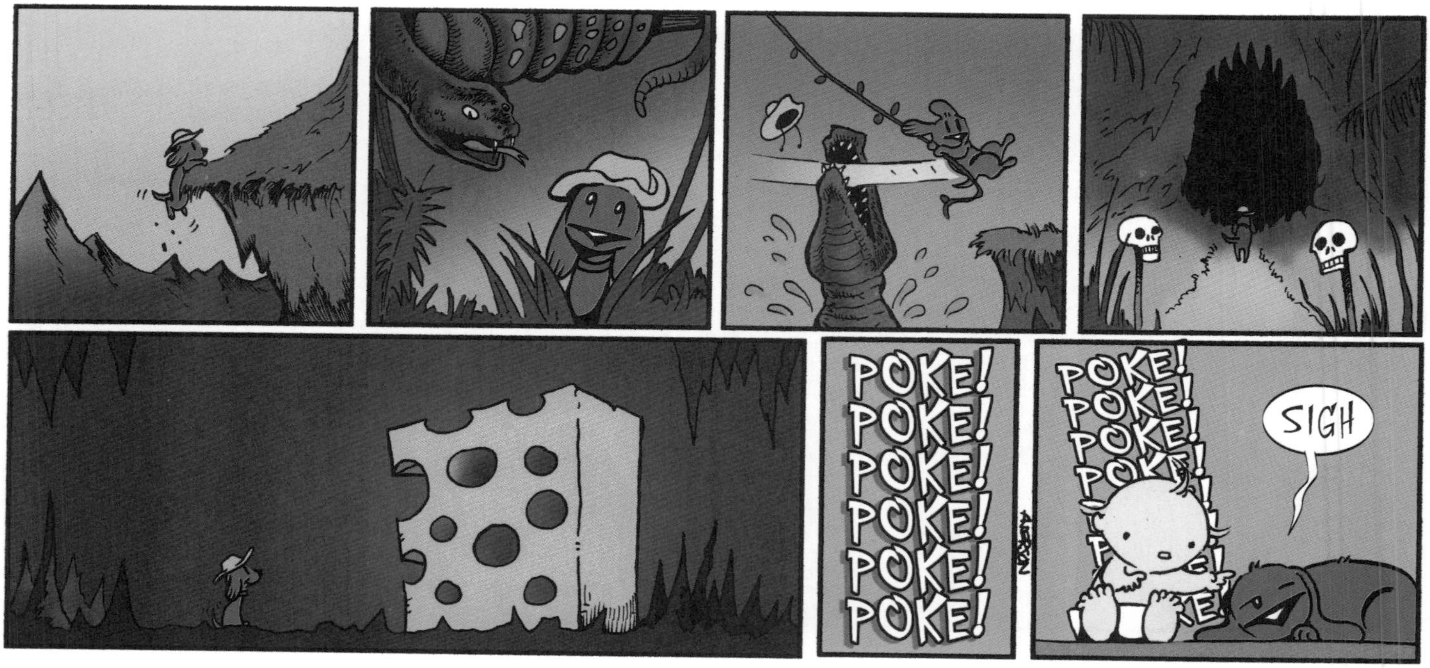
POKE!
POKE!
POKE!
POKE!
POKE!
POKE!
POKE!
POKE!
POKE!
SIGH

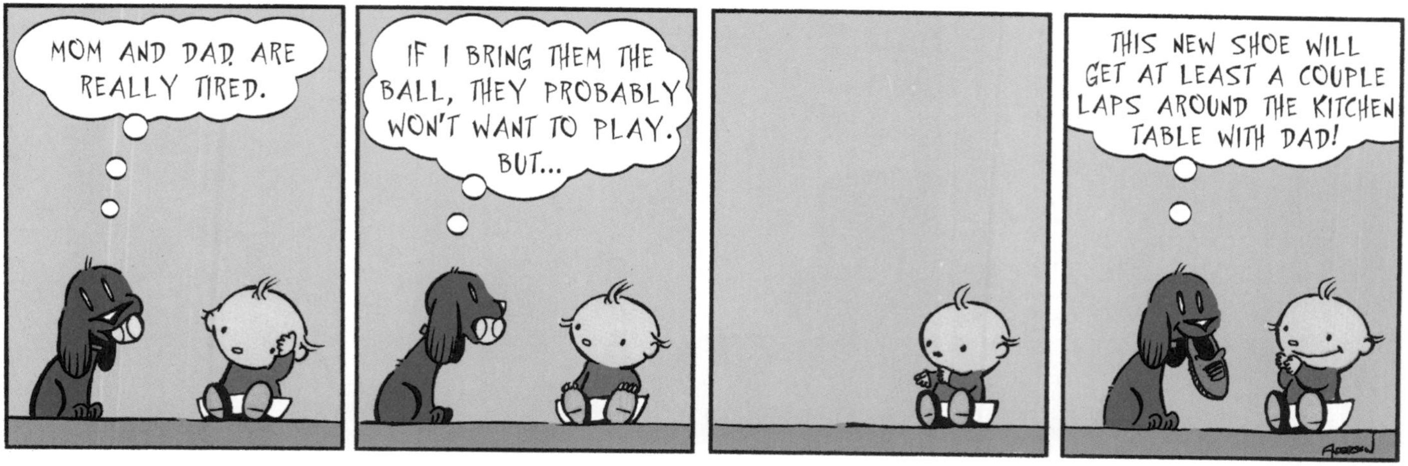
MOM AND DAD ARE REALLY TIRED.
IF I BRING THEM THE BALL, THEY PROBABLY WON'T WANT TO PLAY. BUT...
THIS NEW SHOE WILL GET AT LEAST A COUPLE LAPS AROUND THE KITCHEN TABLE WITH DAD!

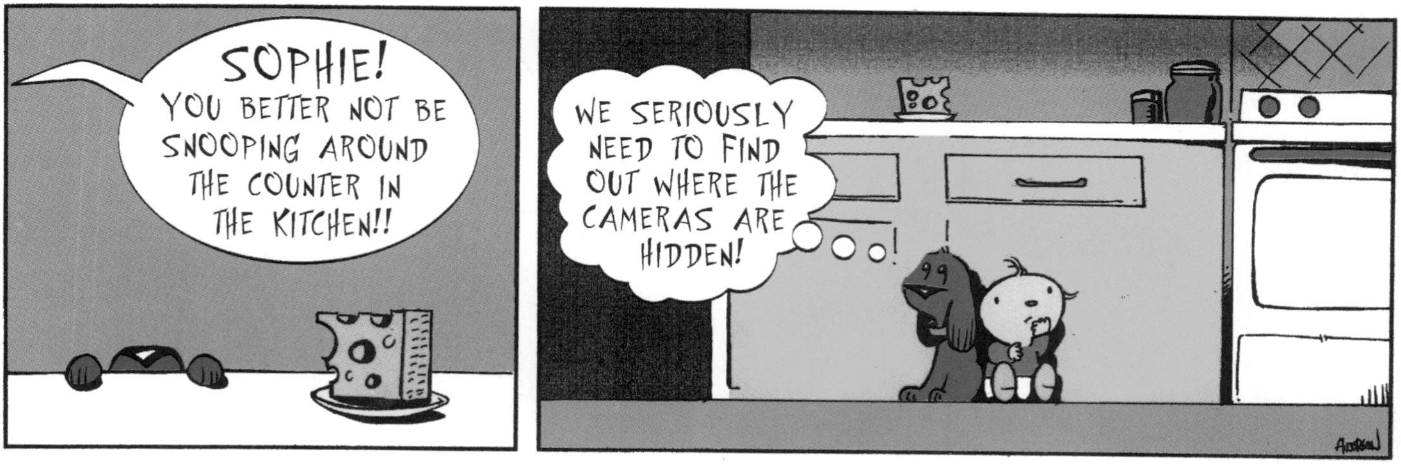
SOPHIE! YOU BETTER NOT BE SNOOPING AROUND THE COUNTER IN THE KITCHEN!!
WE SERIOUSLY NEED TO FIND OUT WHERE THE CAMERAS ARE HIDDEN!

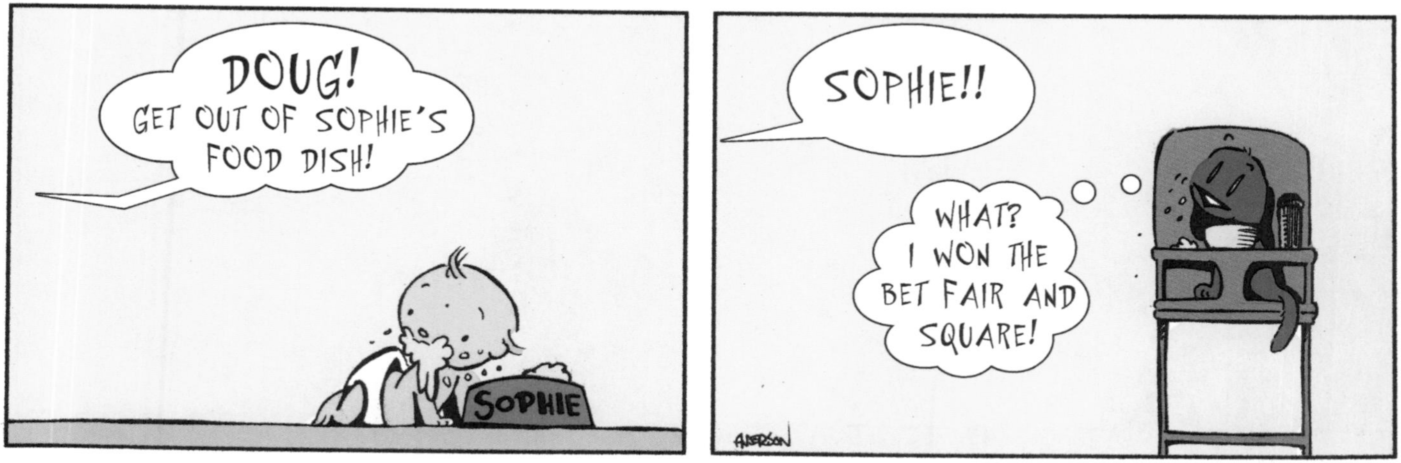
DOUG! GET OUT OF SOPHIE'S FOOD DISH!
SOPHIE
SOPHIE!!
WHAT? I WON THE BET FAIR AND SQUARE!

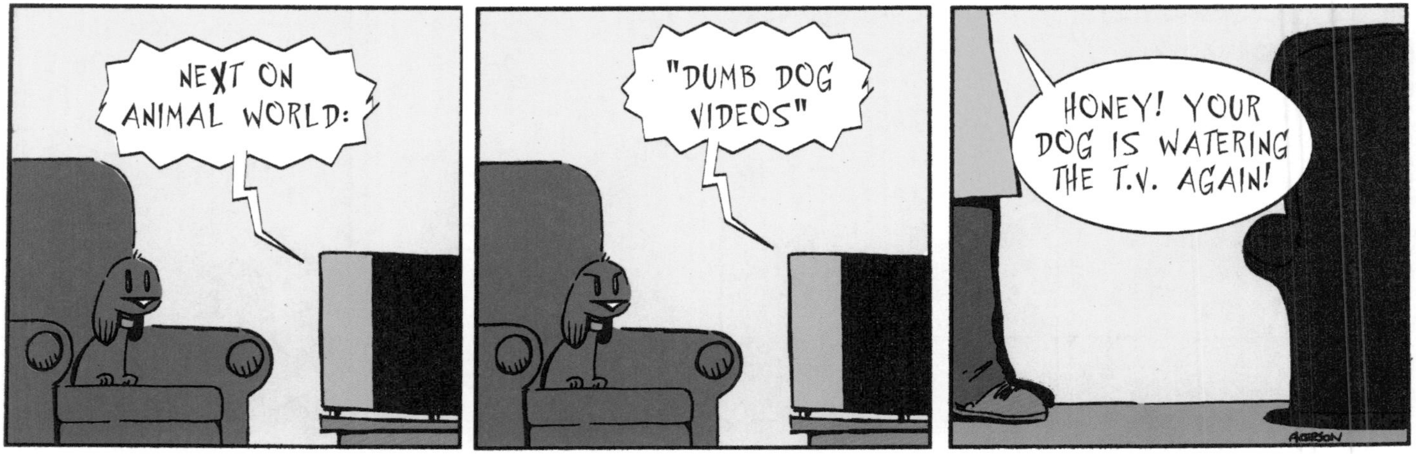
NEXT ON ANIMAL WORLD:
"DUMB DOG VIDEOS"
HONEY! YOUR DOG IS WATERING THE T.V. AGAIN!
ANDERSON

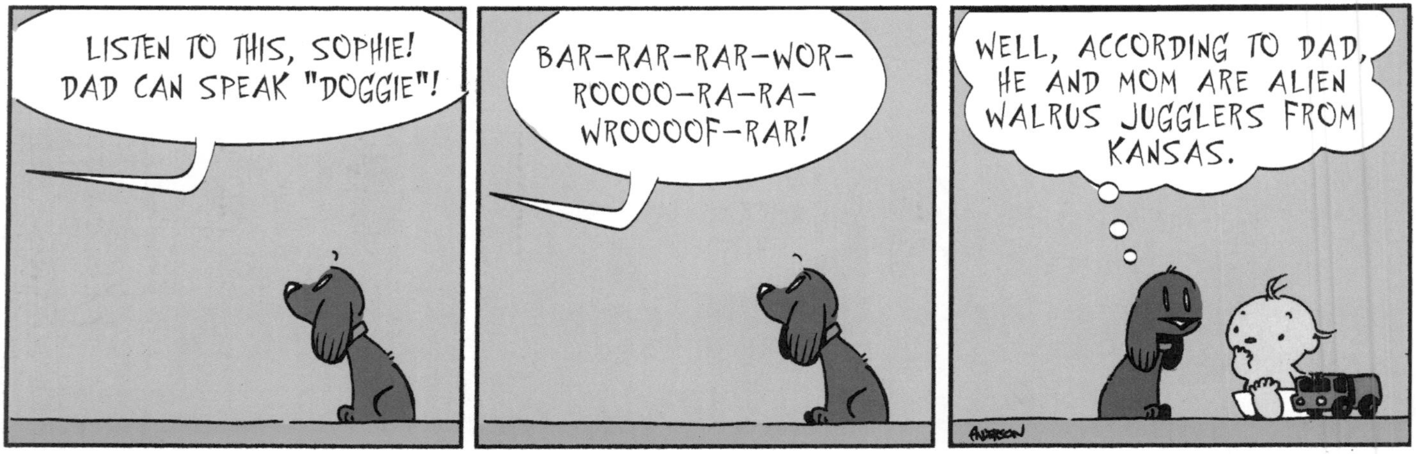
LISTEN TO THIS, SOPHIE! DAD CAN SPEAK "DOGGIE"!
BAR-RAR-RAR-WOR-ROOOO-RA-RA-WROOOOF-RAR!
WELL, ACCORDING TO DAD, HE AND MOM ARE ALIEN WALRUS JUGGLERS FROM KANSAS.
ANDERSON

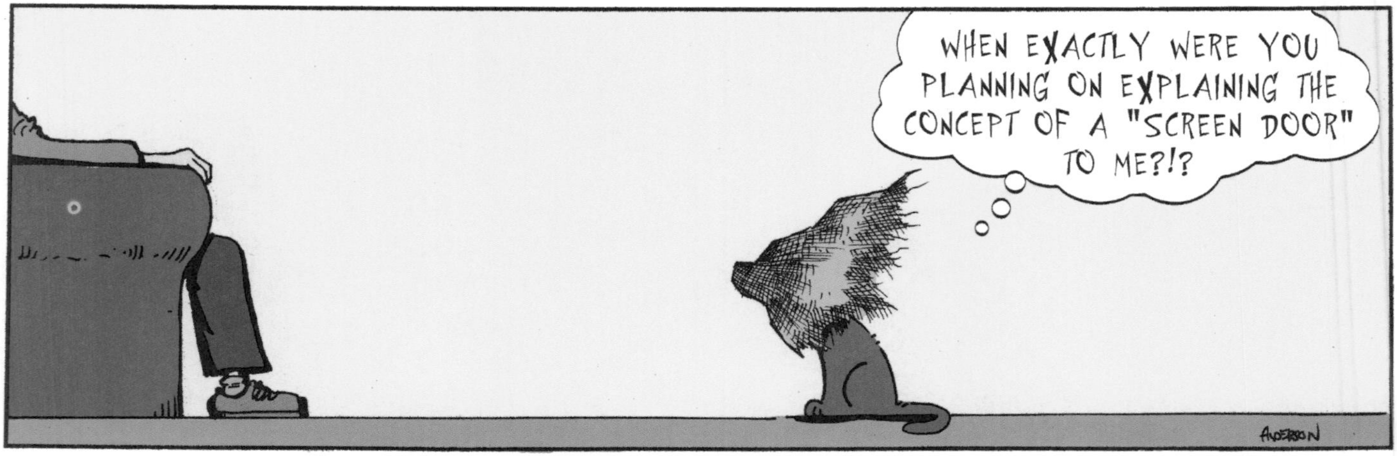
WHEN EXACTLY WERE YOU PLANNING ON EXPLAINING THE CONCEPT OF A "SCREEN DOOR" TO ME?!?
ANDERSON

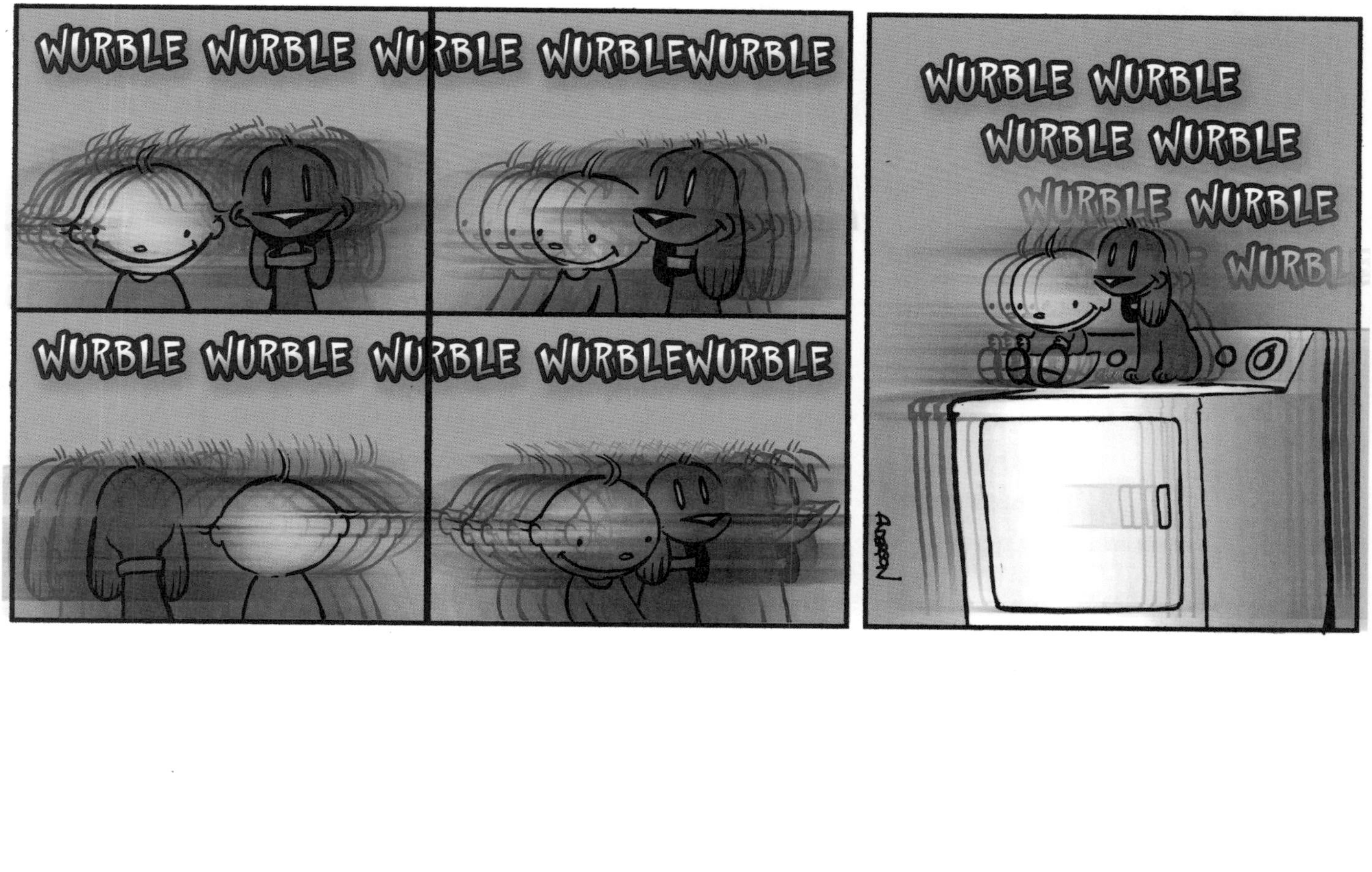
WURBLE WURBLE WURBLE WURBLEWURBLE
WURBLE WURBLE WURBLE WURBLEWURBLE
WURBLE WURBLE
WURBLE WURBLE
WURBLE WURBLE
WURBL

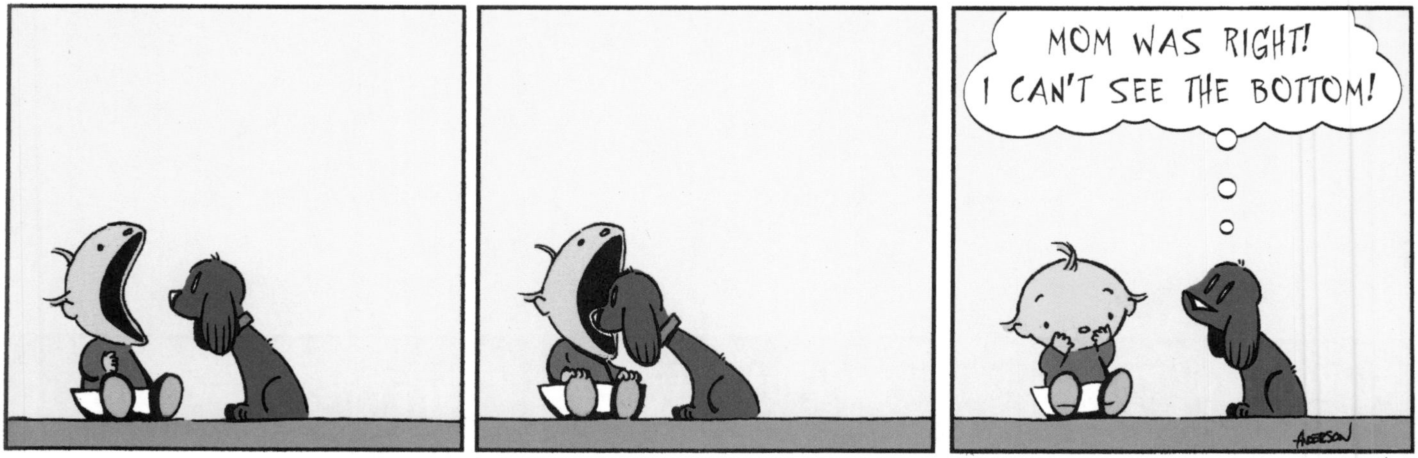
MOM WAS RIGHT! I CAN'T SEE THE BOTTOM!
ANDERSON

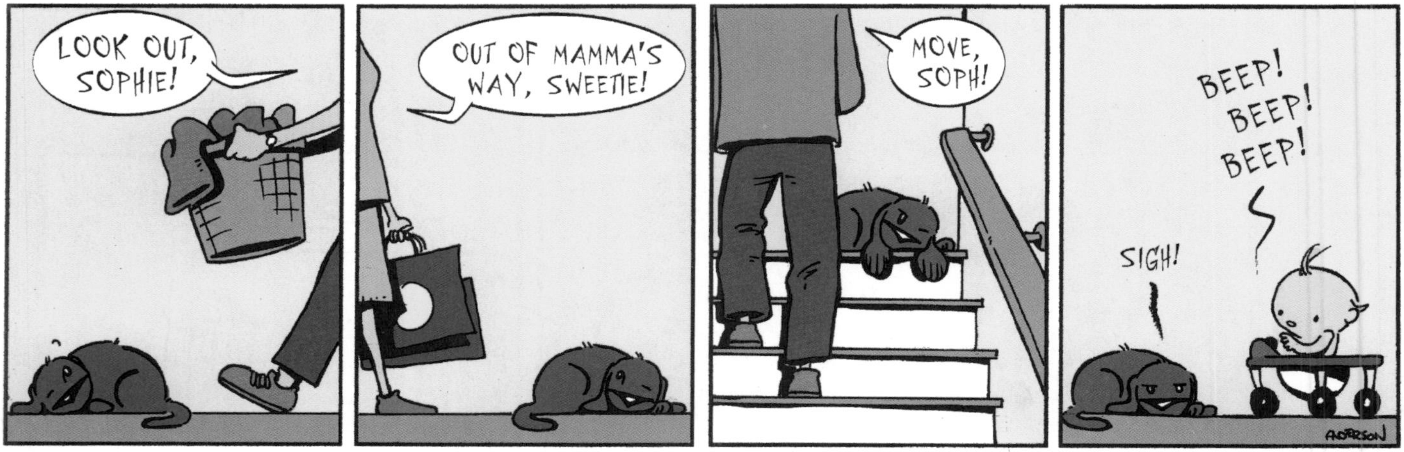
LOOK OUT, SOPHIE!
OUT OF MAMMA'S WAY, SWEETIE!
MOVE, SOPH!
BEEP! BEEP! BEEP!
SIGH!
ANDERSON

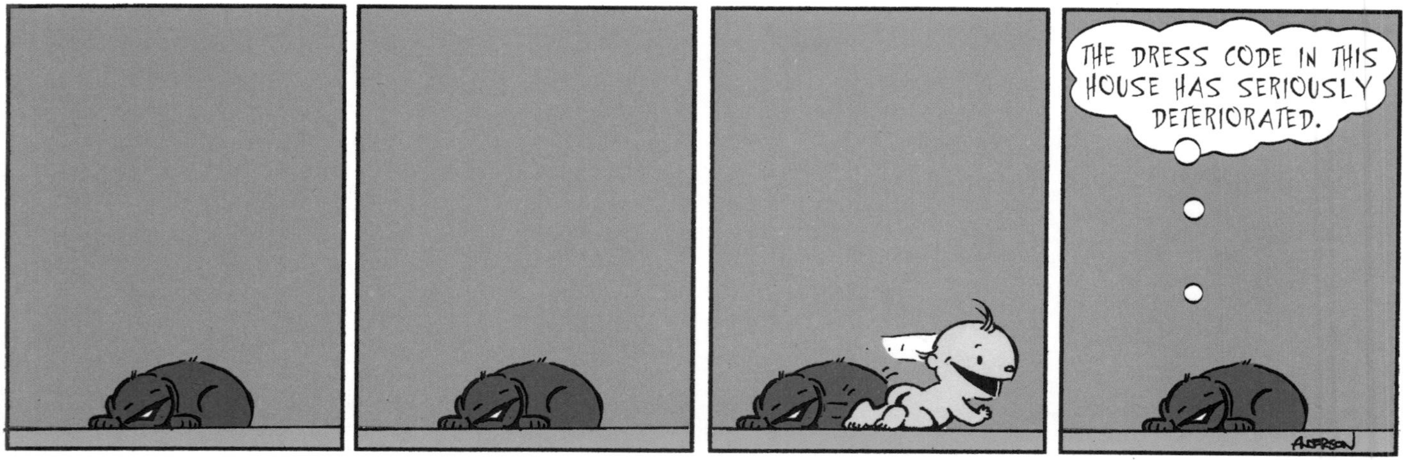
THE DRESS CODE IN THIS HOUSE HAS SERIOUSLY DETERIORATED.
ANDERSON

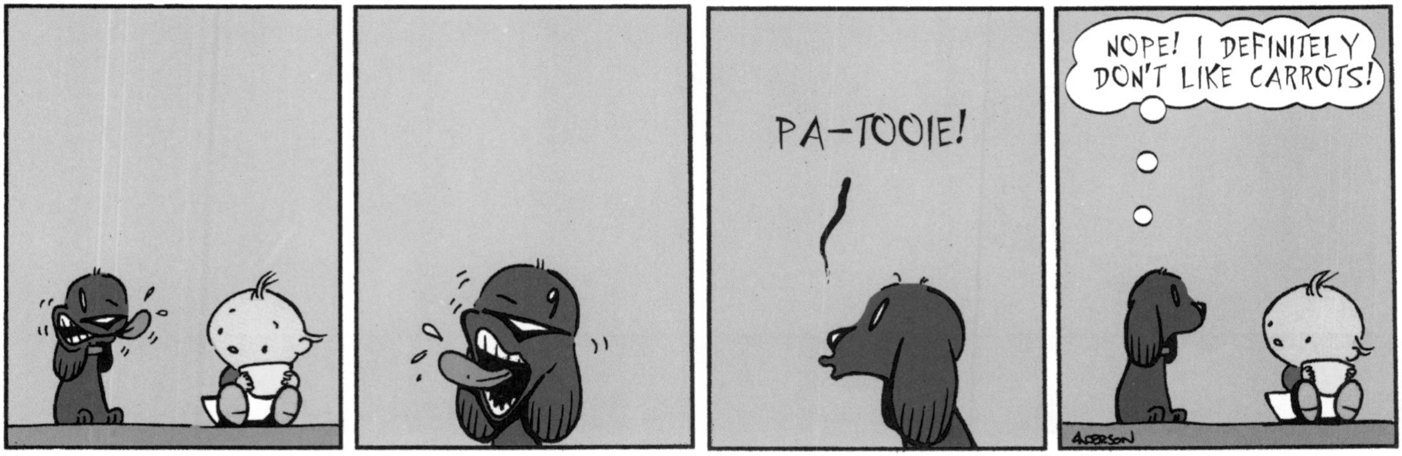
PA-TOOIE!
NOPE! I DEFINITELY DON'T LIKE CARROTS!

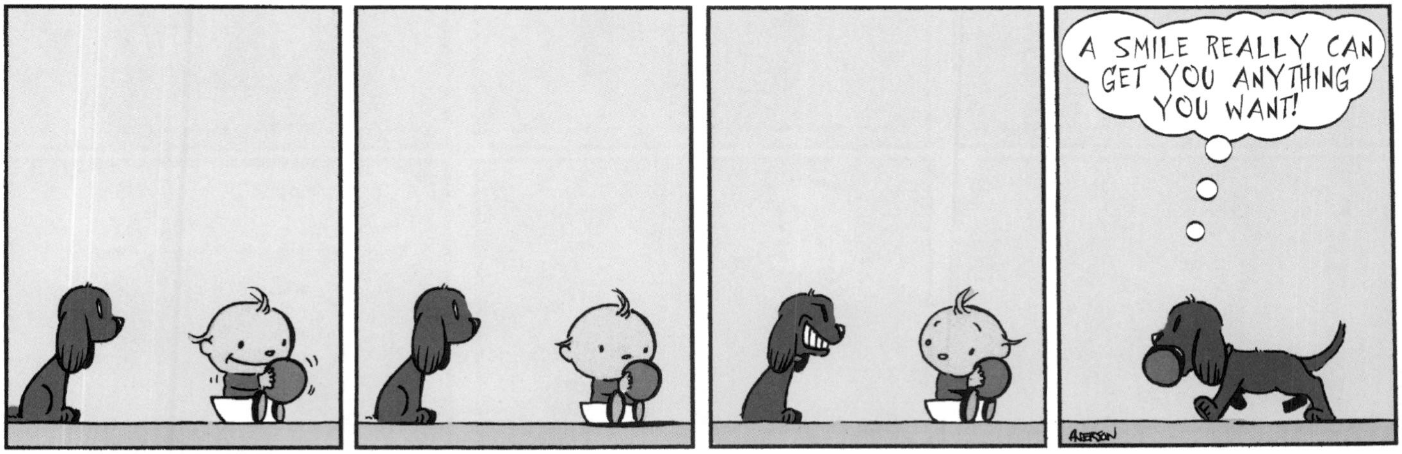
A SMILE REALLY CAN GET YOU ANYTHING YOU WANT!

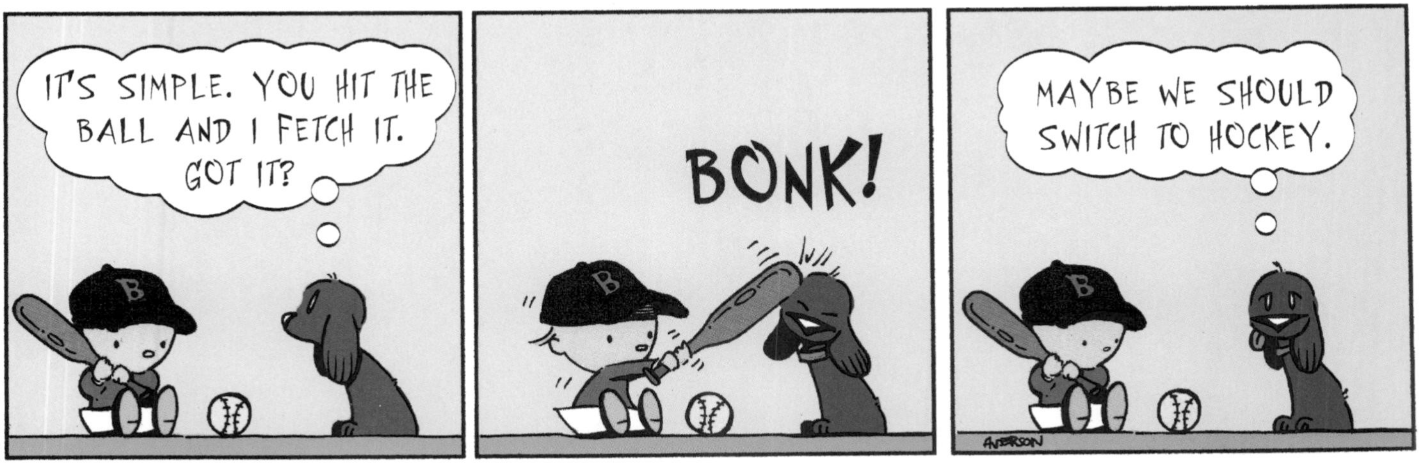
IT'S SIMPLE. YOU HIT THE BALL AND I FETCH IT. GOT IT?
BONK!
MAYBE WE SHOULD SWITCH TO HOCKEY.

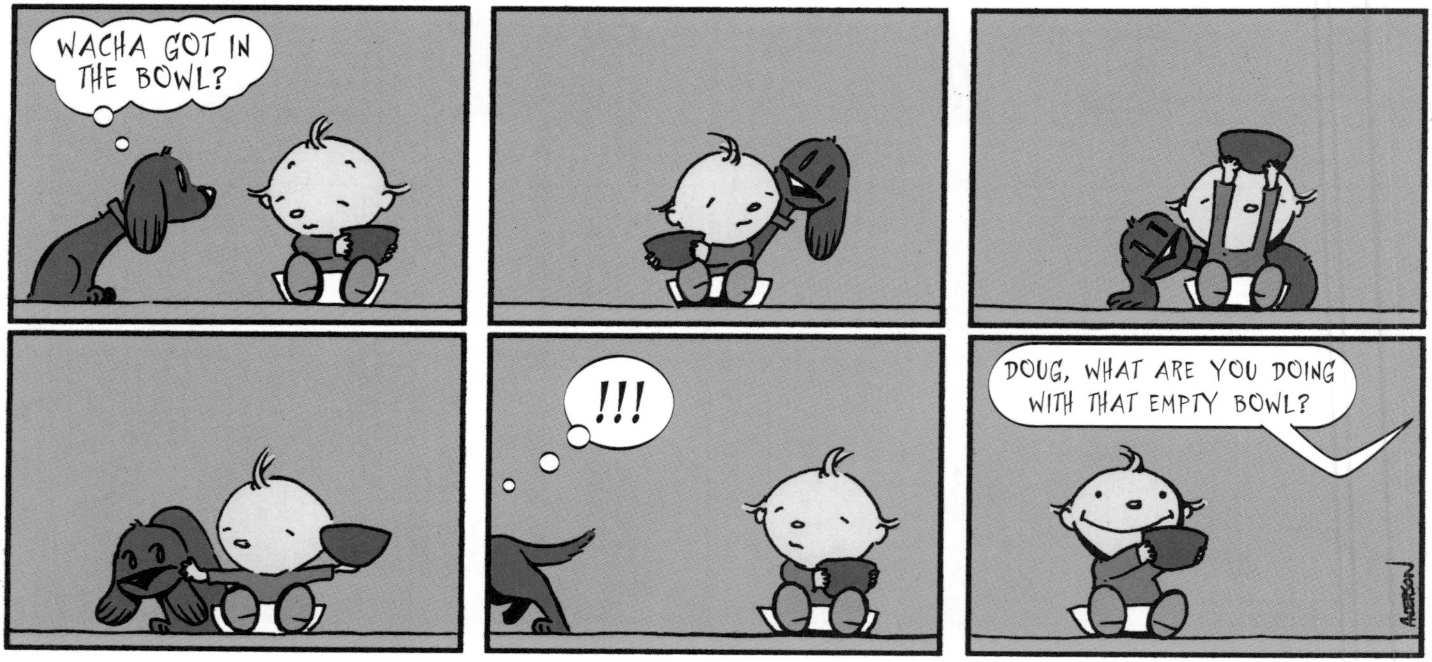
WACHA GOT IN THE BOWL?
!!!
DOUG, WHAT ARE YOU DOING WITH THAT EMPTY BOWL?

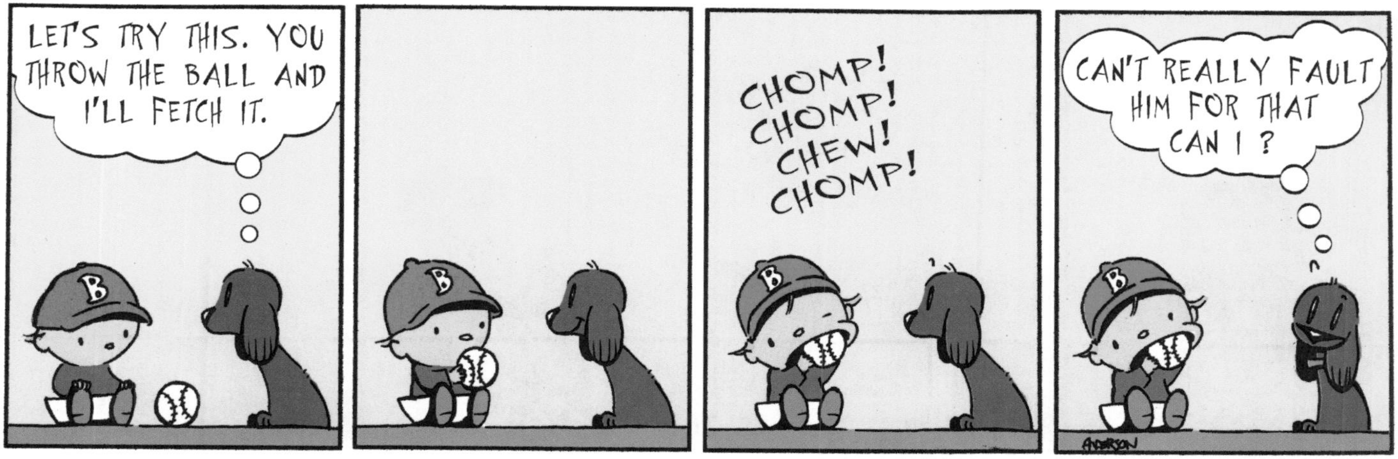
LET'S TRY THIS. YOU THROW THE BALL AND I'LL FETCH IT.
CHOMP! CHOMP! CHEW! CHOMP!
CAN'T REALLY FAULT HIM FOR THAT CAN I ?
ANDERSON

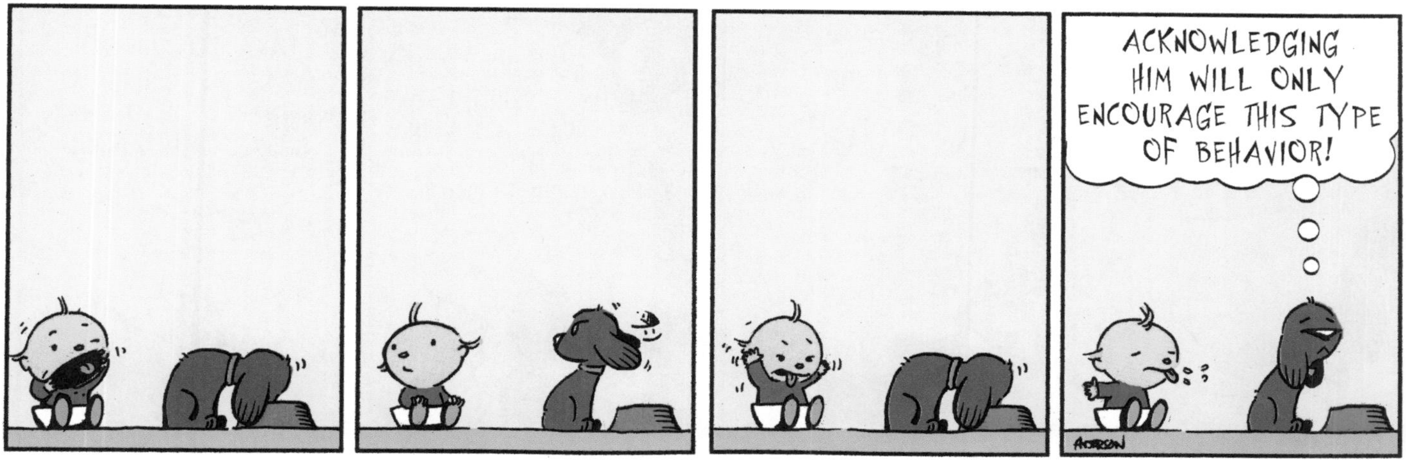
ACKNOWLEDGING HIM WILL ONLY ENCOURAGE THIS TYPE OF BEHAVIOR!
ANDERSON

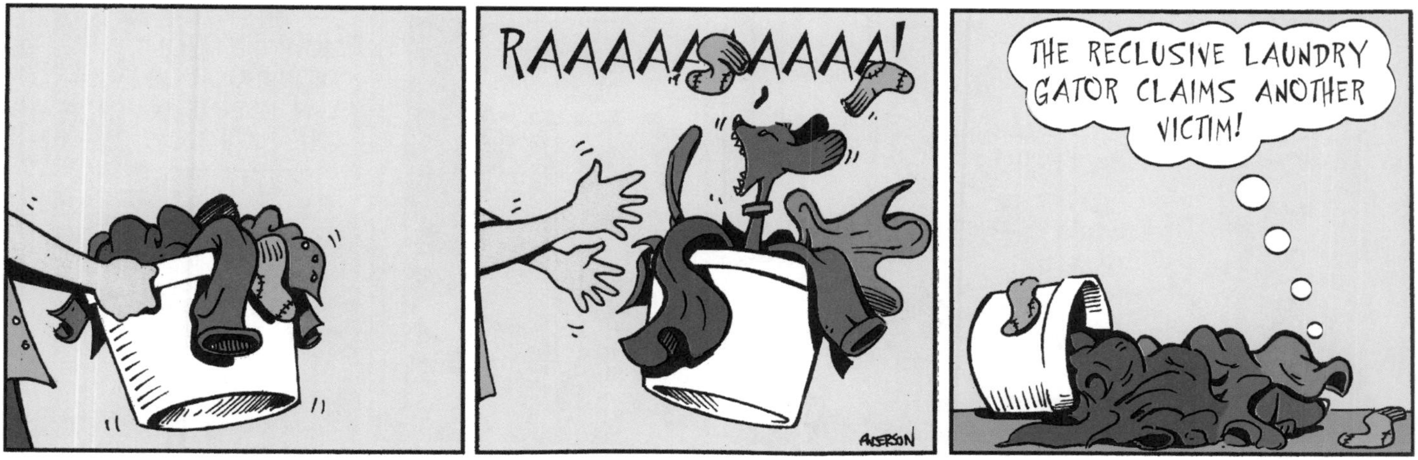
RAAAAAAAAAA!
ANDERSON
THE RECLUSIVE LAUNDRY GATOR CLAIMS ANOTHER VICTIM!

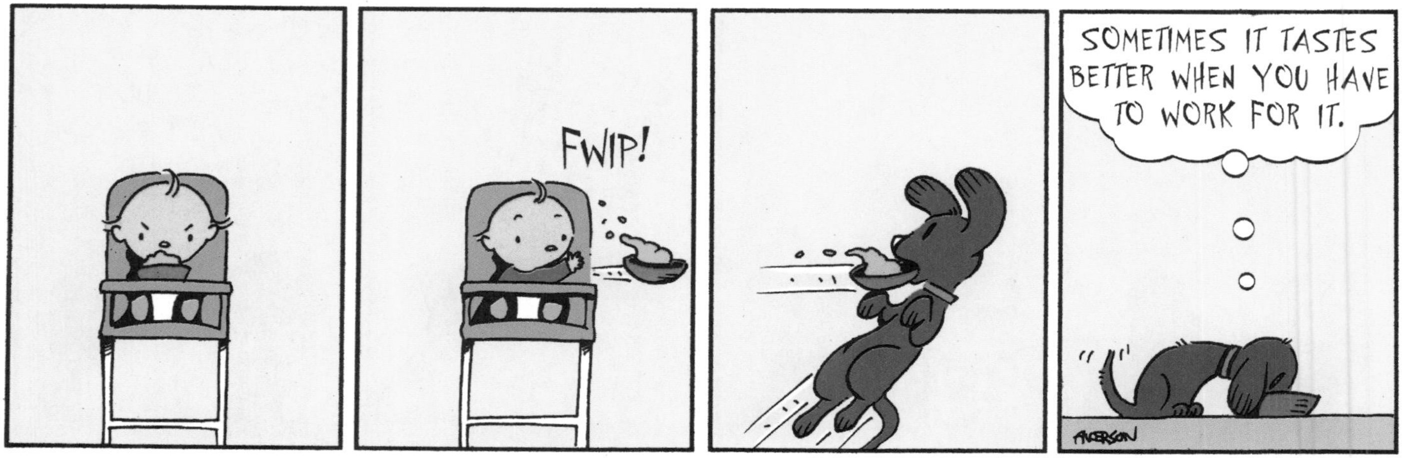
FWIP!
SOMETIMES IT TASTES BETTER WHEN YOU HAVE TO WORK FOR IT.

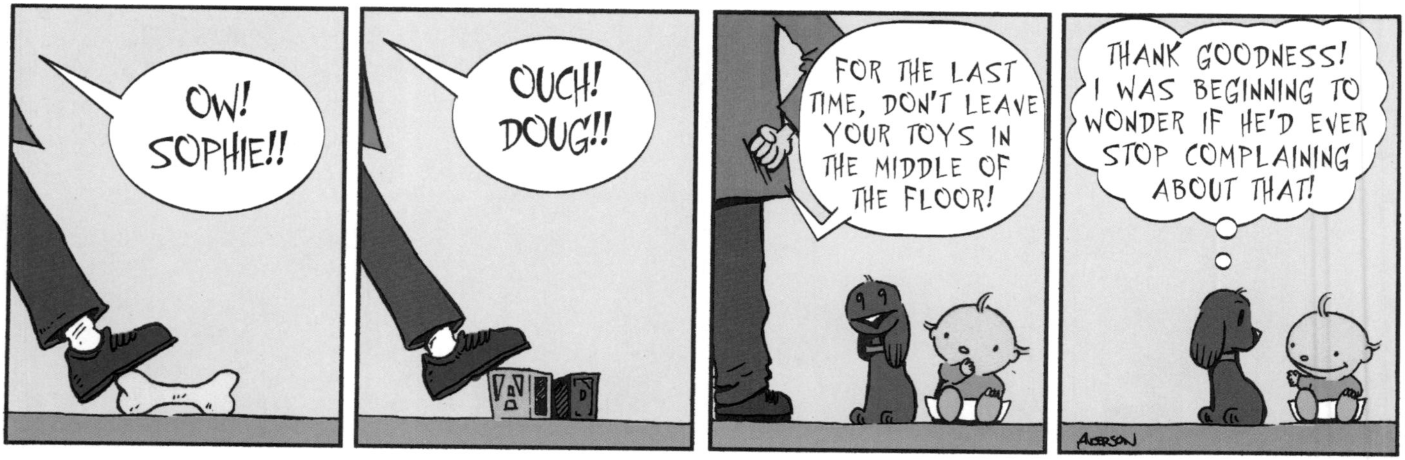
OW! SOPHIE!!
OUCH! DOUG!!
FOR THE LAST TIME, DON'T LEAVE YOUR TOYS IN THE MIDDLE OF THE FLOOR!
THANK GOODNESS! I WAS BEGINNING TO WONDER IF HE'D EVER STOP COMPLAINING ABOUT THAT!

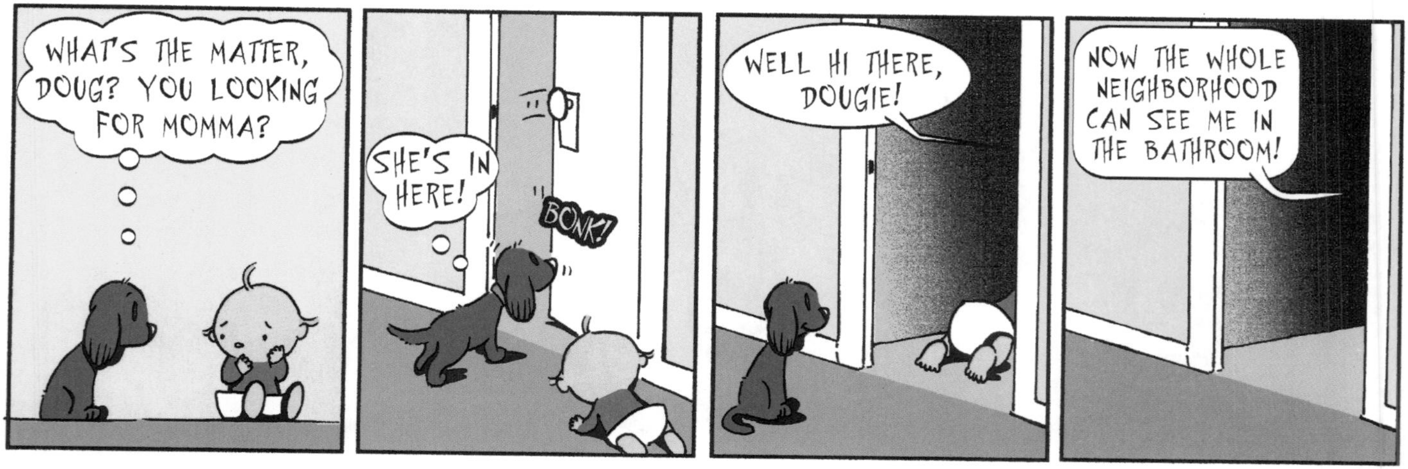
WHAT'S THE MATTER, DOUG? YOU LOOKING FOR MOMMA?
SHE'S IN HERE!
BONK!
WELL HI THERE, DOUGIE!
NOW THE WHOLE NEIGHBORHOOD CAN SEE ME IN THE BATHROOM!

BAM!
BAM! BAM!
RA-OOOO OOOOOOOO
OOR-A
BAM! BAM! BAM! BAM! BAM! BAM!
BAM!
RAF-RAF WROOF-AROOOO
OOOOO AARRR
BAM! BAP!
YAP-YAP YIP-RAR-AAAROOO
RRR
UUUUUF
GUYS, QUIET DOWN! DAD'S STILL SLEEPING!
YA GOTTA WONDER IF STEPHEN TYLER ENCOUNTERED THE SAME OBSTACLES AS A KID.

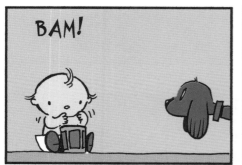

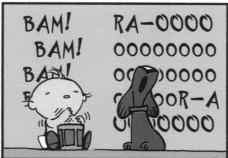

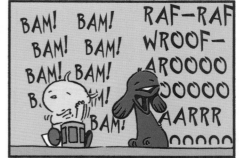

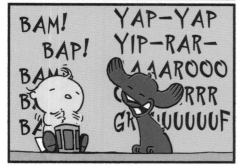

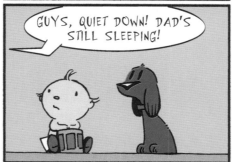

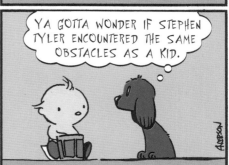

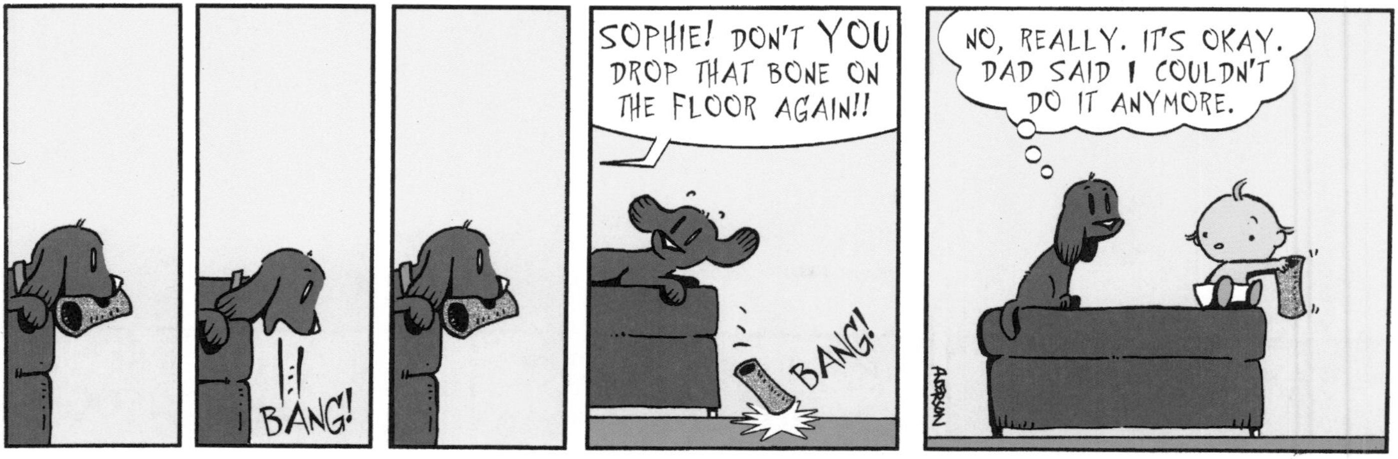
BANG!
SOPHIE! DON'T YOU DROP THAT BONE ON THE FLOOR AGAIN!!
BANG!
NO, REALLY. IT'S OKAY. DAD SAID I COULDN'T DO IT ANYMORE.
ANDERSON

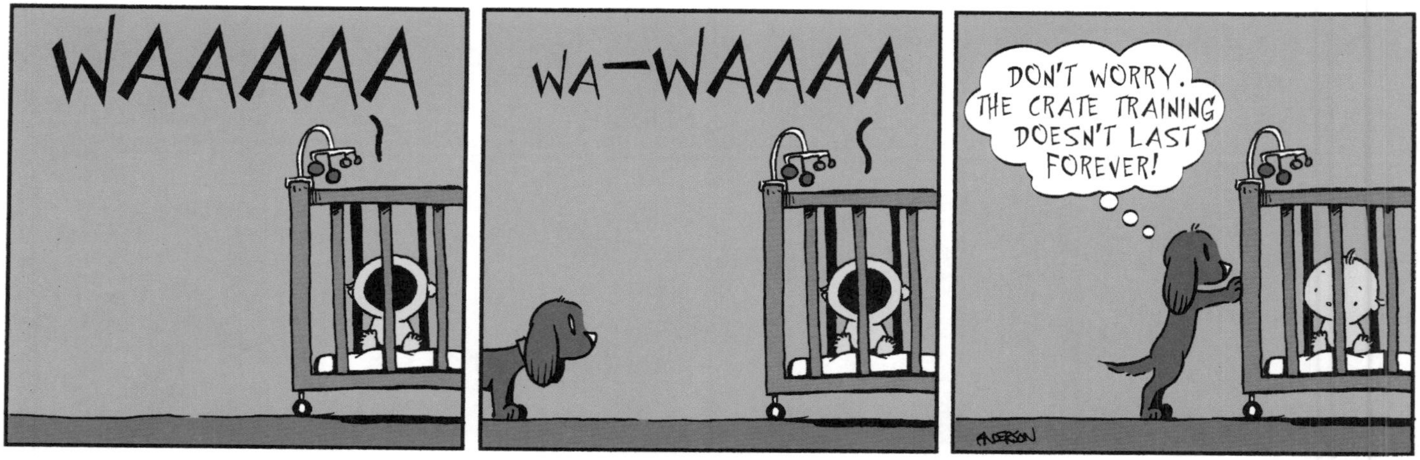
WAAAAA
WA-WAAAA
DON'T WORRY. THE CRATE TRAINING DOESN'T LAST FOREVER!
ANDERSON

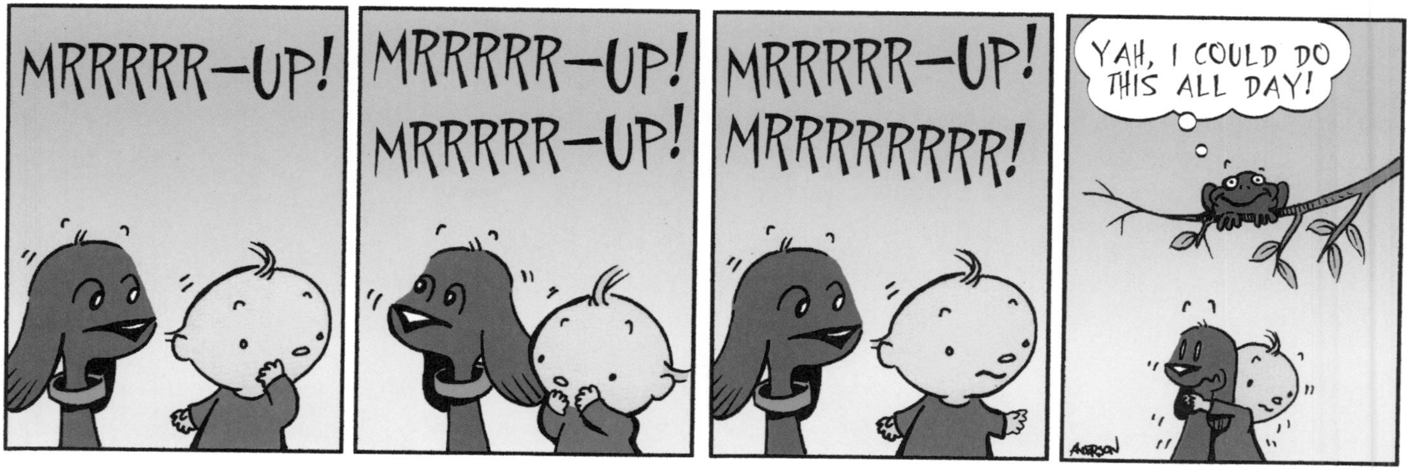
MRRRRR-UP!
MRRRRR-UP!
MRRRRR-UP!
MRRRRR-UP!
MRRRRRRRR!
YAH, I COULD DO THIS ALL DAY!
ANDERSON

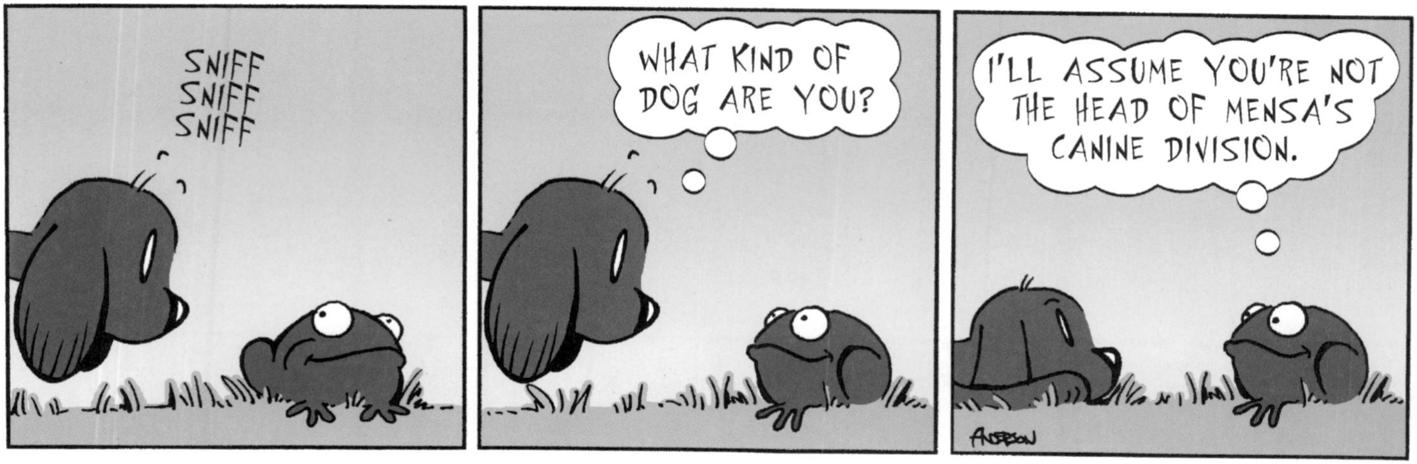
SNIFF SNIFF SNIFF
WHAT KIND OF DOG ARE YOU?
I'LL ASSUME YOU'RE NOT THE HEAD OF MENSA'S CANINE DIVISION.

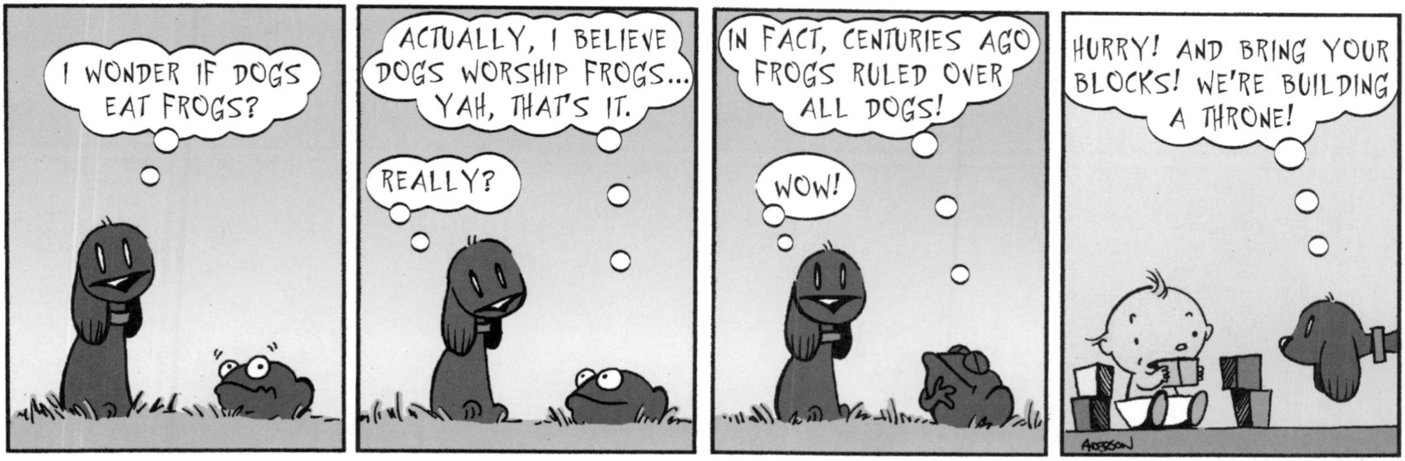
I WONDER IF DOGS EAT FROGS?
ACTUALLY, I BELIEVE DOGS WORSHIP FROGS... YAH, THAT'S IT.
REALLY?
IN FACT, CENTURIES AGO FROGS RULED OVER ALL DOGS!
WOW!
HURRY! AND BRING YOUR BLOCKS! WE'RE BUILDING A THRONE!

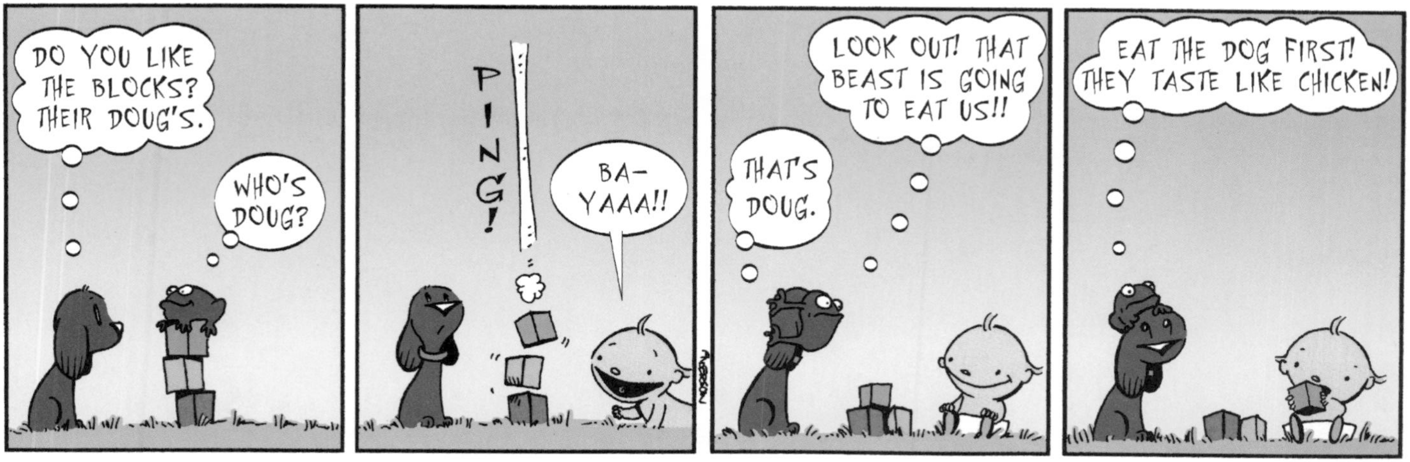
DO YOU LIKE THE BLOCKS? THEIR DOUG'S.
WHO'S DOUG?
PING!
BA-YAAA!!
LOOK OUT! THAT BEAST IS GOING TO EAT US!!
THAT'S DOUG.
EAT THE DOG FIRST! THEY TASTE LIKE CHICKEN!

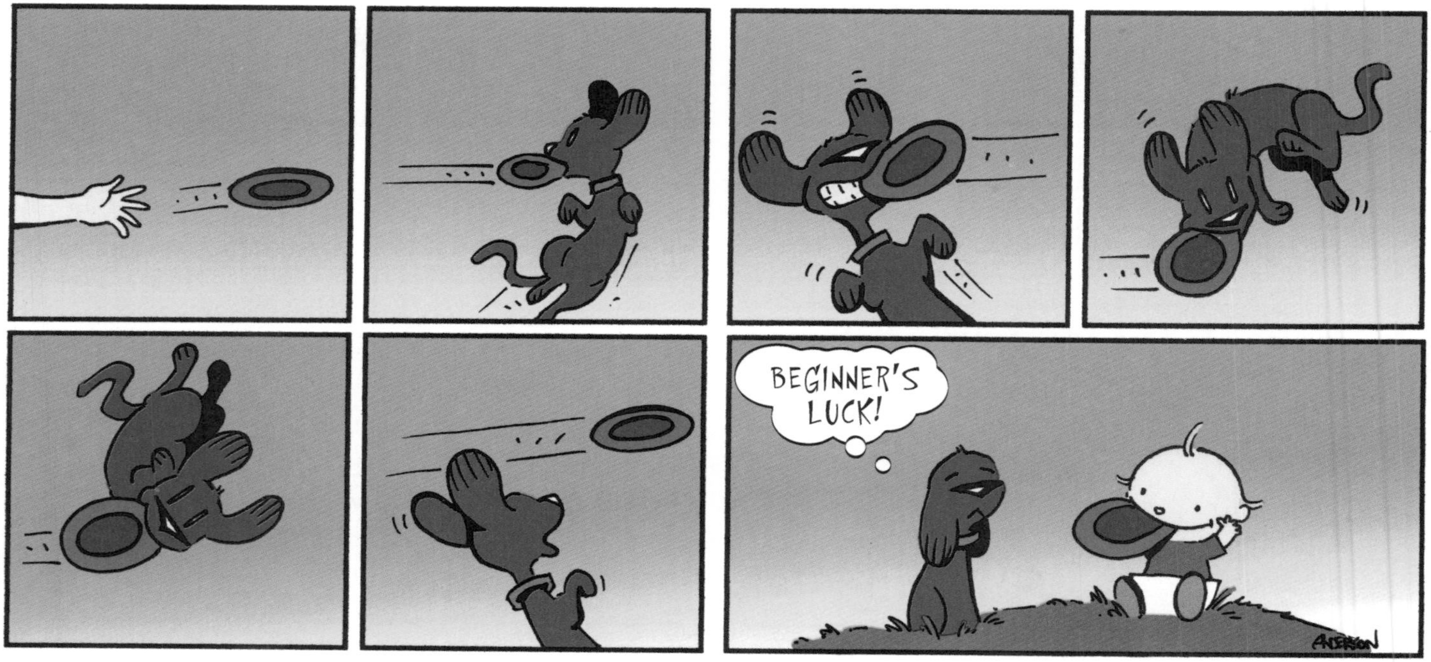
BEGINNER'S LUCK!
ANDERSON

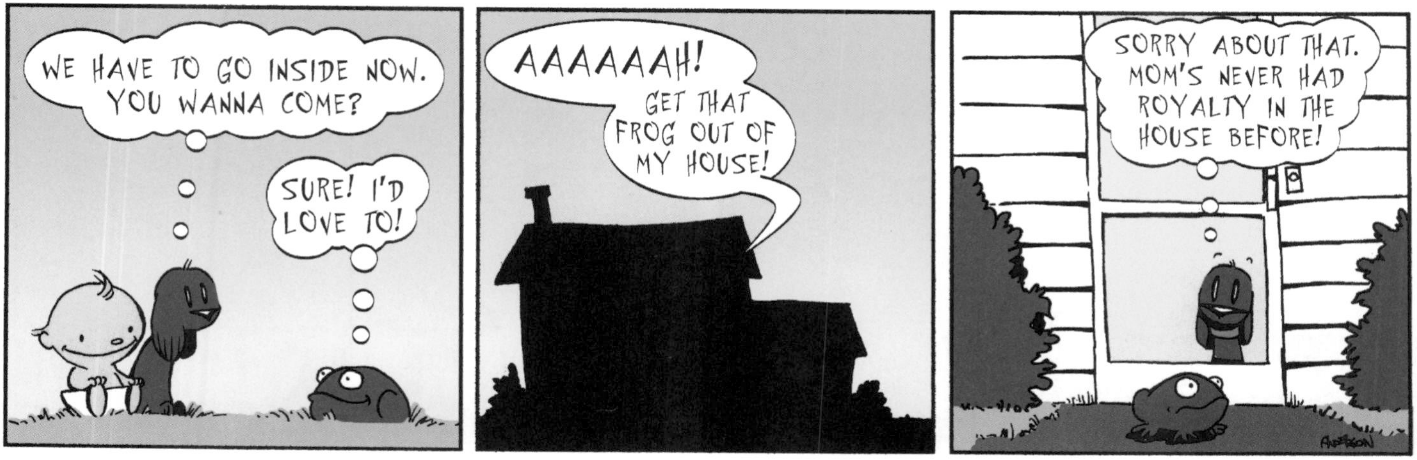
WE HAVE TO GO INSIDE NOW. YOU WANNA COME?
SURE! I'D LOVE TO!
AAAAAAH!
GET THAT FROG OUT OF MY HOUSE!
SORRY ABOUT THAT. MOM'S NEVER HAD ROYALTY IN THE HOUSE BEFORE!
ANDERSON

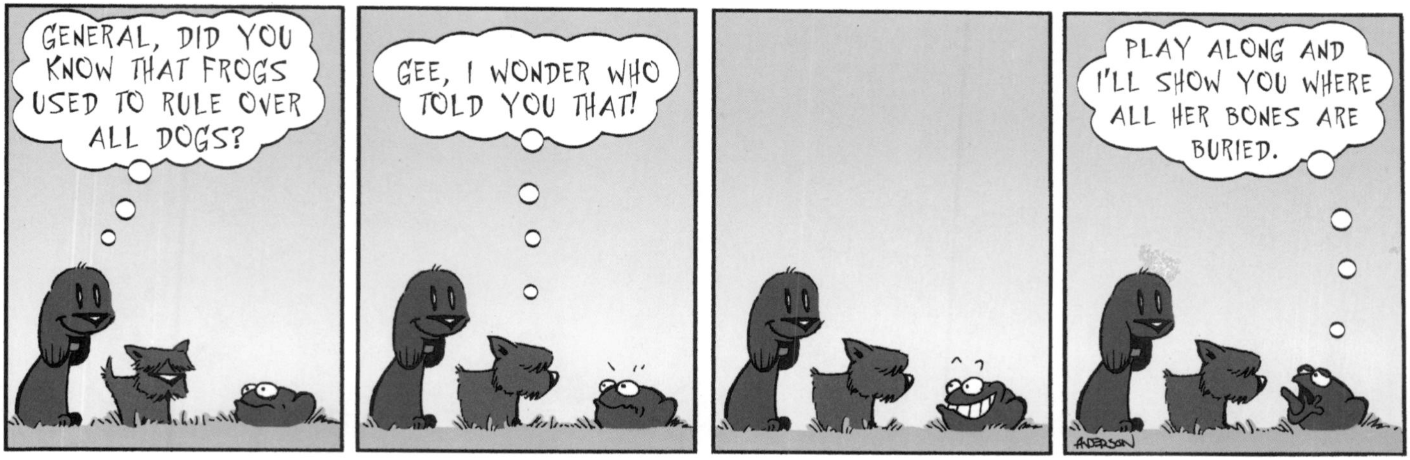
GENERAL, DID YOU KNOW THAT FROGS USED TO RULE OVER ALL DOGS?
GEE, I WONDER WHO TOLD YOU THAT!
PLAY ALONG AND I'LL SHOW YOU WHERE ALL HER BONES ARE BURIED.
ANDERSON

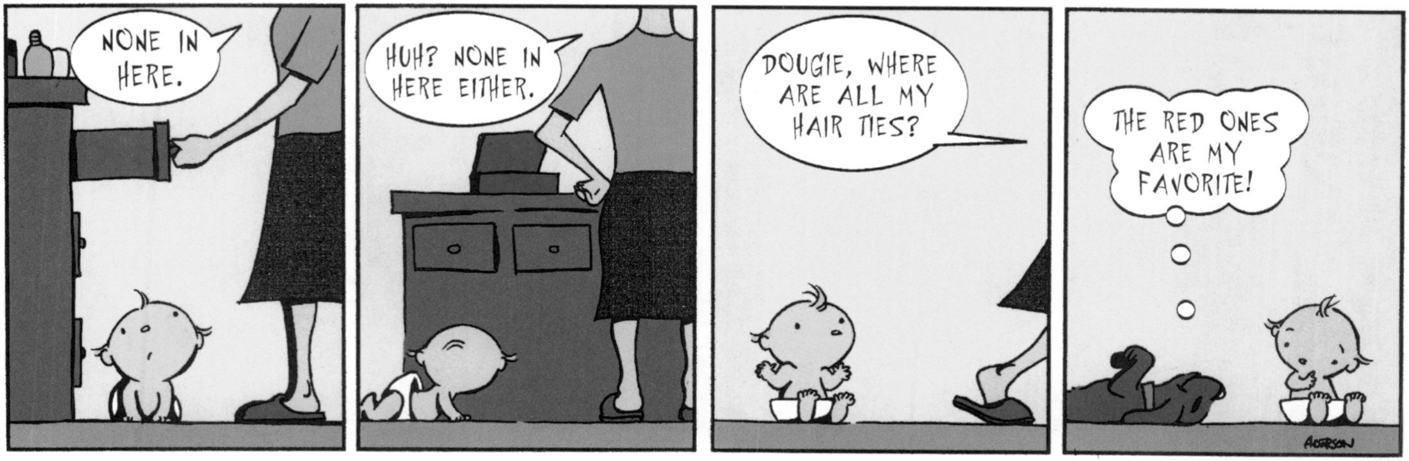
NONE IN HERE.
HUH? NONE IN HERE EITHER.
DOUGIE, WHERE ARE ALL MY HAIR TIES?
THE RED ONES ARE MY FAVORITE!
ANDERSON

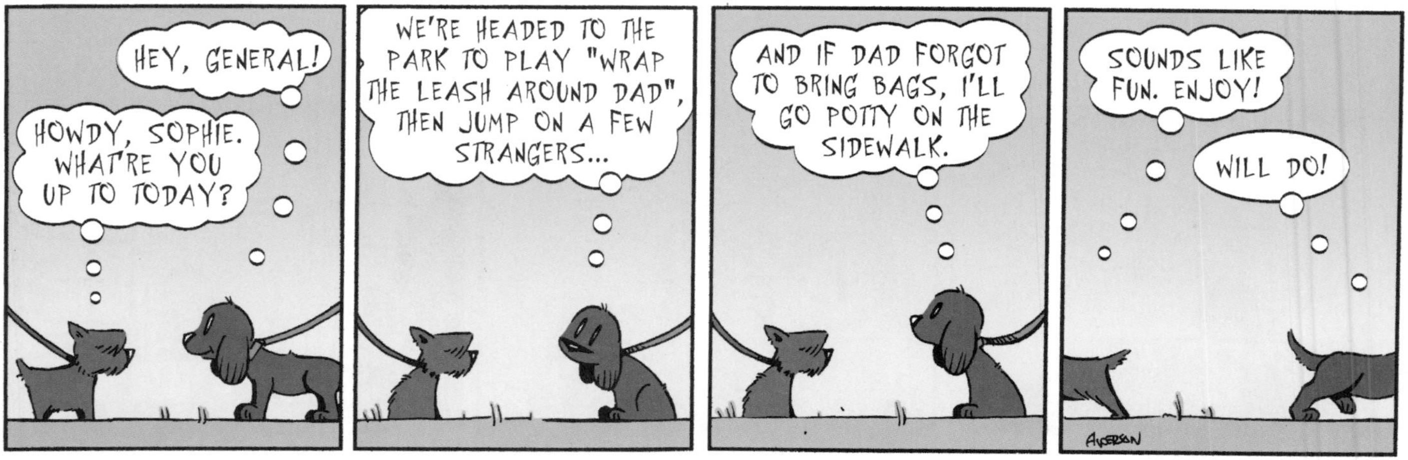
HEY, GENERAL!
HOWDY, SOPHIE. WHAT'RE YOU UP TO TODAY?
WE'RE HEADED TO THE PARK TO PLAY "WRAP THE LEASH AROUND DAD", THEN JUMP ON A FEW STRANGERS...
AND IF DAD FORGOT TO BRING BAGS, I'LL GO POTTY ON THE SIDEWALK.
SOUNDS LIKE FUN. ENJOY!
WILL DO!
ANDERSON

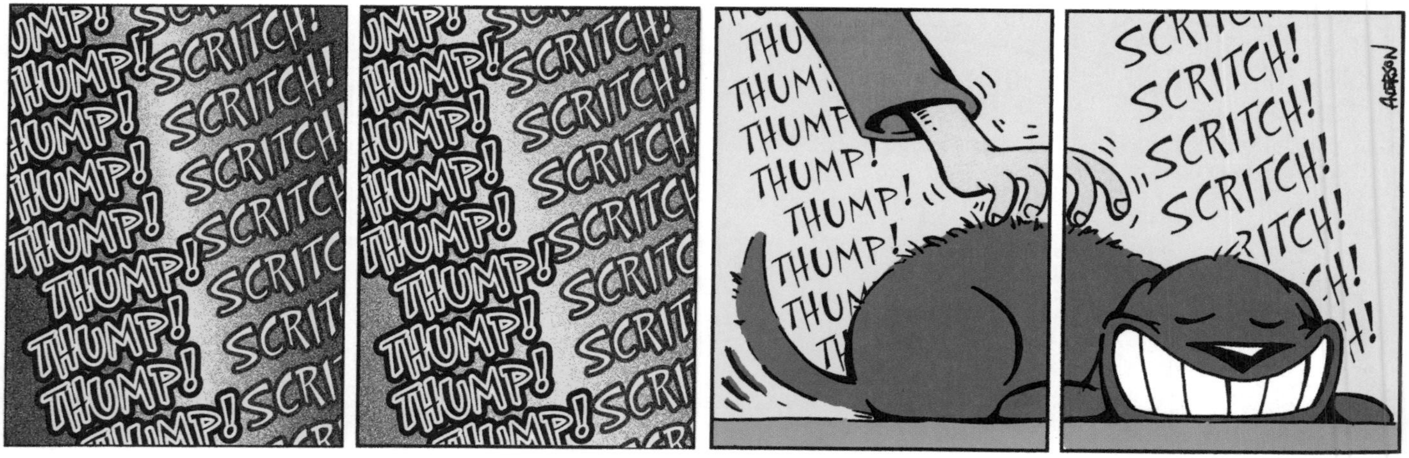
THUMP! SCRITCH!
THUMP! SCRITCH!
THUMP! SCRITCH!
SCRITCH! SCRITCH! SCRITCH!
ANDERSON

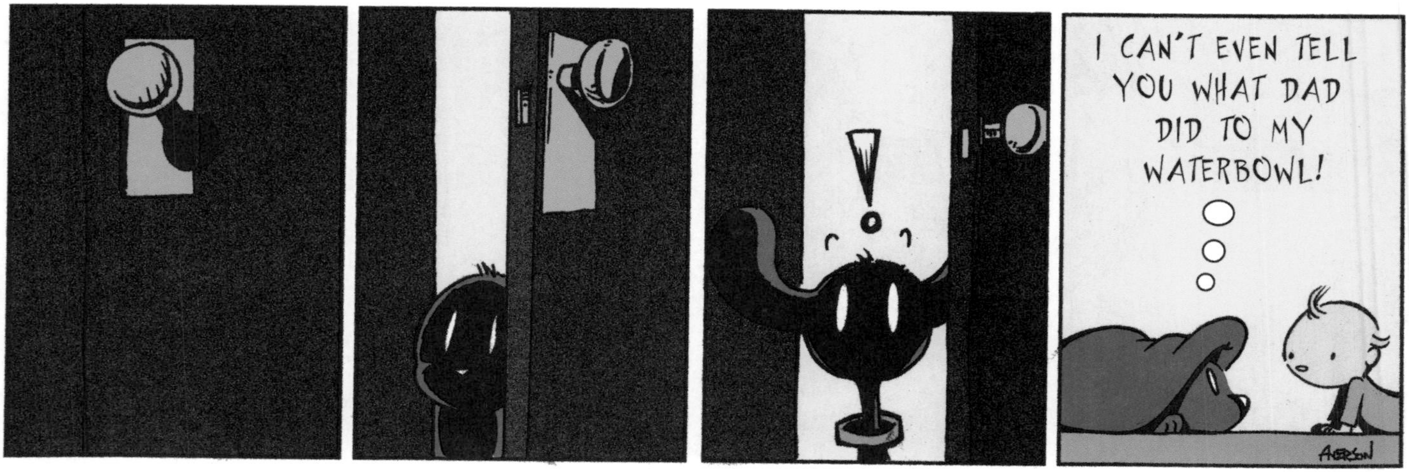
I CAN'T EVEN TELL YOU WHAT DAD DID TO MY WATERBOWL!
ANDERSON

HEY!

NO MORE "BOUNCIES" TILL YOU GUYS BEHAVE!

DAD REALLY KNOWS HOW TO RUIN A GOOD TIME.

ANDERSON

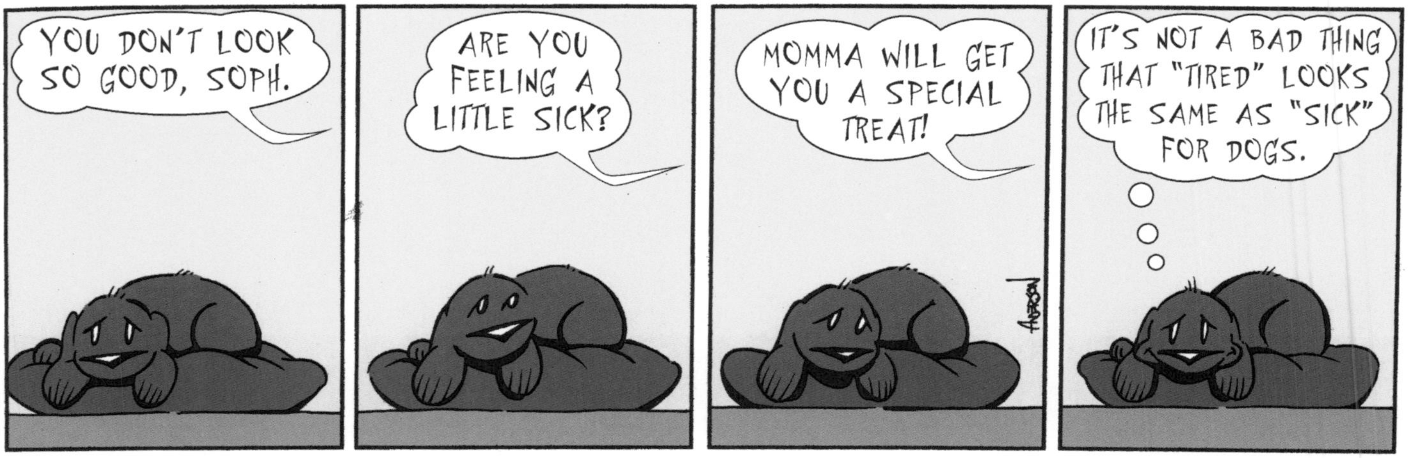
YOU DON'T LOOK SO GOOD, SOPH.
ARE YOU FEELING A LITTLE SICK?
MOMMA WILL GET YOU A SPECIAL TREAT!
IT'S NOT A BAD THING THAT "TIRED" LOOKS THE SAME AS "SICK" FOR DOGS.

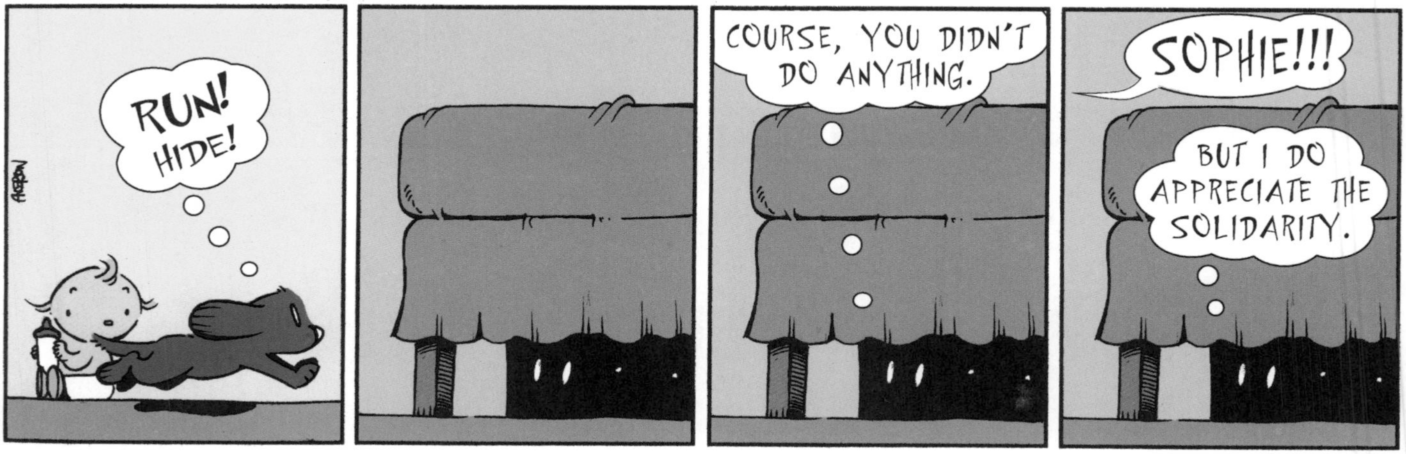
RUN! HIDE!
COURSE, YOU DIDN'T DO ANYTHING.
SOPHIE!!!
BUT I DO APPRECIATE THE SOLIDARITY.

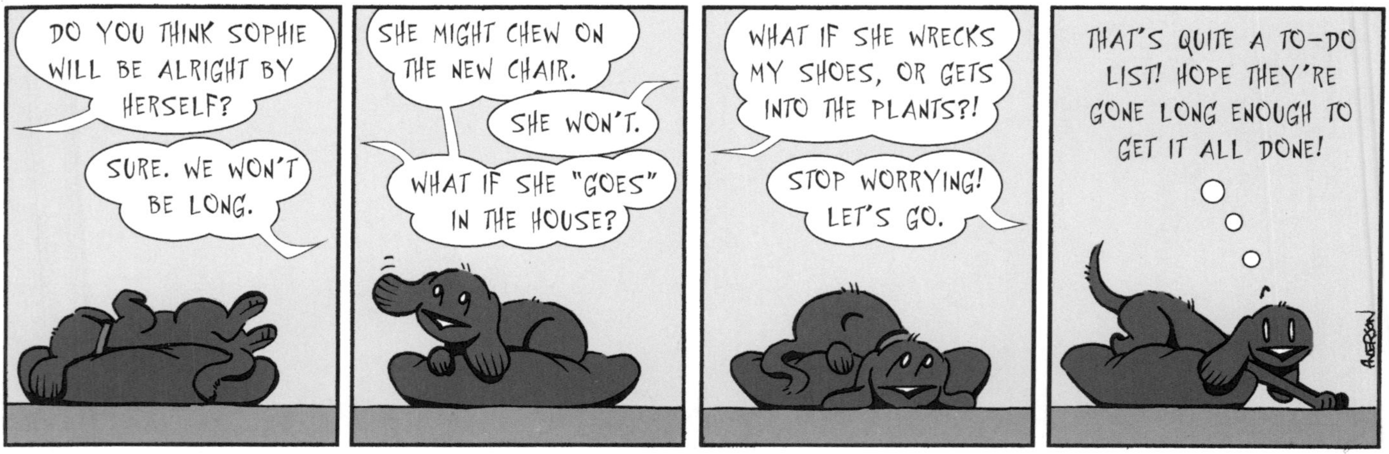
DO YOU THINK SOPHIE WILL BE ALRIGHT BY HERSELF?
SURE. WE WON'T BE LONG.
SHE MIGHT CHEW ON THE NEW CHAIR.
SHE WON'T.
WHAT IF SHE "GOES" IN THE HOUSE?
WHAT IF SHE WRECKS MY SHOES, OR GETS INTO THE PLANTS?!
STOP WORRYING! LET'S GO.
THAT'S QUITE A TO-DO LIST! HOPE THEY'RE GONE LONG ENOUGH TO GET IT ALL DONE!

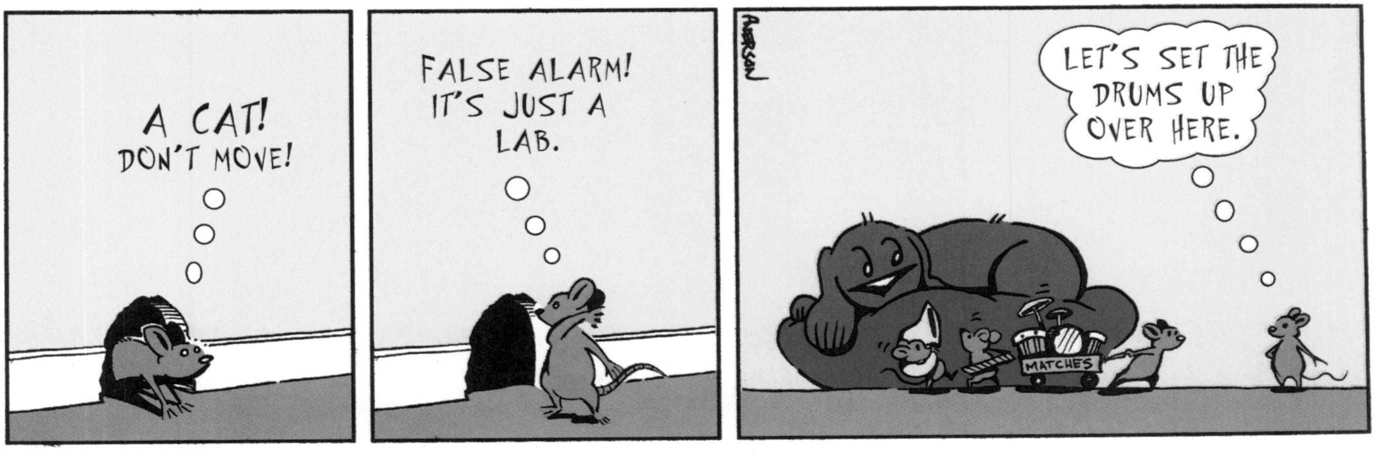
A CAT! DON'T MOVE!
FALSE ALARM! IT'S JUST A LAB.
LET'S SET THE DRUMS UP OVER HERE.
MATCHES

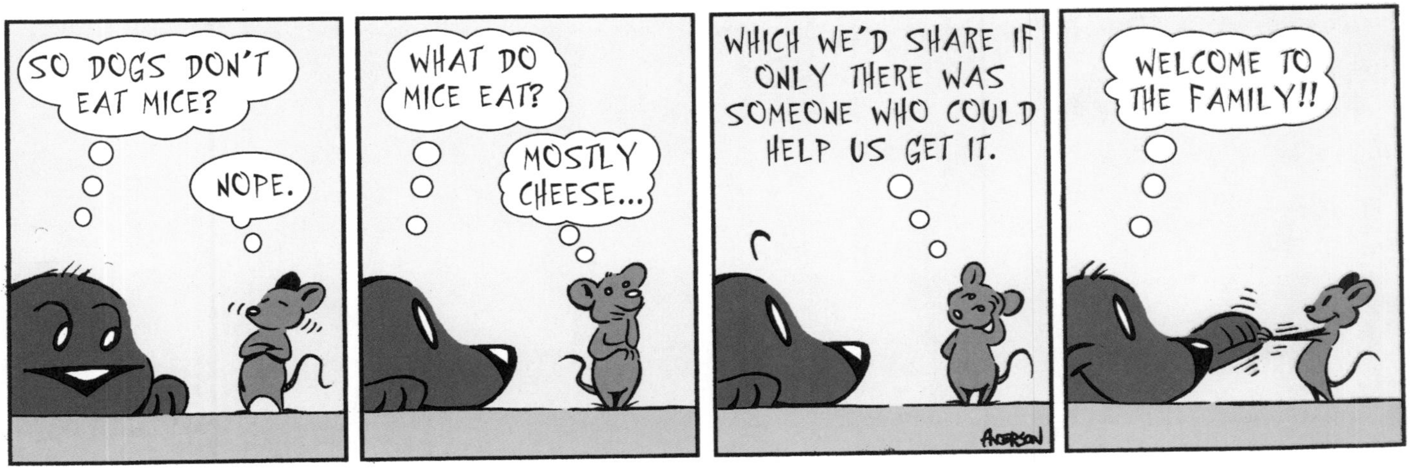
SO DOGS DON'T EAT MICE?
NOPE.
WHAT DO MICE EAT?
MOSTLY CHEESE...
WHICH WE'D SHARE IF ONLY THERE WAS SOMEONE WHO COULD HELP US GET IT.
WELCOME TO THE FAMILY!!

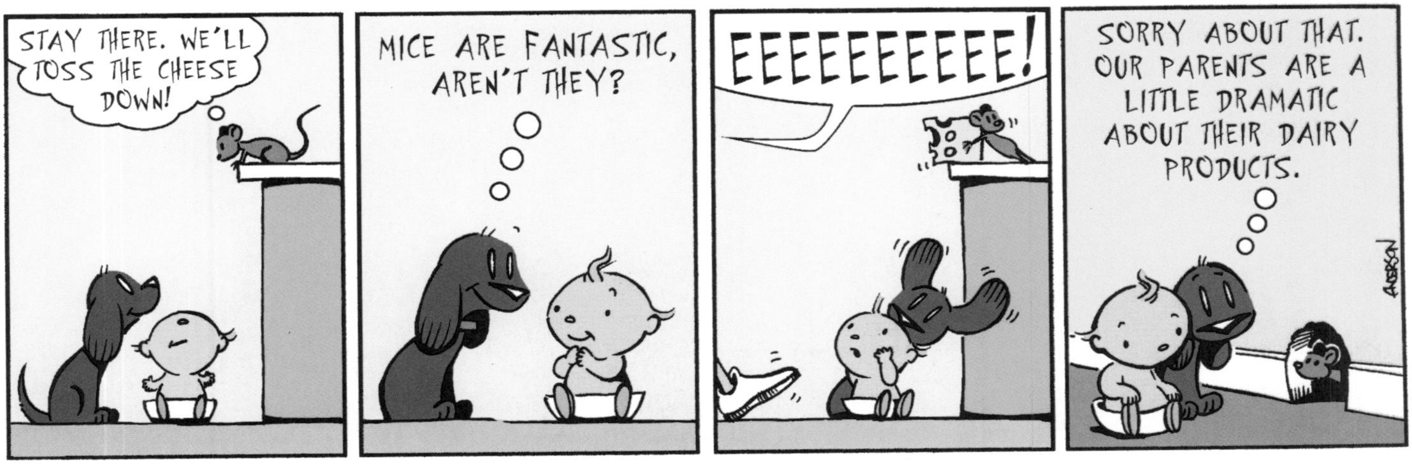
STAY THERE. WE'LL TOSS THE CHEESE DOWN!
MICE ARE FANTASTIC, AREN'T THEY?
EEEEEEEEEEE!
SORRY ABOUT THAT. OUR PARENTS ARE A LITTLE DRAMATIC ABOUT THEIR DAIRY PRODUCTS.

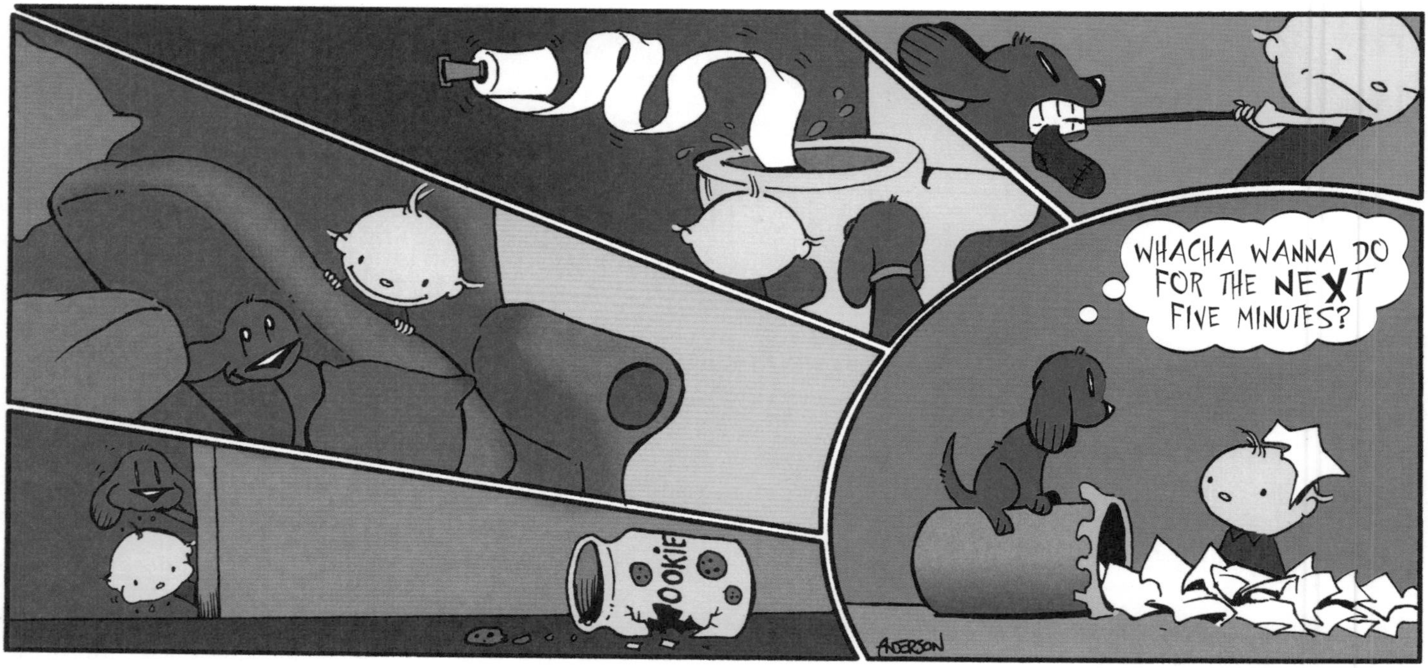
WHACHA WANNA DO FOR THE NEXT FIVE MINUTES?
COOKIE
ANDERSON

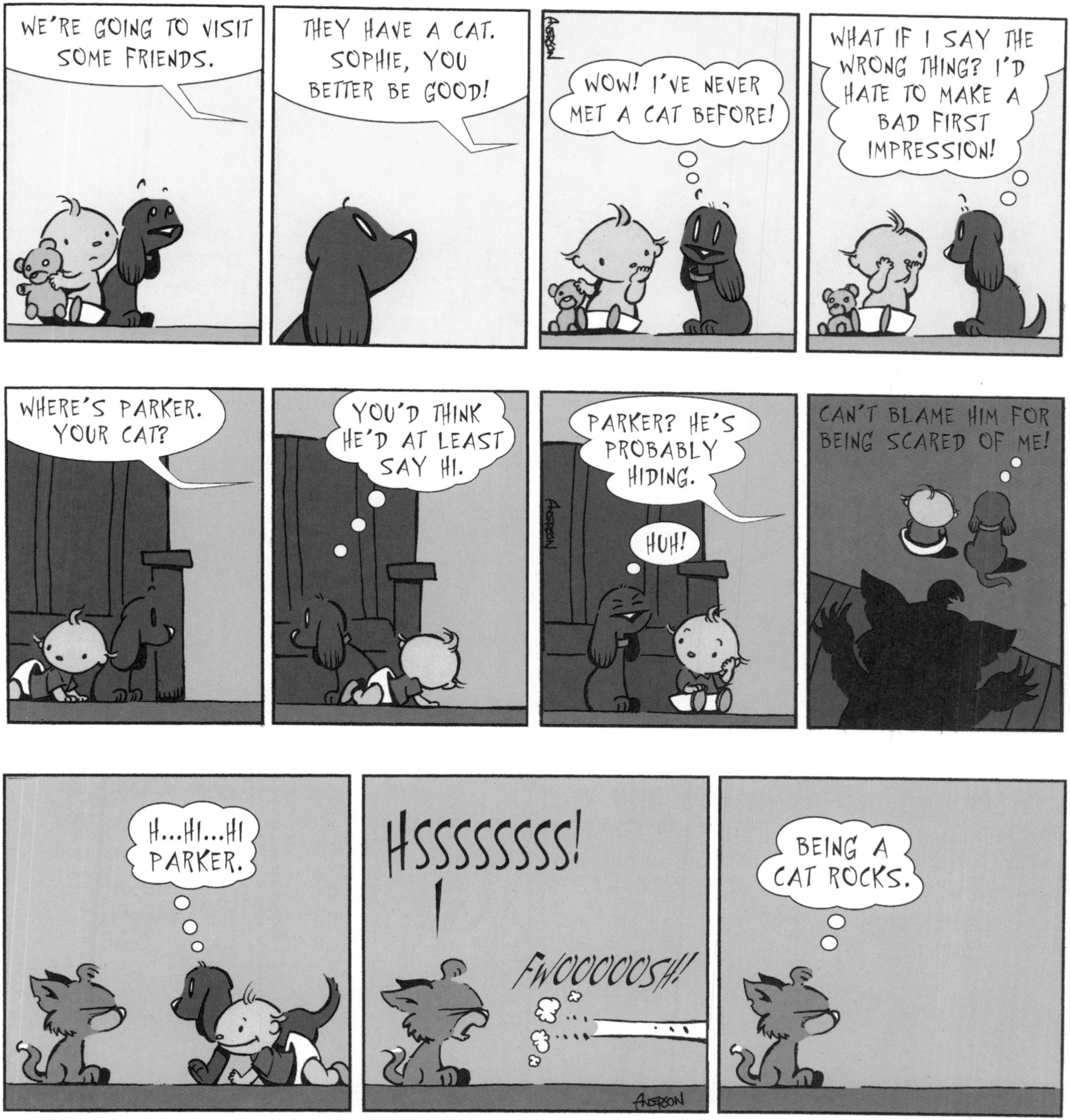

WE'RE GOING TO VISIT SOME FRIENDS.
THEY HAVE A CAT. SOPHIE, YOU BETTER BE GOOD!
WOW! I'VE NEVER MET A CAT BEFORE!
WHAT IF I SAY THE WRONG THING? I'D HATE TO MAKE A BAD FIRST IMPRESSION!
WHERE'S PARKER. YOUR CAT?
YOU'D THINK HE'D AT LEAST SAY HI.
PARKER? HE'S PROBABLY HIDING.
HUH!
CAN'T BLAME HIM FOR BEING SCARED OF ME!
H...HI...HI PARKER.
HSSSSSSSS!
FWOOOOOSH!
BEING A CAT ROCKS.

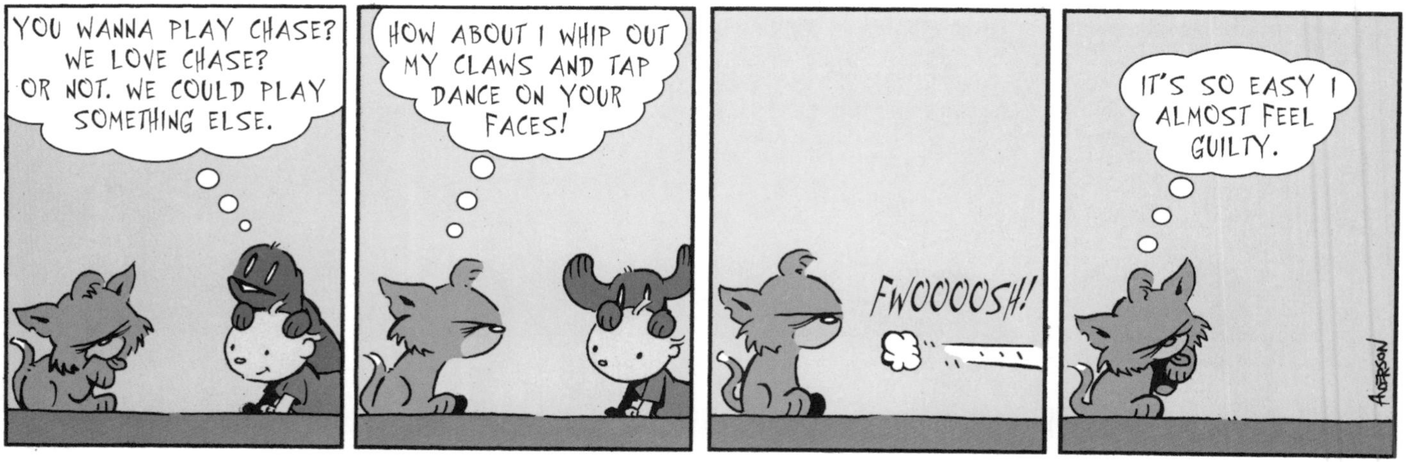
YOU WANNA PLAY CHASE? WE LOVE CHASE? OR NOT. WE COULD PLAY SOMETHING ELSE.
HOW ABOUT I WHIP OUT MY CLAWS AND TAP DANCE ON YOUR FACES!
FWOOOOSH!
IT'S SO EASY I ALMOST FEEL GUILTY.
ANDERSON

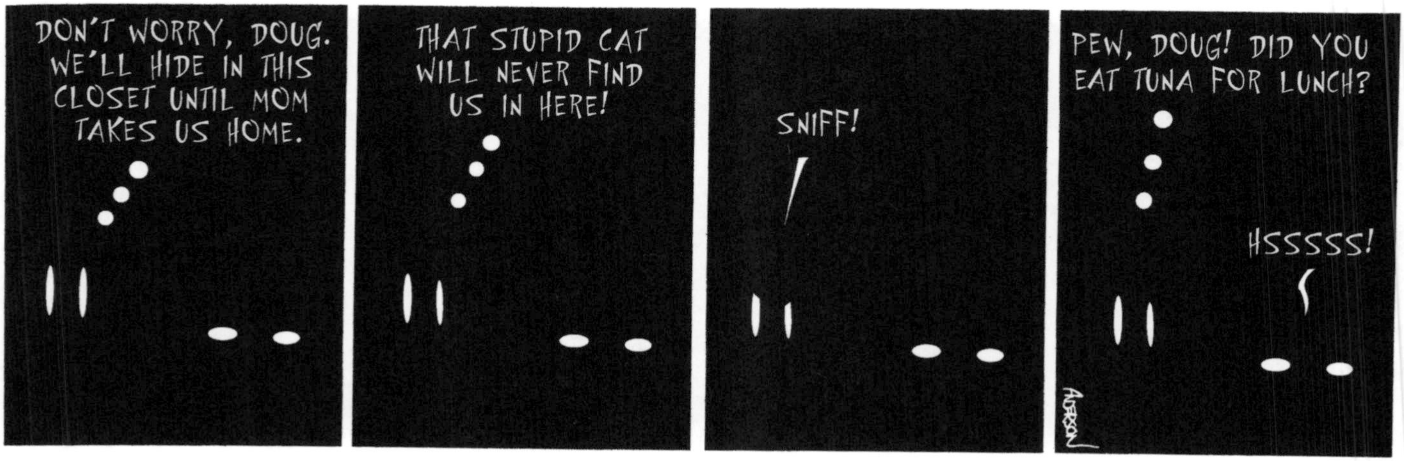
DON'T WORRY, DOUG. WE'LL HIDE IN THIS CLOSET UNTIL MOM TAKES US HOME.
THAT STUPID CAT WILL NEVER FIND US IN HERE!
SNIFF!
PEW, DOUG! DID YOU EAT TUNA FOR LUNCH?
HSSSSS!
ANDERSON

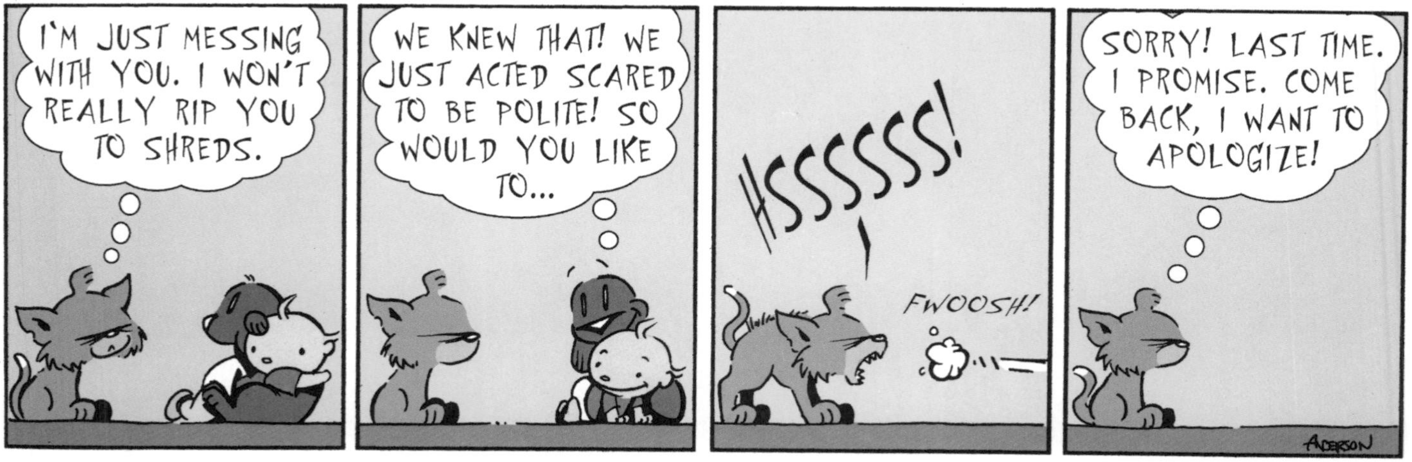
I'M JUST MESSING WITH YOU. I WON'T REALLY RIP YOU TO SHREDS.
WE KNEW THAT! WE JUST ACTED SCARED TO BE POLITE! SO WOULD YOU LIKE TO...
HSSSSSS!
FWOOSH!
SORRY! LAST TIME. I PROMISE. COME BACK, I WANT TO APOLOGIZE!
ANDERSON

WHAT'RE YOU SMILING AT? I'M NOT AFRAID OF DOGS!
OH, I KNOW! YOU SHOULD BE AFRAID OF DOUG.
A BABY! HA! HA! HA! HE'S BALD AND TOOTHLESS! WHY WOULD I FEAR THIS BUTTER BUTT!?!
UURK!!!
OOPS! FORGOT TO MENTION HE'S A HUGGER.

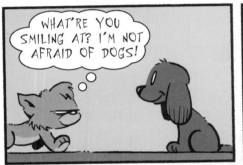

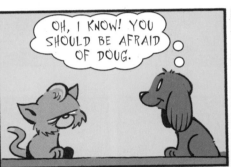

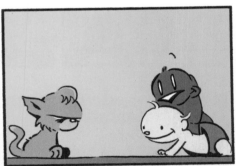

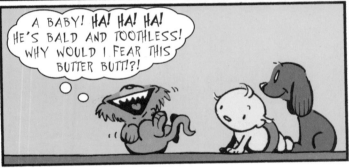

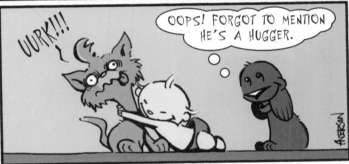

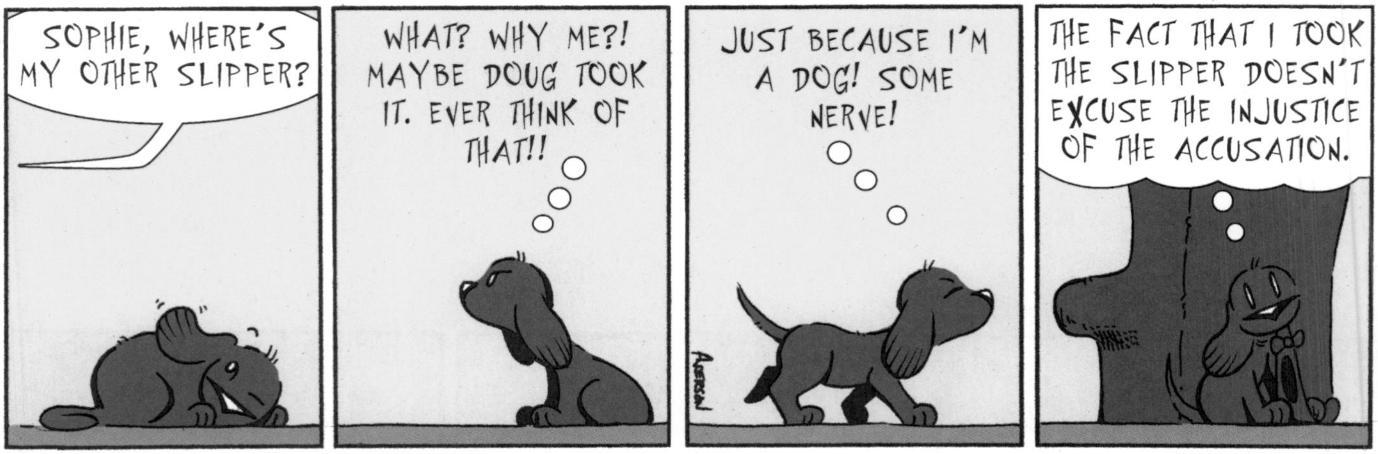
SOPHIE, WHERE'S MY OTHER SLIPPER?
WHAT? WHY ME?! MAYBE DOUG TOOK IT. EVER THINK OF THAT!!
JUST BECAUSE I'M A DOG! SOME NERVE!
THE FACT THAT I TOOK THE SLIPPER DOESN'T EXCUSE THE INJUSTICE OF THE ACCUSATION.

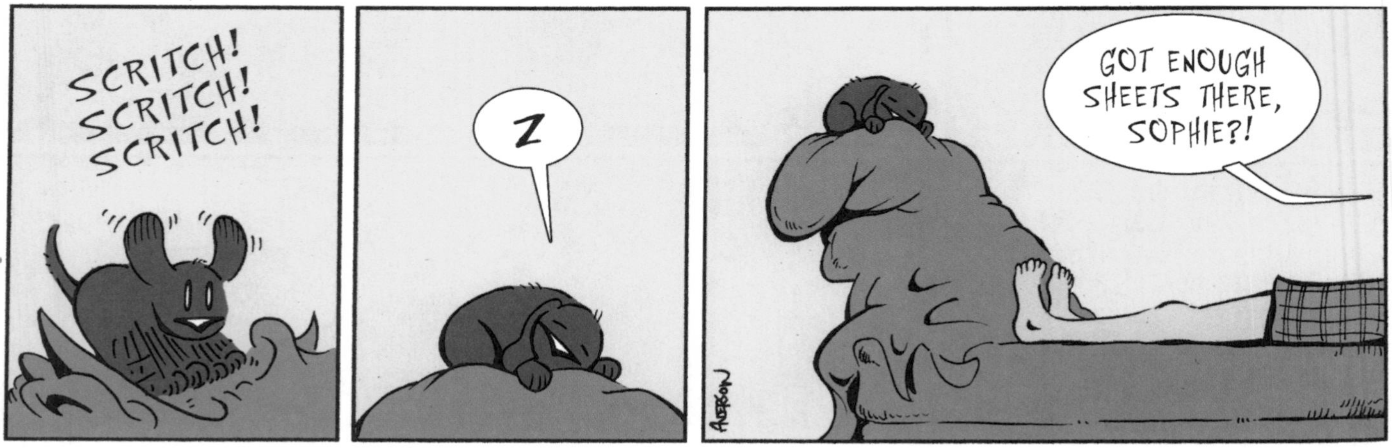
SCRITCH! SCRITCH! SCRITCH!
Z
GOT ENOUGH SHEETS THERE, SOPHIE?!

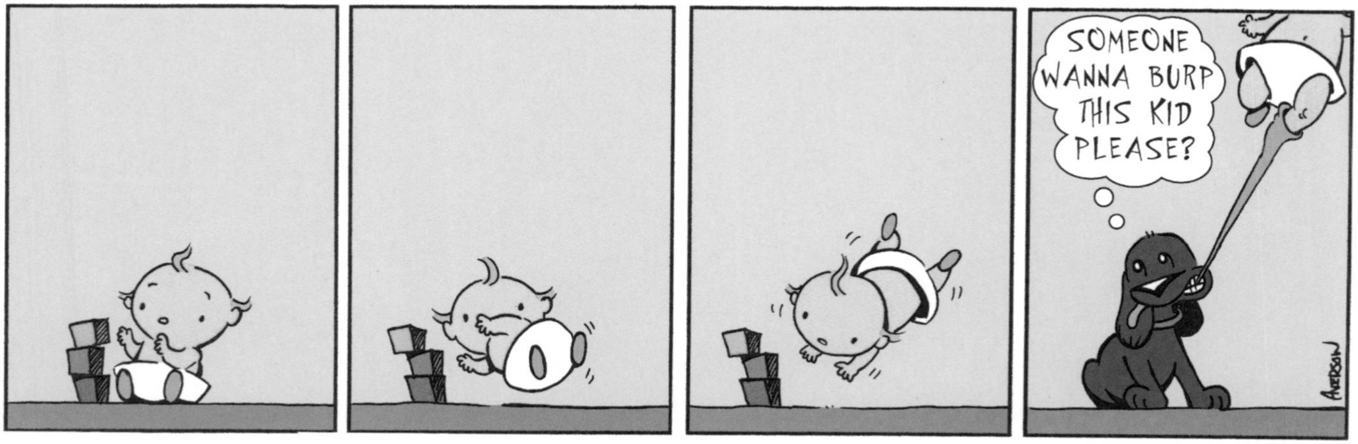
SOMEONE WANNA BURP THIS KID PLEASE?

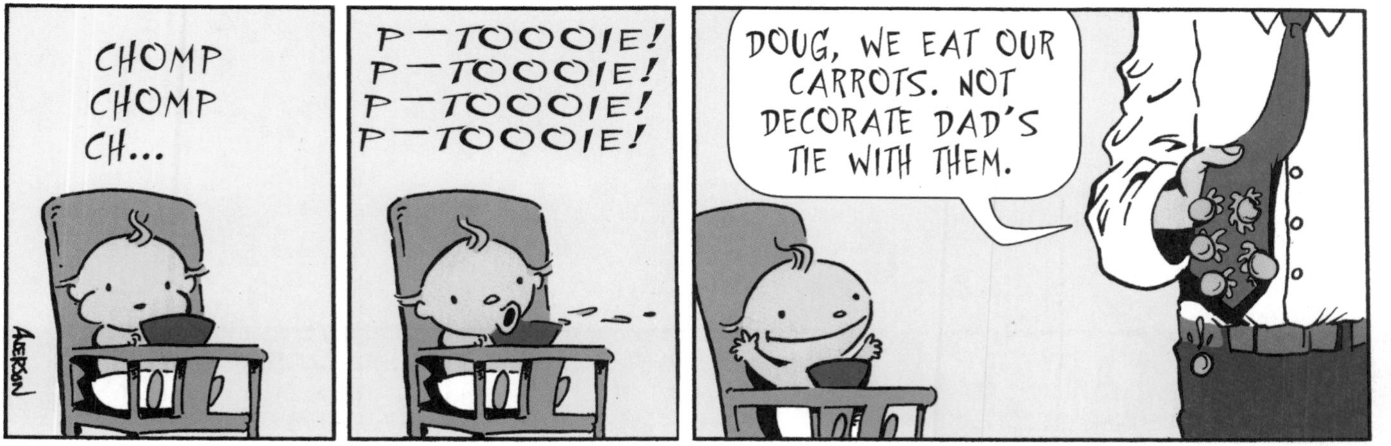
CHOMP
CHOMP
CH...
P–TOOOIE!
P–TOOOIE!
P–TOOOIE!
P–TOOOIE!
DOUG, WE EAT OUR CARROTS. NOT DECORATE DAD'S TIE WITH THEM.

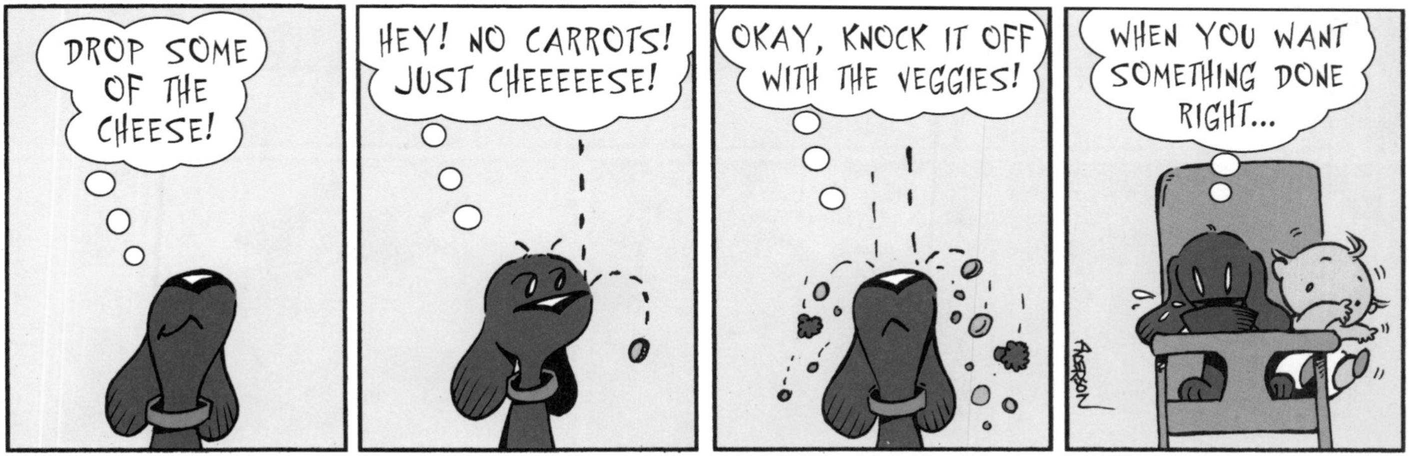
DROP SOME OF THE CHEESE!
HEY! NO CARROTS! JUST CHEEEEESE!
OKAY, KNOCK IT OFF WITH THE VEGGIES!
WHEN YOU WANT SOMETHING DONE RIGHT...

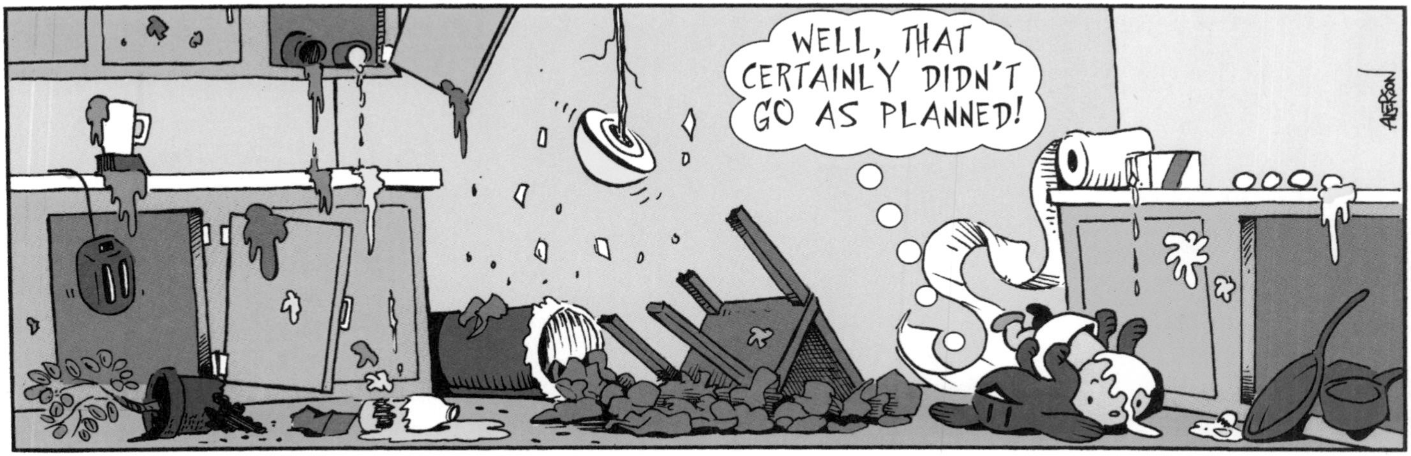
WELL, THAT CERTAINLY DIDN'T GO AS PLANNED!

WE'VE COME TO FAR TO TURN BACK NOW, DOUG.
WE'RE GOING TO CATCH THE MOST FEROCIOUS...
...ALLIGATOR TO ROAM THE EVERGLADES!
SHHH! SOMETHING'S COMING!
RRRRRRRRR!!
THERE HE IS! GET HIM!
HEY!!!

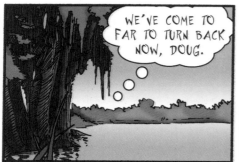

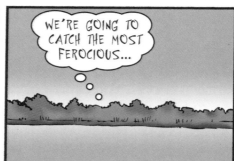

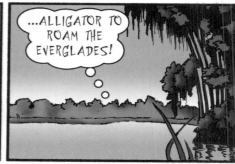

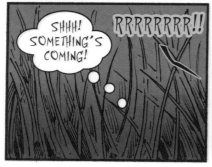

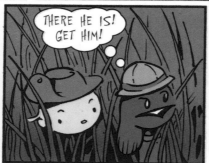

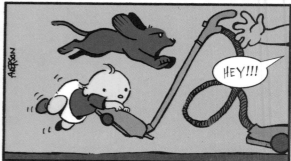

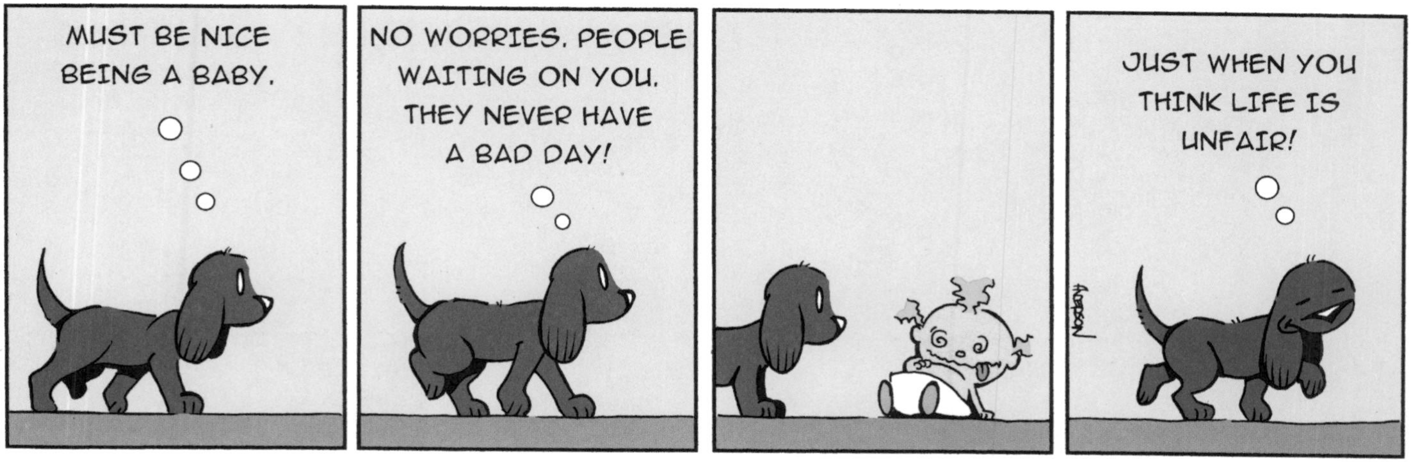
MUST BE NICE BEING A BABY.
NO WORRIES. PEOPLE WAITING ON YOU. THEY NEVER HAVE A BAD DAY!
JUST WHEN YOU THINK LIFE IS UNFAIR!

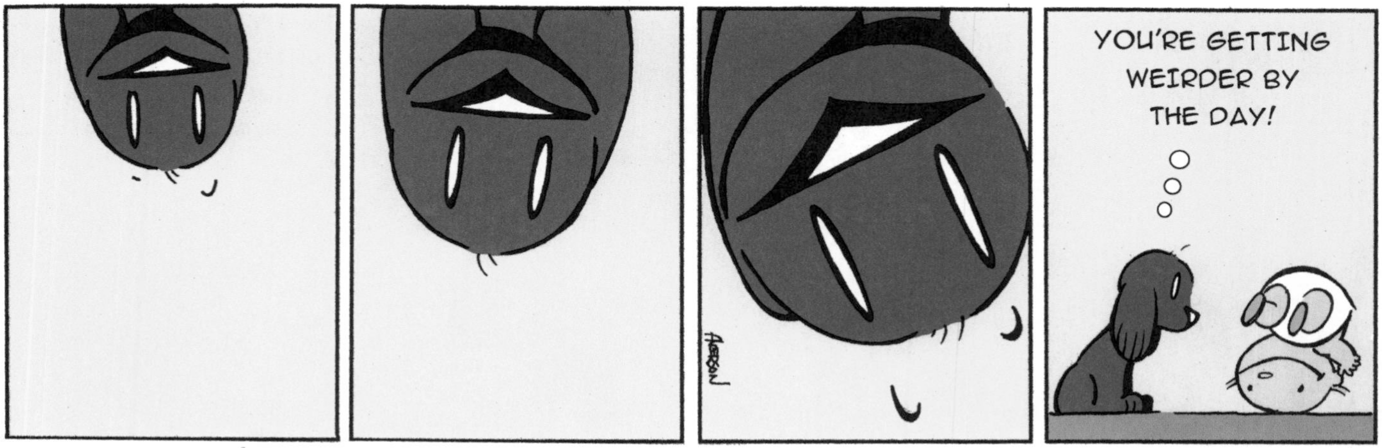
YOU'RE GETTING WEIRDER BY THE DAY!

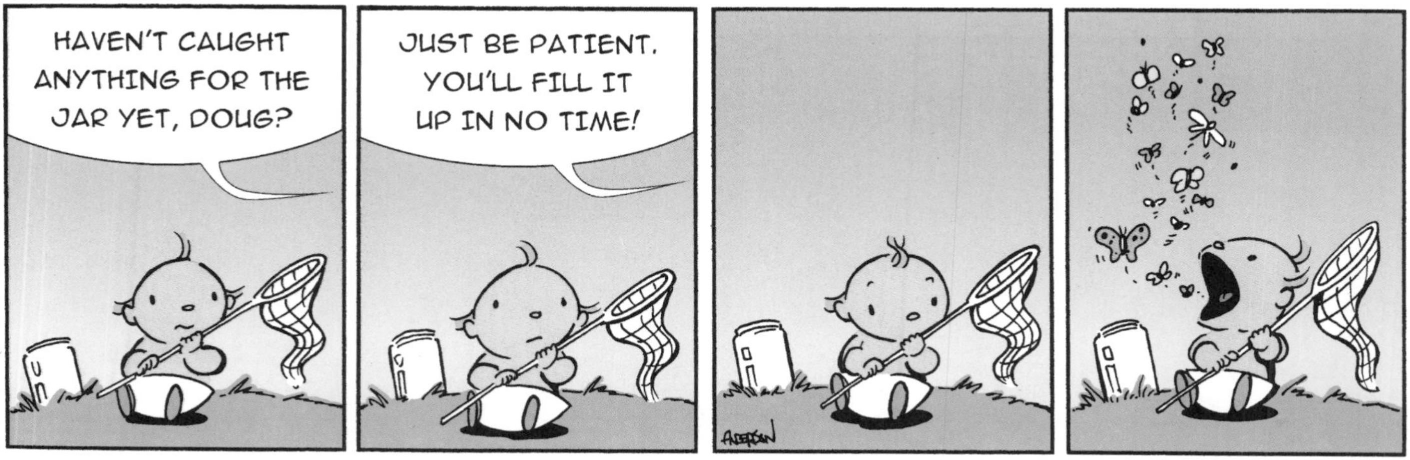
HAVEN'T CAUGHT ANYTHING FOR THE JAR YET, DOUG?
JUST BE PATIENT. YOU'LL FILL IT UP IN NO TIME!

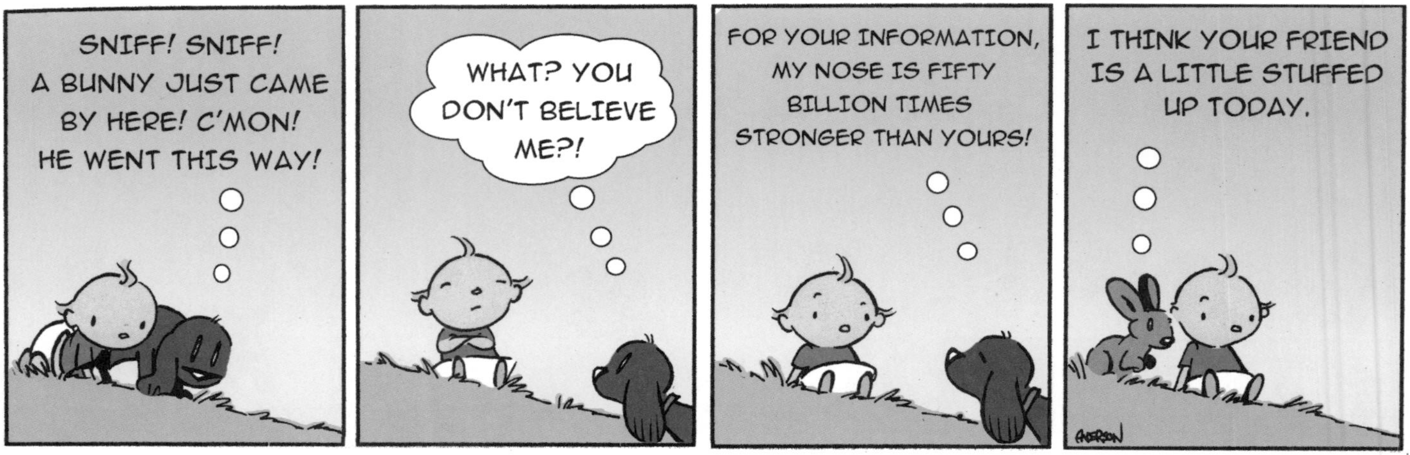
SNIFF! SNIFF! A BUNNY JUST CAME BY HERE! C'MON! HE WENT THIS WAY!
WHAT? YOU DON'T BELIEVE ME?!
FOR YOUR INFORMATION, MY NOSE IS FIFTY BILLION TIMES STRONGER THAN YOURS!
I THINK YOUR FRIEND IS A LITTLE STUFFED UP TODAY.
ANDERSON

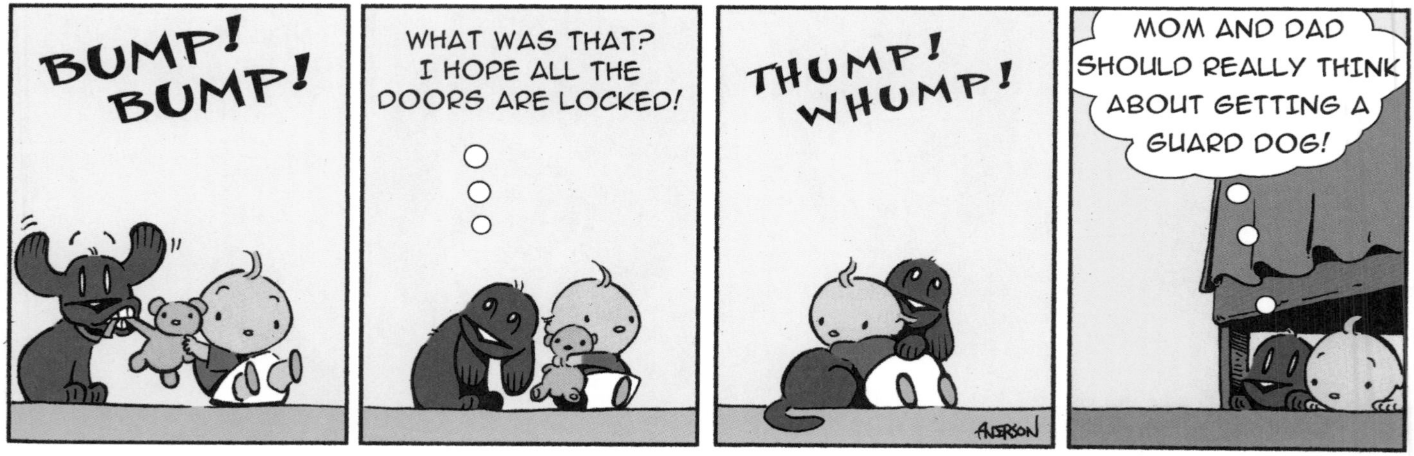
BUMP! BUMP!
WHAT WAS THAT? I HOPE ALL THE DOORS ARE LOCKED!
THUMP! WHUMP!
ANDERSON
MOM AND DAD SHOULD REALLY THINK ABOUT GETTING A GUARD DOG!

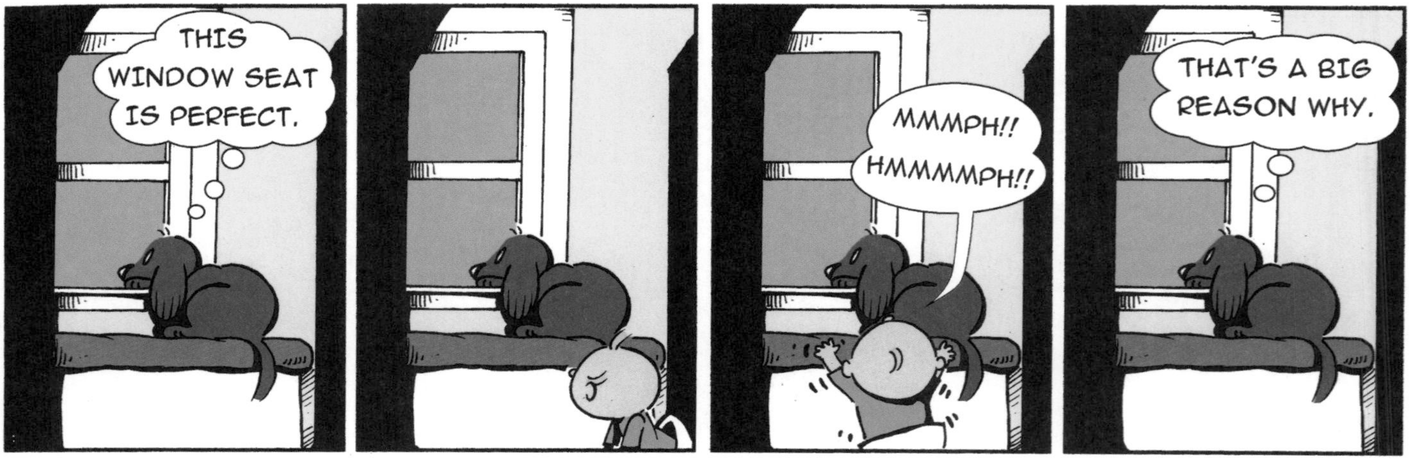
THIS WINDOW SEAT IS PERFECT.
MMMPH!! HMMMMPH!!
THAT'S A BIG REASON WHY.

REMEMBER THAT STORY DAD TOLD US?
ABOUT THE BOY WHO DIVES THROUGH A PUDDLE...
INTO A MAGICAL WORLD OF CANDY TREES AND DOG TREAT CLOUDS?
DAD'S STORIES ARE FULL OF BUNK!

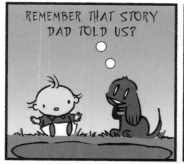

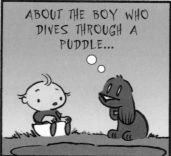

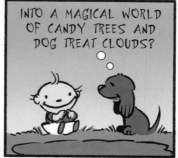

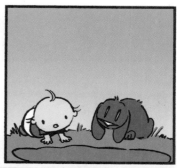

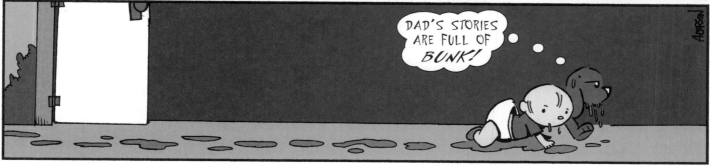

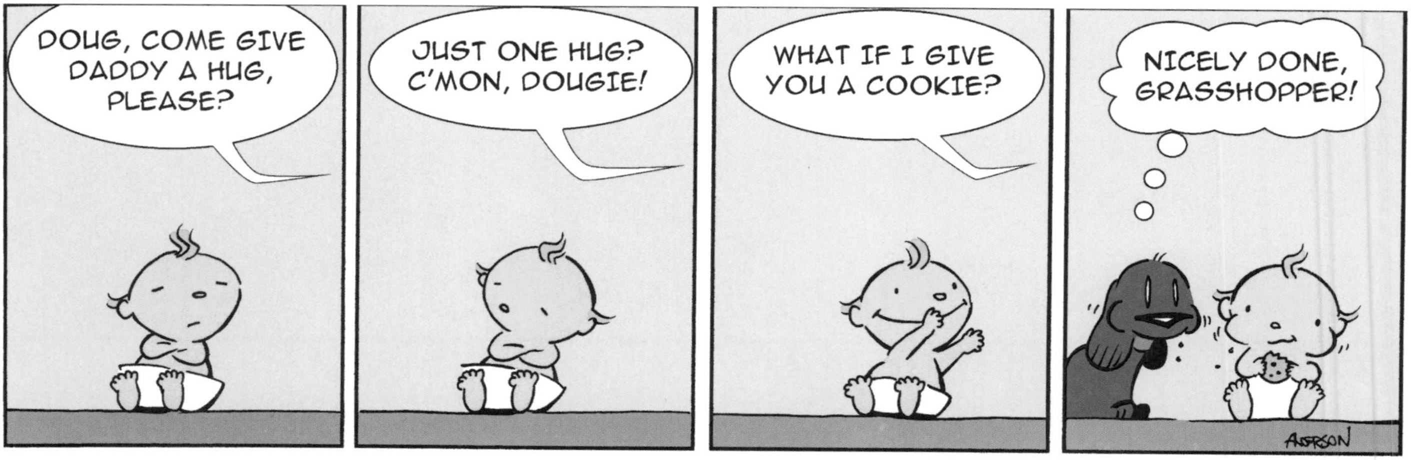
DOUG, COME GIVE DADDY A HUG, PLEASE?
JUST ONE HUG? C'MON, DOUGIE!
WHAT IF I GIVE YOU A COOKIE?
NICELY DONE, GRASSHOPPER!

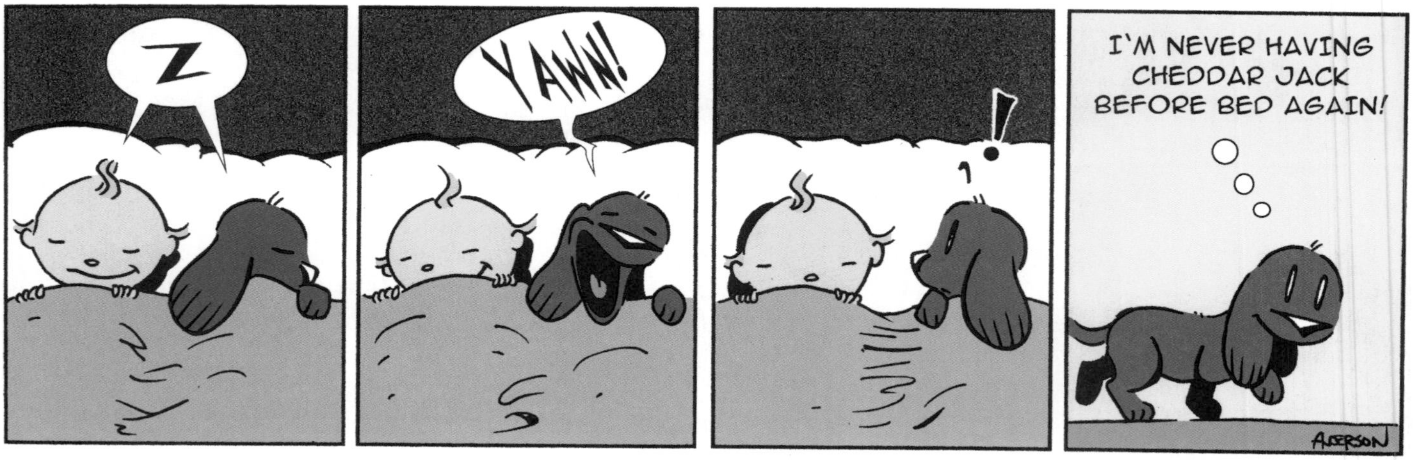
Z
YAWN!
!
I'M NEVER HAVING CHEDDAR JACK BEFORE BED AGAIN!

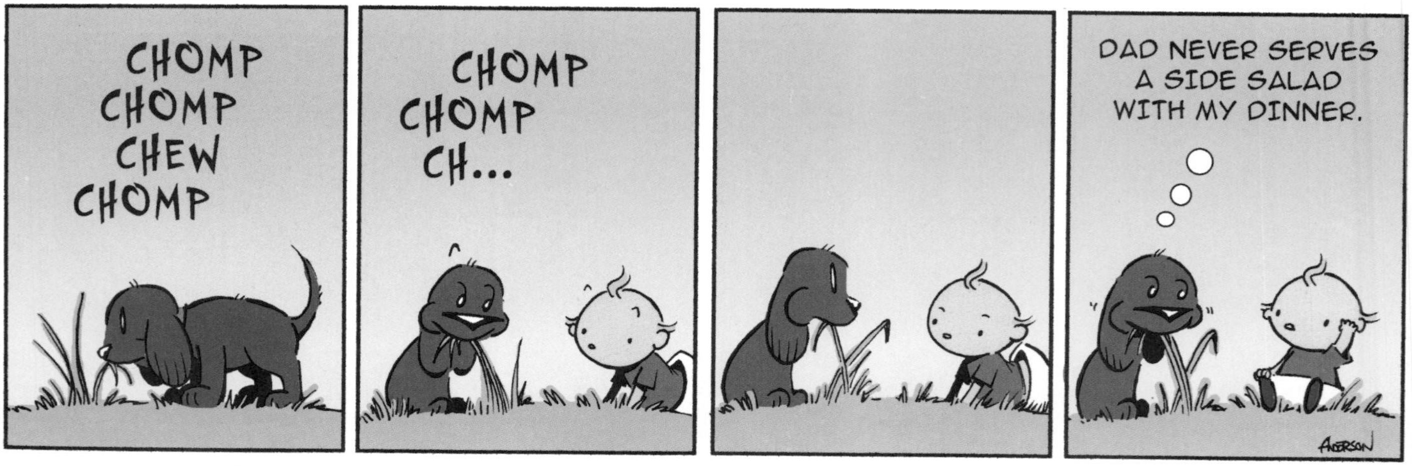
CHOMP CHOMP CHEW CHOMP
CHOMP CHOMP CH...
DAD NEVER SERVES A SIDE SALAD WITH MY DINNER.

BLOOP. BLOOP.
BLOOP. BLOOP.
BLOOP. BLOOP.

BLOOP. BLOOP.
BLOOP. BLOOP.
BLOOP. BLOOP.

BEEP! BEEP!
BEEP! BEEP!
BEEP! BEEP!
BEEP! BEEP!
BEEP! BEEP!
BEEP! BEEP!
BEEP! BEEP!
BEEP! BEEP!
BEEP! BEEP!
BEEP! BEEP!

MOM JUST OPENED THE CHEESE DRAWER!

MOST PEOPLE SURE DON'T APPRECIATE GEOMETRY.

BUT I'LL TELL YOU...

IT SURE WOULD COME IN HANDY FOR DOGS.

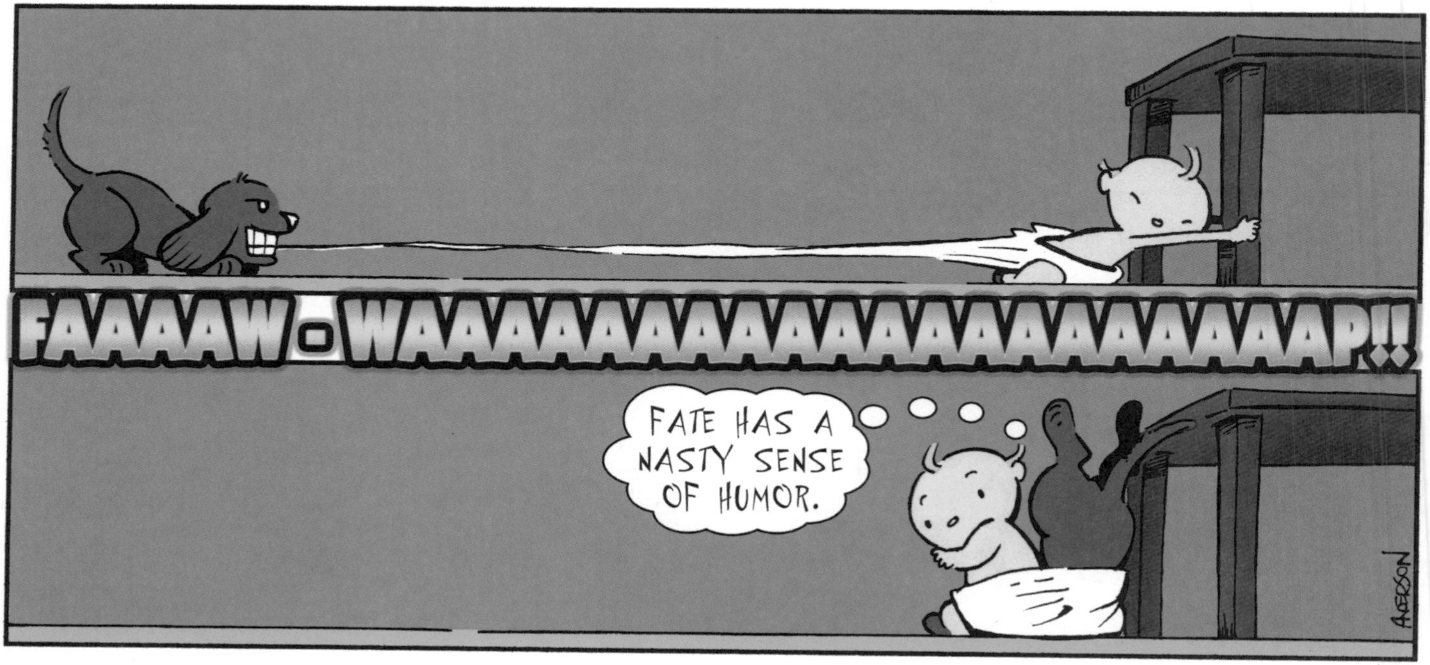

FAAAAW-WAAAAAAAAAAAAAAAAAAAAAAAAP!!
FATE HAS A NASTY SENSE OF HUMOR.
ANDERSON

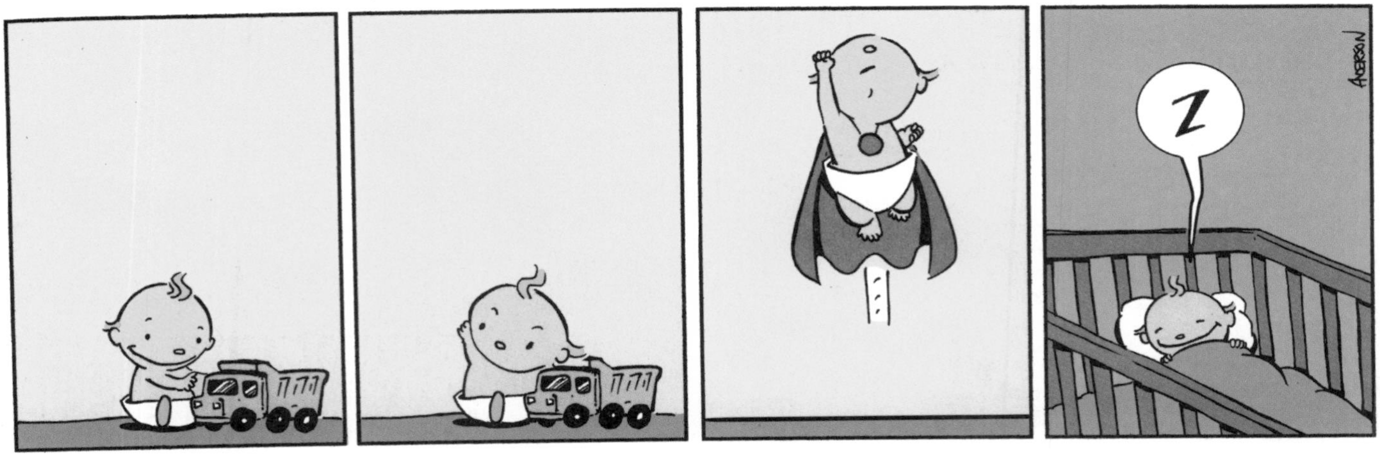
Z

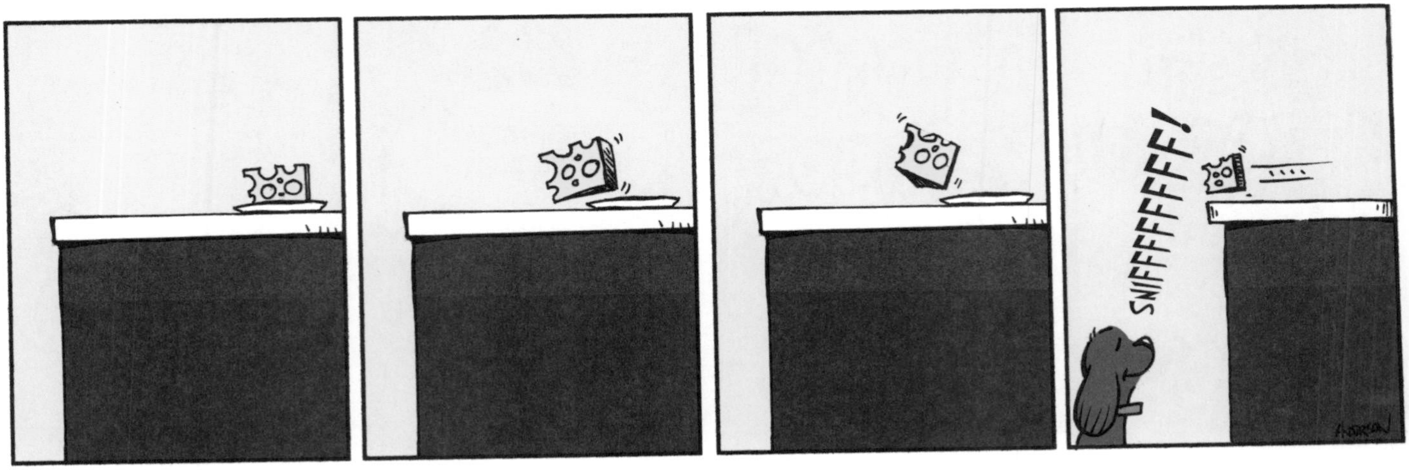
SNIFFFFFFFFF!

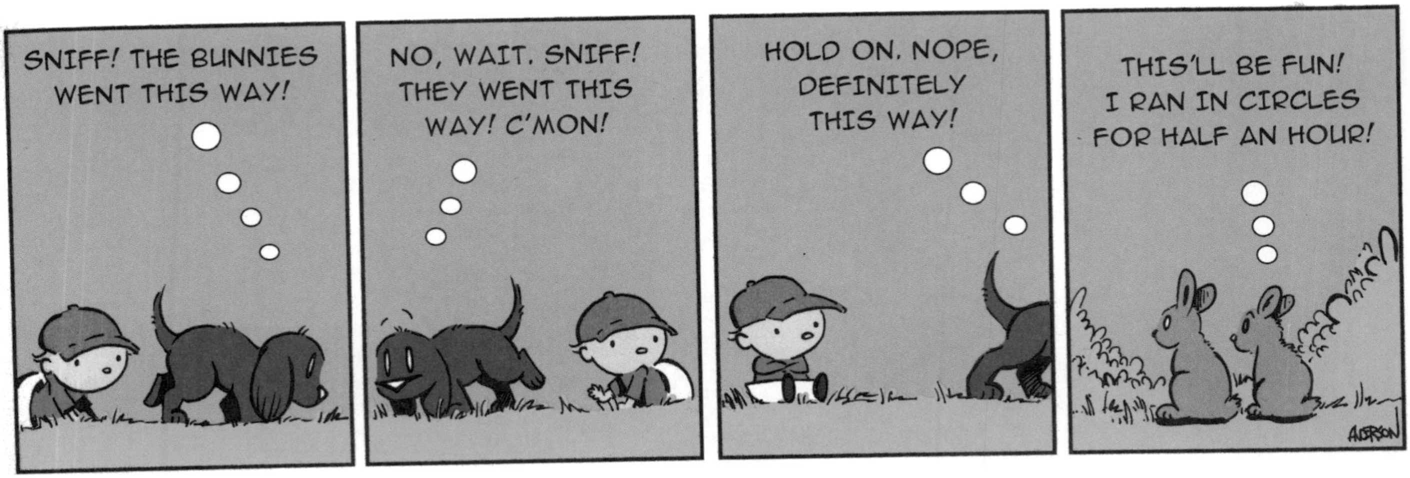
SNIFF! THE BUNNIES WENT THIS WAY!
NO, WAIT. SNIFF! THEY WENT THIS WAY! C'MON!
HOLD ON. NOPE, DEFINITELY THIS WAY!
THIS'LL BE FUN! I RAN IN CIRCLES FOR HALF AN HOUR!

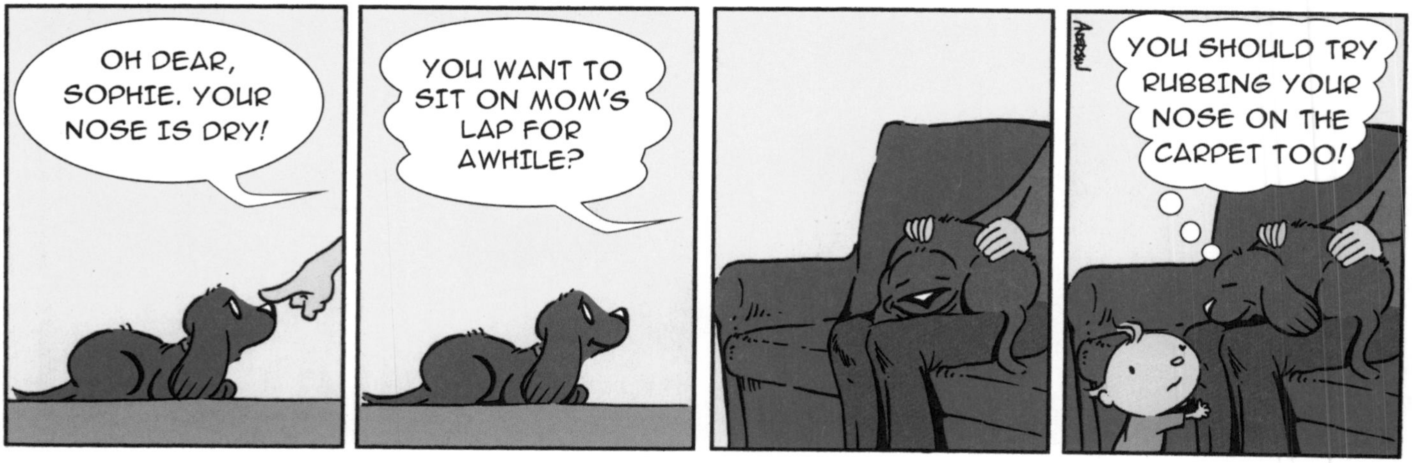
OH DEAR, SOPHIE. YOUR NOSE IS DRY!
YOU WANT TO SIT ON MOM'S LAP FOR AWHILE?
YOU SHOULD TRY RUBBING YOUR NOSE ON THE CARPET TOO!

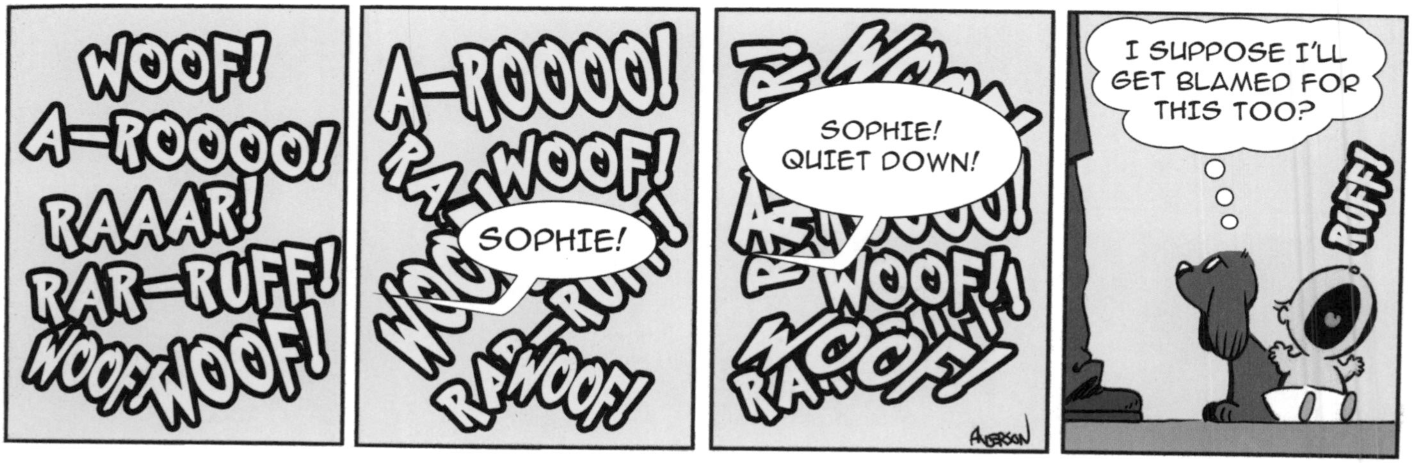
WOOF!
A-ROOOOO!
RAAAR!
RAR-RUFF!
WOOFWOOF!
A-ROOOOO!
WOOF!
SOPHIE!
SOPHIE! QUIET DOWN!
WOOF!
I SUPPOSE I'LL GET BLAMED FOR THIS TOO?
RUFF!

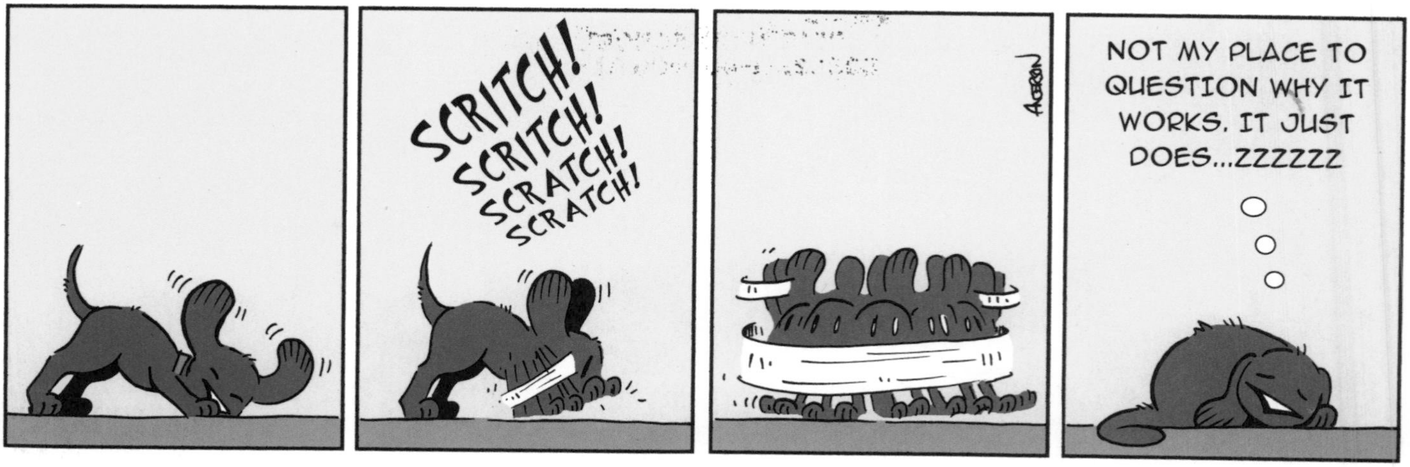
SCRITCH!
SCRITCH!
SCRATCH!
SCRATCH!
NOT MY PLACE TO QUESTION WHY IT WORKS. IT JUST DOES...ZZZZZZ